Amici

Volume 1

A TEXT FOR BEGINNERS IN ITALIAN
Second Edition

Fernando Mallozzi
Onondaga Community College

Annamaria Moneti
Syracuse University

Alfred J. Valentini
T. R. Proctor Senior High School
Utica College of Syracuse University

Original Art Work by **Luciana Mallozzi**

MVM Publishers
707 Sumner Avenue
Syracuse, New York 13210

ISBN# 0-9637279-4-X

Printed in the United states of America by Hamilton Printing Company, Rensselear, NY

TABLE OF CONTENTS

ABOUT THE BOOK

Amici: Volume 1, Second Edition, is a textbook for the teaching of Italian that presents authentic language and culture in a natural and non-threatening way. In revising and up-dating the text (originally published in 1993), the authors have addressed more extensively several fundamental concerns, in particular:

- to soften classroom anxiety;
- to present *real* language and culture and *real* linguistic functions as implied by native speakers of today;
- to involve students in active participation;
- to fulfill performance objectives in the four skill areas of listening, reading, writing and speaking as outlined in local and state syllabi, as well as state and national frameworks and standards.

To soften the classroom anxiety, the authors have avoided the "displacement" of the learner, that is: the language is initially absorbed in an environment familiar to the students, by means of the friendship that develops between two boys, an American and an Italian who is visiting the United States. John and Renzo learn from each other, naturally, as any student would in the same situation. They also learn from other characters that appear in the ongoing story, young and adult, male and female.

The ***SITUATIONS*** that introduce each chapter are "slices of life"; characters' utterances reflect the principles of *authentic discourse*. The setting favors the production of language by means of *comprehensible input*. The presence of adults allows for the change of language register required by authentic Italian communication. New to this edition of the text are the ***PERFORMANCE ACTIVITIES,*** which appear in the final section of each chapter. These guided activities consist of:

- **E ora in italiano:** a review dialogue presented entirely in Italian designed to reiterate language and structures previously introduced in the chapter;
- **Ascoltiamo:** practice in listening comprehension, from simple utterances to complete situations;
- **Leggiamo:** exercise designed to develop and enhance reading comprehension;
- **Scriviamo:** writing exercises that include short messages and notes, postcards and letters, to family and friends;
- **Parliamo:** suggested situations that provide opportunities to develop speaking competence

The ***LANGUAGE*** is that of the educated native speaker, made as simple as accuracy allows. The vocabulary, our **PAROLE DA RICORDARE**, is introduced as needed in real-life terms, hence, not necessarily according to a preset outline. The vocabulary expansion is organized on the basis of semantic clusters in order to facilitate mnemonic retention. New, or expanded clusters comprise vocabulary for school, jobs, food and meals, the human body and additional descriptive adjectives. All vocabulary has been checked for frequency according to the study of Prof. Tullio De Mauro, University of Rome, Italy (*Guida all'uso delle parole*, Editori Riuniti, 1985).

The ***LANGUAGE STRUCTURE***, our ***BUILDING BLOCKS***, is streamlined to the essentials necessary for correct expressions. Discrete points are presented individually and practiced immediately.

EXERCISES, our **PROVIAMOCI**, offer a variety of teaching suggestions, from spelling checks to reading comprehension and completion, interviews and peer practice, as well as the "cooperative learning" approach and other classroom activities. Further features provide self-testing and cumulative reviews. Discourse is as complete as possible, in that it "makes sense" and is appropriate (depending on the format of the exercise). As students progress in their learning, sentences become longer and more sophisticated, continuously reinforcing the acquisition of the second language. Opportunities to develop students' ability to function in new situations and think for themselves are constantly presented. Again, this edition's new feature, ***PERFORMANCE ACTIVITIES***, offers ample opportunities for student performance in the four skill areas, using both individual and group approaches.

The ***ITALIAN CULTURE*** is woven into all sections of the text, in that every language exchange, idiomatic form and activity reflect it. Authentic photographs and "realia" provide visual stimulus. ***ABOUT ITALY***, in English in this first volume, offers information pertinent to the Italian way of life, especially that of young people, and promotes understanding between the two cultures.

Amici is accompanied by a *Workbook* with many reinforcement exercises, and a *Teacher's Guide* that provides extra information, suggestions, quizzes and exams.

ACKNOWLEDGEMENTS

The authors wish to thank their colleagues, the "practitioners," for their input and suggestions in producing this new, expanded edition. Additional thanks go to those same colleagues and the thousands of students around the country who have made *Amici: Volume 1* a success.

Finally, the authors wish to recognize the support and encouragement given them by their families through the "gestation" of this volume, especially: Janet Mallozzi, Giancarlo Moneti and Maria Rita Valentini.

CAPITOLO UNO: CHI SEI?
CHAPTER ONE: WHO ARE YOU?

FUNCTIONS

Personal identification
Greetings

LANGUAGE

Come ti chiami?
Mi chiamo...
Dove, chi
Sono, sei, è
Pronunciation
Numbers 1-10
Italian names

ABOUT ITALY

Famous Italians
Italy and the Italian cities

SITUATION

While cutting the grass one afternoon, John Wright notices a soccer ball coming over his backyard fence. Suddenly, a boy about the same age as John hops over the fence to retrieve the ball. The stranger sees John and says:

STRANGER:	**Ciao!**
JOHN:	Hi!
STRANGER:	**Mi chiamo Renzo. E tu chi sei?**
JOHN:	Huh?
STRANGER:	(*points to himself*) **Sono Renzo**. (*points to John*) **Come ti chiami?**
JOHN:	Oh! You are Renzo! (*points to himself*) My name is John.

Mrs. Romano, John's neighbor, calls out from her yard.

MRS. R.:	Renzo! **Dove sei?**
RENZO:	**Sono qui, Zia!**
MRS. R.:	(*coming over to the fence*) **Ah, sei lì!** Buon giorno, John. I mean hello, John. This is my nephew, Renzo, from Rome.
JOHN:	Pleasure to meet you Renzo!
RENZO:	**Piacere,** John!
MRS. R.:	Renzo is staying with me this summer. You'll hear a lot of Italian.

Renzo and his aunt go back toward their house.

MRS. R.:	Goodbye, John!
RENZO:	**Arrivederci,** John!

Capitolo Uno: Chi Sei?

PAROLE DA RICORDARE

NOUNS

il giorno the day
la zia the aunt

PRONOUNS

chi who

OTHERS

dove where

lì there
qui here

VERBS

è s/he, it is
sei you are
sono I am, they are

ADJECTIVES

buono good

USEFUL EXPRESSIONS

Arrivederci!	Good bye!
Buon giorno!	Good day!
Ciao!	Hi/Bye! (familiar)
Come ti chiami?	What is your name?
Dov'è ...	Where is ...
Mi chiamo...	My name is... (I call myself...)

PROVIAMOCI

A. Matching - Match the Italian expression with its English equivalent.

1. Ciao!
2. Dove sei?
3. Mi chiamo.
4. Sono qui!
5. Chi sei?
6. Buon giorno!

a. Who are you?
b. I am here!
c. Hi/Bye!
d. Good day!
e. Where are you?
f. My name is...

B. Conversation - Supply the Italian dialogue for the following situations.

1. The two boys are greeting each other.

2. One boy tells who he is and asks for the other boy's name.

3. Mrs. Romano calls Renzo, who answers from the backyard.

C. Informal introductions - Introduce yourself to a classmate.

Ex.: Student #1: Mi chiamo ... e tu chi sei (*or* come ti chiami)?
Student #2: Mi chiamo (*or*, sono) ... e [*to next student*] tu chi sei?
[*And so on, around the room*]

D. Clarification - Let's pretend your teacher has trouble remembering names.

Ex.: Teacher: Tu chi sei? [*Indicates student*]
Student: Sono ...
Teacher: Chi è? [*Indicates that student to the class*]
Class: È ...

E. Finding someone - Continue the role-playing with your teacher.

Ex.: Teacher: Dov'è ... ?
Student: [*Raises hand*] Sono qui, professore/professoressa!
Or, another student can indicate the student named and say: " È qui!"

F. Completion - Fill in the missing parts of the conversations below.

X: [Hi!] ...
Y: ...

X: Mi chiamo ... e ... ?
Y: Mi chiamo ...

X: [Y], dove ...?
Y: ... qui.
X: Ah, sei ... !

PRONUNCIATION

The pronunciation of Italian is very simple: only a few sounds require your attention. The vowels are pronounced as follows:

a - like the **a** in the musical notes "l**a**" or "f**a**"
e - like the **e** in "w**e**st" or the **e** in "sl**e**igh"
i - like the **i** in "mach**i**ne"
o - like the **o** in "f**o**ught" or the **o** in "R**o**me"
u - like the **u** in "cl**u**e"

PROVIAMOCI

A. Repeat the following words after your teacher.

ciao	Renzo	sei	dove	tu	blu
sono	lì	Roma	nipote	studente	zia
uno	chi	mi	lui	lei	professore

B. Repeat the following groups of letters after your teacher. Notice the effect of the letter "h".

co	[**co**coa]	**ca**	[**ca**r]	**cu**	[**coo**l]
ci	[a**chi**eve]	**ce**	[**che**st]		
chi	[**key**]	**che**	[**ca**pe]		

C. Now read the following words, then copy them and underline the sounds introduced above.

amico	ciao	calcio	scusi	cestino	casa
chiamo	caro	chiaro	perché	anche	cinque

HOW DO ITALIANS GREET PEOPLE?

Italians are very fond of their titles and use them all the time. Here is what a young person like you would say.

DAY TIME	**Buon giorno, signora!**	Good day, madame! (formal)
	Buon giorno, professore/ssa!	Good day, teacher! (formal)
	Buon giorno, dottore!	Good day, doctor! (formal)
	Ciao, Maria!	Hi, Mary! (familiar)
	Salve!	Hi!/ Hello!
	Buon giorno!	Good day/Hello! (universal)
EVENING	**Buona sera, dottore!**	Good evening, doctor! (formal)
	Buona sera, Maria!	Good evening, Mary!
	Ciao, Pietro!	Hi, Peter! (familiar)
	Buona sera, signora!	Good evening, madame!
	Buona sera!	Good evening!
LEAVING	**ArrivederLa, signora!**	Goodbye, madame!
	ArrivederLa, professore/ssa!	Goodbye, teacher!
	Arrivederci!	Goodbye! (familiar)
	Ciao, Maria!	'Bye, Mary! (familiar)
	A più tardi	See you later (when you "will" see someone later)
	A presto!	See you soon! (familiar)
	A domani!	See you tomorrow! (familiar)
	Ci vediamo!	See you later! (any time)
BED TIME	**Buona notte!**	Good night! (universal)

1. There is no equivalent to, "Good afternoon!" For an Italian, it is simply day as long as there is daylight.
2. The family name of the person greeted is not mentioned unless s/he is not aware of your presence and you want to call his/her attention.
3. "Ciao," is only used for family members and peers.

PROVIAMOCI

What would you say when ...?

A. ... you meet the following people in the morning:

1. your teacher in the hall
2. your family doctor
3. Mrs. Rossi, the school librarian
4. you friend, Giovanni
5. Mr. Tedeschi, the baker

B. ... you meet the same people in the evening

C. ... you are taking leave from:

1. professor Verdi after a conference
2. your family doctor
3. Mrs. Cecchini, a friend of your parents
4. your friend, Paola
5. Mr. Tedeschi after buying bread

THAT'S ITALIAN!

After Renzo has returned to the Romano yard with the ball, John hears, "*uno, due, tre, quattro, cinque, sei, sette, otto, nove, dieci...*" and wonders what is going on over the fence. He climbs up a tree to get a look and sees Renzo, a girl and a younger boy bouncing the soccer ball off their knees, feet and heads, without ever letting it touch the ground. John notices that Mrs. Romano keeps count of the successful hits by counting on her hands from thumb to little finger. How strange! That must be the way Italians count on their fingers!

I NUMERI DA UNO A DIECI

[NUMBERS FROM ONE TO TEN]

0 = **zero**

1 = **uno**	6 = **sei**
2 = **due**	7 = **sette**
3 = **tre**	8 = **otto**
4 = **quattro**	9 = **nove**
5 = **cinque**	10 = **dieci**

SOME MATHEMATICAL OPERATIONS

Quanto fa ...	How much is ...	**fa**	makes, equals
più	plus, more	**meno**	minus, less

An example of a simple mathematical question in Italian might be:

Quanto fa due più cinque? How much is two plus five?

To answer that question, one would say:

Due più cinque fa sette. Two plus five equals seven.

An example of a simple subtraction problem might be:

Quanto fa otto meno tre? How much is eight minus three?

The answer is expressed as:

Otto meno tre fa cinque. Eight minus three equals five.

PROVIAMOCI

A. Quanto fa? - In Italian ask a partner each of the following mathematical problems. Your partner should respond with the appropriate Italian solution.

a. 3 + 2 = b. 5 - 4 = c. 7 - 2 = d. 1 + 4 =

e. 10 - 6 =	f. 6 - 3 =	g. 8 + 1 =	h. 7 + 3 =
i. 6 + 1 =	j. 3 + 3 =	k. 9 - 6 =	l. 5 + 5 =

B. Express in writing the following numbers (use individual digits).

1. The number of the Italian classroom 2. Your telephone number 3. The number of faces on a cube 4. The number of players on a basketball team 5. The number of people in your immediate family

DO YOU RECOGNIZE THESE ITALIAN NAMES?

ragazzi [*boys*]		ragazze [*girls*]	
Adamo	Lorenzo	Andreina	Lorenza
Alfredo	Luca	Anna	Lucia
Alberto	Luigi	Barbara	Luciana
Andrea	Massimo	Carla	Luisa
Carlo	Matteo	Caterina	Margherita
Cristoforo	Marco	Chiara	Marina
Daniele	Michele	Cristina	Nicoletta
Davide	Nicola	Diana	Paola
Domenico	Paolo	Elena	Patrizia
Edoardo	Patrizio	Elisabetta	Piera
Enrico	Pietro	Enrica	Roberta
Francesco	Raimondo	Francesca	Rosa
Franco	Riccardo	Franca	Susanna
Giorgio	Roberto	Giorgia	Teresa
Gregorio	Stefano	Laura	Viviana

PERFORMANCE ACTIVITIES

E ORA, IN ITALIANO *[AND NOW, IN ITALIAN]*

In this section, you will see a situation similar to the one at the beginning of each chapter. Now the conversation is ALL in Italian. Can you guess what it means?

Dott. Gallo:	Buon giorno, Lucia.
Sig.ra Romano:	Oh, buon giorno.
Dott. G.:	Chi è questo [*this*] ragazzo?
Sig.ra R.	È Renzo.
Dott. G.:	Salve, Renzo, piacere!
Renzo:	Piacere.
Dott. G:	(*notices his watch*) Mamma mia!
	Sono le sei[*It is six o'clock*]! A presto, Lucia!
Sig.ra R:	Arrivederci, Armando!
Renzo:	ArrivederLa!

ASCOLTIAMO *[LET'S LISTEN]*

Listen as your teacher reads aloud a series of statements or questions. After hearing each one, choose the most appropriate answer from the choices offered below.

1. a. È Carlo
   b. Buon giorno, professore.
   c. Sono Anna Cassell.
2. a. Sono Marco.
   b. Sono qui.
   c. Buona sera
3. a. È lì.
   b. Sono qui.
   c. È buono.
4. a. cinque
   b. sei
   c. uno
5. a. due
   b. quattro
   c. tre
6. a. Buona notte.
   b. Buon giorno.
   c. Buona sera, ingegnere.

PARLIAMO *[LET'S TALK]*

A. Get acquainted with your classmates. Turn to the student next to you and introduce yourself with the expression:

Ciao, mi chiamo ... e tu chi sei?

The second student will then respond.

B. You see a new exchange student from Italy in the hallway at school. Say hello, introduce yourself and ask her name.

C. Now the bell rings and you and your new Italian friend are separated by the crowd of rushing students. What do you say to locate her? What does she answer?

SCRIVIAMO *[LET'S WRITE]*

Express in writing the following:

1. Say goodbye to your best friend.
2. Greet Mrs. DiCaprio at the supermarket (in the afternoon).
3. Say "hi" to Maria.
4. Greet your teacher in the morning.

ABOUT ITALY

A. FAMOUS ITALIANS

a. Jig-saw learning - Working in small groups, students will research and become experts on one of the following famous Italians. When ready, each member of the group will report to a different group.

1. Giovanni Boccaccio
2. Giovanni Cabot(o)
3. Camillo Cavour
4. Benvenuto Cellini
5. Donatello
6. Giuseppe Garibaldi
7. Lorenzo De Medici
8. Niccolò Machiavelli
9. Maria Montessori
10. Raffaello Sanzio
11. Amerigo Vespucci
12. Antonio Vivaldi

Giuseppe Garibaldi

Giuseppe Verdi

b. Matching: Can you identify the famous personalities below? Match each name to the appropriate accomplishment in the list that follows the names.

1. Guglielmo Marconi
2. Giuseppe Verdi
3. Dante Alighieri
4. Marco Polo
5. Enrico Fermi
6. Arturo Toscanini
7. Enrico Caruso
8. Galileo Galilei
9. Michelangelo Buonarroti
10. Leonardo Da Vinci

a. A Venetian merchant and explorer who traveled to China in 1260.

b. He wrote the poetic masterpiece, *The Divine Comedy*, which helped establish his native Tuscan dialect as the literary language of Italy.

c. An Italian Renaissance artist and scientist.

d. The supreme Renaissance artist. He created monumental works in painting, sculpture and architecture.

e. The foremost composer of Italian romantic opera.

f. A pioneer of modern astronomy. He invented the telescope.

g. The father of the wireless. He detected radio waves across the Atlantic in 1901.

h. He is considered one of the greatest operatic tenors of all time.

i. One of the finest and most admired musical conductors.

j. He conducted experiments in radioactivity, for which he received the Nobel Prize for physics in the year 1938.

Michelangelo Buonaroti's *Pietà* is one of the treasures of the Vatican. Can you name some other works by this great artist?

B. THE COUNTRY

The evening after his first meeting with Renzo, John looks up Italy in his mom's old college books. He finds that it is a boot-shaped peninsula in the middle of the Mediterranean Sea. He recognizes the names of many cities, countries, seas, even though some of their Italian names are somewhat different from English.

CITIES

Torino	Napoli
Genova	Bari
Milano	Potenza
Verona	Taranto
Vicenza	Cosenza
Venezia	Catanzaro
Trieste	Reggio Calabria
Bologna	Palermo
Pisa	Messina
Firenze	Catania
Ancona	Agrigento
Perugia	Siracusa
Pescara	Cagliari
Roma	

COUNTRIES

Francia
Svizzera
Austria
Slovenia
San Marino
Città del Vaticano

SEAS

Mar Ligure
Mar Tirreno
Mar Mediterraneo
Mare Ionio
Mare Adriatico

a. Answer the following questions.

1. Can you give the English names of the cities given on the map?
2. Do you know any other famous places in Italy?
3. What are some products that come from Italy?
4. Do you know which cities are associated with the following famous places?
   The Colosseum • The Leaning Tower • The Grand Canal • The "David"

b. Working in pairs, try to find as many answers as you can.

1. The capital of Italy is ...
2. Two large islands in Italy are ... and ...
3. The city of canals and gondole is called ...
4. A famous tower is still leaning in ...
5. The romance between Romeo and Juliet unfolded in ...
6. An active volcano near Naples is ...
7. The Italian city which was the cradle of the arts is ...
8. Columbus was born in ...
9. One of the most industrial cities in Italy is ...

c. Complete the following in Italian.

1. La Torre Pendente [*leaning*] è a ...
2. Il Vesuvio è a ...
3. Il Colosseo è a ...
4. Il Davide è a ...

d. Jig-saw learning: Working in small groups, students will research and become experts on one of the Italian cities found on the previous map. When ready, each member of the group will report to a different group.

Pisa, and its *Piazza dei Miracoli,* is one of the fascinating cities of Italy.

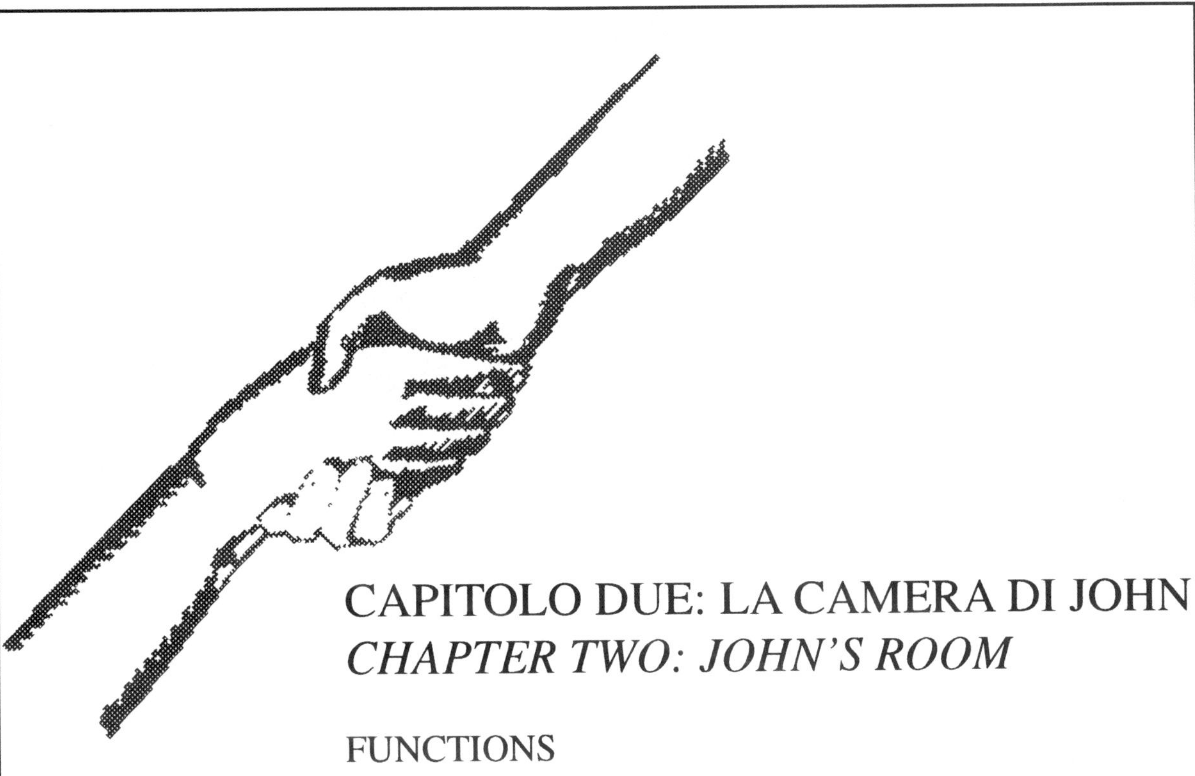

CAPITOLO DUE: LA CAMERA DI JOHN
CHAPTER TWO: JOHN'S ROOM

FUNCTIONS

Getting to know people and things

LANGUAGE

Pronunciation
Indefinite articles
Singular nouns
In a teenager's room
In the classroom
Questo, questa
Che cos'è?

ABOUT ITALY

Made in Italy

SITUATION

It is a lazy summer day at the Wright home. The doorbell rings and John answers. When he opens the door he is greeted by Mrs. Romano and Renzo.

MRS. R: Hi, John!
RENZO: **Salve**, John!
JOHN: Buon giorno!
MRS. R.: **Benissimo**! [*Very well*] John, you're speaking Italian already!

(*Mrs. Wright enters the room.*)

MRS. W.: Ciao, Lucia! Questo è Renzo? Buon giorno, Renzo. Io sono **la mamma di** [*the mother of*] John.
RENZO: **Piacere, signora.** [*Pleased to meet you, Ma'am*]
JOHN: Mom, I didn't know you spoke Italian!
MRS. W.: I studied it in college for my degree. Lucia, let's have some coffee. John, you still have to clean your room.

(*When the boys enter the room, John begins to pick up things. As he does so, he says the name of each item in English. Renzo tells him the word in Italian.*)

JOHN: This is a book.
RENZO: This is a book. Questo è un libro.
JOHN: Questo è un libro. This is a photograph.
RENZO: This is a photograph. Questa è una fotografia.
JOHN: Questa è una fotografia. This is a baseball glove.
RENZO: A baseball glove. Un guanto da baseball.

JOHN: You're kidding! Un guanto da "baseball"?
RENZO: (*laughing*) Sì, **bravo**! [*good/clever*]

(*The boys continue this game including the items listed below.*)

un'aranciata	an orange soda	**un poster**	a poster
un armadio	a closet/wardrobe	**una rivista**	a magazine
un calendario	a calendar	**una scrivania**	a desk
un calcolatore	a calculator	**una sedia**	a chair
un computer	a computer	**uno specchio**	a mirror
un comò	a dresser	**uno stereo**	a stereo
una finestra	a window	**una sveglia**	an alarm clock
una lampada	a lamp	**un tappeto**	a rug
un letto	a bed	**un telefonino**	a cellular phone
un modellino	a model	**un videogioco**	a video game
una porta	a door	**uno zaino**	a backpack

(*At a certain point, the boys begin to quiz each other to test their memories.*)

JOHN: OK, Renzo, what's this?
RENZO: This is a bed. **Sono bravo, eh?** [*I am good, right?*] **Cos'è questa?** [*What is this?*] (*indicates a chair*)
JOHN: Huh? Oh, questa è una sveglia.
RENZO: No, non è una sveglia; è una sedia. **Ripeti, per favore.** [*Repeat, please.*]
JOHN: Sedia.
RENZO: **Perfetto. C'è** [*there is*] una finestra?
JOHN: (*points to the window*) Sì, questa è una finestra!

PAROLE DA RICORDARE

NOUNS

il libro	the book
la mamma	the mother
la signora	the lady, ma'am

USEFUL EXPRESSIONS

Benissimo!	Very well!
Bravo!	Good!/ Well done!
C'è	There is
Cos'è?	What is it?
Per favore	Please
Piacere!	Pleased to meet you

ADJECTIVES		VERBS		PRONOUNS	
perfetto	perfect	**ripeti**	repeat	**questo**	this (masc.)
				questa	this (fem.)

PROVIAMOCI

A. Picture recall: Students will prepare a series of flash cards by drawing pictures of items found in John's room. Working in pairs, students will drill partners in identifying the illustrated items.

B. What would you say? Choose an appropriate response from the new vocabulary expressions.

1. A performer has just done an outstanding job.
2. You are looking at an unfamiliar object.
3. You need someone to do something for you.
4. You have just met somebody.
5. Your Italian friend offers to take you to a rock concert.

C. What is missing?

a. Provide the missing letters in the following expressions.

1. Pia_ere!
2. una s_dia
3. un gu_nto da baseball
4. un'aran_iata
5. una sve_lia
6. un lib_o.
7. Perfet_o!
8. un com_
9. uno z_ino
10. una scrivan_a

b. Provide the missing word.

1. un guanto... baseball
2. Buon ...!
3. ... favore.
4. ... è una fotografia.
5. La signora Wright è la ... di John.

D. What can it be? Give the appropriate response in Italian.

1. You use it to listen to tapes and CD's.

2. You sit on it.
3. You sleep on it.
4. You would like one for the wall of your room.
5. You switch it on when it's dark.
6. You look at yourself in it.
7. It wakes you up in the morning.
8. You open it when it's warm outside.
9. You carry your books to school in it.
10. You store your clothes in it.
11. You'd rather step on this than a cold floor in the morning.
12. You use it to check your math.
13. You use it to communicate when not at home.
14. You need a computer to play with it.
15. You open it when you hear the bell ring.
16. You drink it.

E. Make a list of the things in your room (In Italian, of course!) and compare it with a classmate's.

PRONUNCIATION

go (**go**pher)	**ga** (ci**gar**)	**gu** (la**goon**)
gi (**Gi**na)	**ge** (**ge**m)	
ghi (**gea**r)	**ghe** (**ge**t)	
gn (lasa**gn**a)		

PROVIAMOCI

Repeat the following words after your teacher.

signora	mangiare	ragù	righe	lavagna
gente	paghi	gatto	lago	leghe
gusto	pagina	gesso	Gino	gentile

PROVERBI

Nella guerra d'amor, vince chi fugge.
Impara piangendo, riderai guadagnando.
Denari di gioco van come fuoco

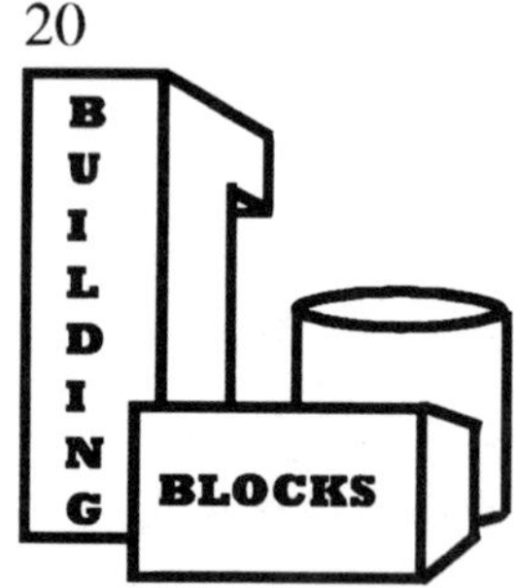

Indefinite articles and singular nouns

Did you notice that the words **a** and **an** in English can be **un, uno, una** or **un'** in Italian? The reason for so many choices is that indefinite articles reflect the gender of the noun they refer to. In Italian some nouns are masculine, others are feminine. Most masculine nouns are easy to spot because they end in **o**. Most feminine nouns end in **a**. A few nouns end in **e**. At the moment you may not be able to determine their gender but the accompanying article will help tell you. Let's try.

un	before masculine nouns beginning with a consonant or a vowel	un letto un poster un esame [*an exam*] un amico [*a friend*]
uno	before masculine nouns beginning with **z** or **s** followed by a consonant	uno stereo uno specchio uno zaino
una	before feminine nouns beginning with a consonant	una sedia una finestra una studentessa
un'	before feminine nouns beginning with a vowel	un'amica un'opera un'automobile

Generally, words borrowed from other languages ending in a consonant are masculine: un bar, uno sport, un film, un poster, un computer, un week-end etc..

Un weekend da non perdere!

Il leader del nuovo millennio!

L'Italia in blue jeans!

Lo shock dell'anno!

PROVIAMOCI

A. What would you use? Working independently, determine which article (**un, uno, una** or **un'**) each noun requires. Then compare your decisions with a partner and discuss your choice.

1.  ... modellino	8.  ... lampada
2.  ... poster	9.  ... zaino
3.  ... armadio	10.  ... porta
4.  ... specchio	11. 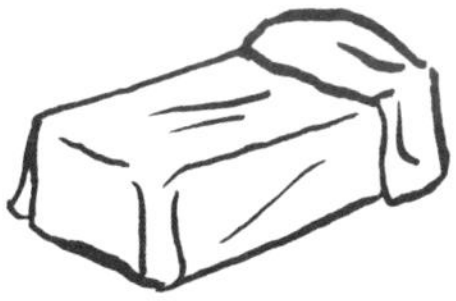 ... letto
5.  ... stereo	12.  ... finestra
6.  ... sedia	13.  ... computer
7.  ... scrivania	14.  ... comò

B. Identify the Items in the bedroom shown here

C. With a partner draw and label in Italian a picture of an ideal teenager's bedroom.

CLASSROOM VOCABULARY

Here is a list of things in a classroom that will help you to accomplish the following activities.

un banco	student desk	**una lavagna**	a blackboard
una bandiera	a flag	**una lavagna luminosa**	an overhead projector
un cancellino	an eraser	**un libro**	a book
una carta geografica	a map	**una matita**	a pencil
una cattedra	a teacher's desk	**un orologio**	a clock
un cestino	a waste basket	**una penna**	a pen
una finestra	a window	**un quaderno**	a notebook
un foglio di carta	a sheet of paper	**una riga**	a ruler
un gesso	a (piece of) chalk	**un voto**	a grade

A. Write the names of classroom items on individual 3x5 cards. Shuffle the cards and place them face down on a desk. Take turns with classmates drawing cards and placing each next to the appropriate item in the classroom.

B. ***Che cos'è?*** - With a partner play the game that Renzo and John play in the dialog using items around the classroom.

C. Draw a floor plan of the classroom and label the various items in Italian. Do a similar floor plan of your own room at home.

D. Using photographs of bedrooms and classrooms play the "Che cos'è?" game with a partner.

PERFORMANCE ACTIVITIES

E ORA, IN ITALIANO

Mrs. Romano is talking to Robertino, Renzo's little brother, as he plays with his toys.

Sig.ra R.: Robertino, che cos'è questo?
Robertino: È il modellino di una nave spaziale [space ship] di *Guerre stellari* [*Star Wars*].
Sig.ra R.: Ah, sì è un film di George Lucas.
Robertino: Questa è una rivista di cinema.
Sig.ra R.: E questo è Harrison Ford un attore di *Guerre stellari.*
Robertino: Questo è un CD di musica del film.
Sig.ra R.: Bene! C'è uno stereo in camera. Ascoltiamo questo CD

ASCOLTIAMO

Listen as your teacher reads aloud a series of statements or questions. After hearing each one, choose the most appropriate answer from those offered below.

1. a. Benissimo. b. Buongiorno, signora. c. Piacere, signora.
2. a. Piacere, signora. b. Mi chiamo Renzo. c. Sono qui.
3. a. Ciao! b. Sono John. c. Mi chiamo Renzo.
4. a. Perfetto! b. Sono bravo! c. È un guanto da baseball.
5. a. Una fotografia b. A domani! c. Una finestra.
6. a. A presto! b. Salve! c. È lì.
7. a. Per favore. b. A domani! c. Buona notte.
8. a. Buon giorno! b. Chi sei? c. Ci vediamo!

PARLIAMO

A. Working with a partner, complete the exchanges of the following conversation and then say the lines aloud as each of you takes one of the roles.

Paolo: Ciao!
Anna; _______
Paolo: Come ti _________?
Anna: Mi chiamo Anna, e tu chi _______?
Paolo: Sono_______.

B. With your partner, figure out what questions or statements resulted in the following responses.

1. ___?	Sono qui.
2. ___?	Mi chiamo Enzo.
3. ___?	È lì.
4. ___!	Buona sera.
5. ___!	Buon giorno, John.
6. ___!	Arrivederla, signora!

C. Role playing: Using the following situations as points of departure, try to carry out a conversation in Italian with a partner for at least four exchanges.

Your Italian friend pays a visit. You show him/her your room. Take turns asking and answering what things are called in your respective languages.

Your Italian teacher is testing you to see if you can identify different things in the classroom.

SCRIVIAMO

A. Unscramble the sentences below, write them out and translate.

1. Renzo io sono
2. un questo libro è
3. favore per ripeti
4. finestra c'è una
5. John chiamo mi

B. Numbers

a. Answer the following questions in complete Italian sentences.

1. Quanto fa otto meno tre?
2. Quanto fa nove più uno?
3. Quanto fa sette meno tre?
4. Quanto fa due piu sei?

b. Write out the following statements in Italian supplying the missing number.

1. Cinque più ___ fa nove.
2. Sette meno ___ fa quattro.
3. Nove meno uno fa ___.
4. Due più sei fa ___.
5. ___ meno tre fa sette.

ABOUT ITALY

Made in Italy

Renzo likes to pick up objects and say in English what they are. In a shoe box he finds John's collection of **automobiline** [*toy cars*], many of which are replicas of Italian-made vehicles. He enjoys teaching John the exact pronunciation of each: una **Ferrari**, una **Lancia**, una **Lamborghini**, un'**Alfa Romeo**, una **Maserati**, una **Fiat** and a truck by **Iveco**.

Then the boys decide to explore the house in search of Italian products. In the kitchen they find olive oil, aromatic vinegar, canned tomatoes, spaghetti and so on. But that is easy! They try the bathroom. Yes, look! There are Italian ceramic tiles on the floor, and, on the window, lace curtains that Mrs. Wright bought in **Abruzzi** (a region of Italy) many years ago.

What about the living room? There is a flower vase of lead crystal, and a Florentine (from the city of Florence) tray. Mr. Wright's favorite lounge chair is upholstered in soft Italian leather.

In Mrs. Wright's bedroom they find a pair of **Ferragamo** shoes and a **Fendi** silk scarf, but don't expect to find much in Mr. Wright's study. Suddenly, Renzo spots an **Aurora** pen and a new pair of reading glasses with frames by **Luxottica**. In the meantime John looks at the computer and remembers that the tellers at his family's bank use computer terminals made by **Olivetti**. As they end their hunt for Italian products, the boys discover an old **Benetton** sweater half hidden under John's bed.

Renzo knows that in his house in Rome John would find many American things: his Timberlands, his Levi's, his father's set of Parker pens, his mother's beauty products, his sister's CD collection, his little brother's Disney videos (dubbed in Italian), a Texas Instruments calculator, a Stetson cowboy hat he could not resist buying and (who knows?) if he wins **la lotteria**, John will find a Harley Davidson in the garage.

A few questions for you

A. What do we know? Can you name any Italian-made items from your home?

B. Can you put the following Italian brand names, products and terms in the appropriate categories?

Music	**Food**	**Clothing**	**Automobiles**

Fila, opera, Ferrari, ricotta, Benetton, soprano, aria, Gucci, Alfa Romeo, cappuccino, Maserati, pasta, Versace, radicchio, viola, Lamborghini, stanza, Armani, crescendo, zucchine, Ferragamo, mozzarella, concerto, Krizia,

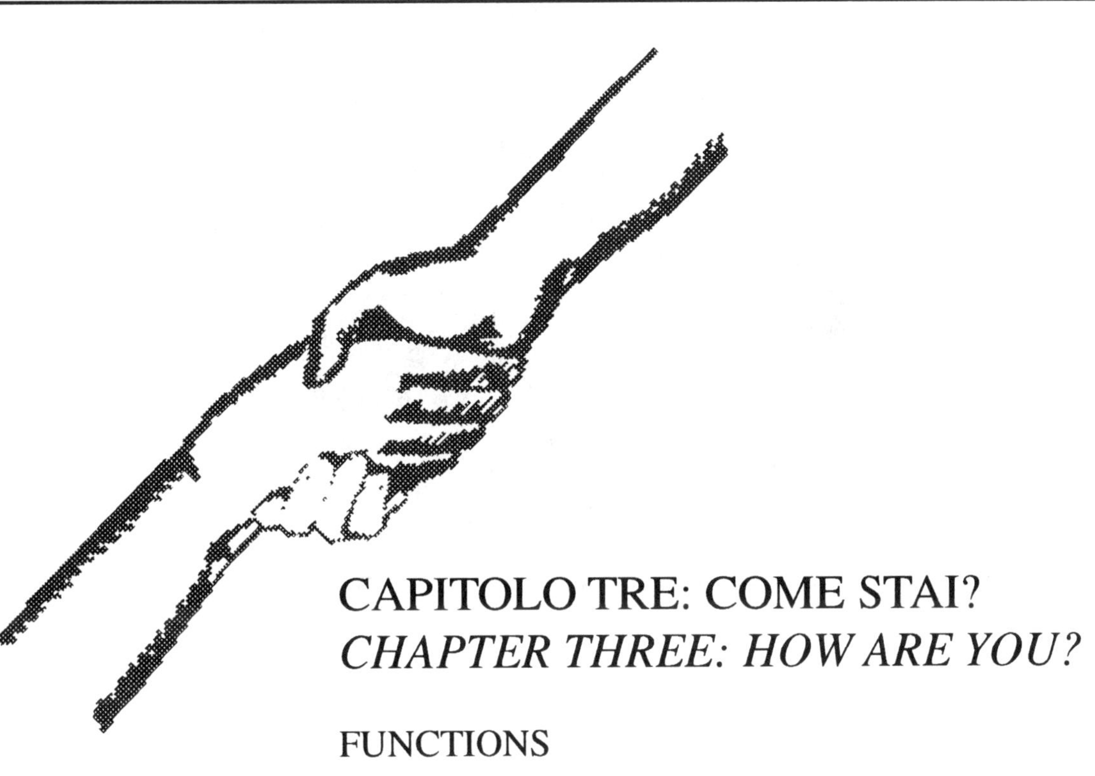

CAPITOLO TRE: COME STAI?
CHAPTER THREE: HOW ARE YOU?

FUNCTIONS

Formal greetings and titles
Expressing physical states

LANGUAGE

Subject pronouns
Avere and idioms
Negative statements

ABOUT ITALY

Origin of titles

SITUATION

John thinks that since Renzo is so good with a soccer ball, he would be terrific in a "Hacky sac" showdown. He plans to invite him to play in a match against Jeff Golden. John is greeted at the door of the Romanos by Mrs. Romano.

MRS. R:	Ciao, John! **Benvenuto**.
JOHN:	Buon giorno, signora!
MRS. R.:	Bravo! You are speaking Italian. (*She calls Renzo.*) Renzo, dove sei?
RENZO:	(*Shouts from the top of the stairs*) Sono qui, zia. Oh, ciao, John. Come va?
JOHN:	Mi chiamo John! (*Mrs. R. and Renzo laugh*)
MRS. W.:	No, John, Renzo didn't ask your name. He said, "How is it going?"
JOHN:	Oh (*laughs*), but I don't know how to answer that yet.
MRS. R.:	Well, you could say, **bene**, which means "well," **molto bene**, which means "very well," then there is **non c'è male**, which means "not bad." Oh yes, there is also **così, così**, which means "so-so." Remember to say **grazie**, which means "thanks," in order to be polite.
JOHN:	Molto bene, grazie. E tu?
MRS. R.:	Non c'è male grazie. Come sei bravo!
JOHN:	(*To Mrs.R.*) Buon giorno, signora. Come va?
MRS. R.:	Bene grazie. But listen, when speaking to adults you should say, "**Come sta?**" It is more formal. Remember that, **"Come va?"** and especially, **"Ciao!"** are only for family, friends and peers.
JOHN:	(*Practicing*) Come sta?
MRS. R.:	(*Pretending to answer a stranger*) Molto bene, grazie. E **Lei**?
JOHN:	Lei?
MRS. R.:	Lei is the formal way of saying "tu."
JOHN:	OK.

MRS. R.: At this point, instead of "OK" you can say: ***Va bene!***
JOHN: Va bene.

PAROLE DA RICORDARE

NOUNS

la signora	Mrs., lady

PRONOUNS

Lei	you (polite)

ADJECTIVES

benvenuto	welcome
bravo	good/ well done!

USEFUL EXPRESSIONS

Come sta?	How are you? (polite)
Come stai?	How are you? (familiar)
Come va?	How is it going?
Così, così	So-so
Grazie	Thank you
Non c'è male.	Not bad.
Va bene.	All right, OK

ADVERBS

bene	well
molto	very

Come stai?/Come sta? is a real question which indicates genuine interest in the well being of a person. It is essentially used when people have not seen each other for a while.

PROVIAMOCI

A. How do you say it in Italian?

a. A friend is visiting you.

1. Say "hello" and "welcome."
2. Ask him/her how it is going.
3. Now your friend asks you. Answer saying that "it is not bad" and thank him/her.
4. Your friend has won a school prize. Say, "How good you are!"
5. Your friend's mother comes to visit your mother. Greet her and ask her how she is.

b. You and your friend meet at the park. Provide the suggested exchanges in Italian.

You: (Greet your friend)
S/He: (Greets you)

You: (Ask how s/he is)
S/He: (Says s/he is not doing so well and asks about you)
You: (Say that you are very well, thank you)
S/He: (Says "fine" and "good bye")
You: (Reply, "See you soon!")

B. Role Playing - Working in pairs, act out the encounter in the above exercise with your friend, then switch roles.

GREETINGS WITH TITLES

As you learned in Chapter 1, the use of titles is much more common in Italian than in English. For instance: anyone holding a university degree expects to be addressed with the title of dottore/dottoressa by those who are not close friends.

Buon giorno, signora	Come sta, dottore?
Buon giorno, professore.	Benissimo, grazie, avvocato. E Lei?

The simplest way is to say only: **buon giorno, buona sera, arrivederLa**. Remember that the family name is generally not used.

SOME FORMS OF ADDRESS:

signore	Mr./Sir	**direttore/direttrice**	Director
signora	Mrs./Madame	**ragioniere**	Accountant
signorina	Miss	**avvocato**	Lawyer/Attorney
dottore/ dottoressa	Doctor	**ingegnere**	Engineer
		architetto	Architect
professore/ professoressa	Professor	**onorevole**	Honorable

PROVIAMOCI

A. Formal greetings - What would Italians say in these situations?

1. Dr. Biondi greets Mrs. Rossi, a professor of history, in the evening.
2. Dr. Foschi greets Mrs. Argenti, who lives next door, in the afternoon.

3. Mrs. Argenti greets Mrs. Rossi, her son's teacher, in the morning.
4. Professor Lucini says good bye to his lawyer.
5. Two ladies, who live in the same apartment building, meet in the elevator.
6. Dottor Marci meets professor Bondi on the elevator in the evening.

B. Group activities

a. On 3x5 cards, students make signs stating different Italian titles. The cards are then distributed at random. Students greet each other, assuming the identity of their particular sign.

b. Create teacher/student exchanges using the following as a model.

Teacher:	C'è un [title]__qui?
Student:	Ecco [*here is*] un [title]__. - Or - Io sono [title]__.

C. Role playing

a. Role play a formal meeting of two adults. Carry the conversation as far as you can go with what you have learned.

b. Repeat the exercise above, but make the characters two young people.

c. Now try the exchange with one character as an adult and the other as a young person.

The verb AVERE *[to have]*

The verb **avere**, which means "to have," is very important. Here it is in all its forms in the present tense.

io	**ho**	I have	noi	**abbiamo**	we have
tu	**hai**	you have	voi	**avete**	you (plural) have
lui/lei	**ha**	he/she has	loro	**hanno**	they have
Lei	**ha**	you have (polite, sing.)	Loro	**hanno**	you (polite, plural)

The subject pronoun is not always required in Italian; the form of the verb indicates who or what the subject is.

Ex.: Hai un foglio di carta? Do you have a sheet of paper?

PROVIAMOCI

A. Restate the sentence with each new subject, making necessary changes in the verb.

Ex.: Rocco ha uno stereo. - Io - Io **ho** uno stereo.

1. lui
2. tu
3. lei
4. noi
5. loro
6. voi
7. io e lui
8. tu e lei
9. Maria e Giovanna

B. Restate the sentence with each new form of the verb, using an appropriate subject pronoun.

Ex.: Luisa ha uno zaino. - ho - **Io** ho uno zaino.

1. avete
2. ha
3. hai
4. hanno
5. abbiamo
6. ho

C. Show and tell - Create sentences based on the drawings below suggesting what each person has for "show and tell".

Ex.:

Io

Io **ho** un libro.

Tu

Io e Alfredo

Lui

Loro

Voi

Chi

Tu e Renzo

John

Idioms with "AVERE"

Avere is used in many common expressions such as:

avere caldo	to feel warm	**avere freddo**	to feel cold
avere fame	to be hungry	**avere sete**	to be thirsty
avere ragione	to be right	**avere torto**	to be wrong
avere paura	to be afraid	**avere voglia di**	to feel like (doing/having something)
avere sonno	to be sleepy		
avere bisogno di	to need	**avere pazienza**	to be patient
avere...anni	to be...years old	**avere fretta**	to be in a hurry

PROVIAMOCI

A. Who are we talking about? - Complete each of the following with the appropriate subject pronoun.

1. ___ ho pazienza, ma [*but*]___hai fretta.
2. ___ ha paura.
3. ___ abbiamo ragione e ___ hanno torto.
4. Avete freddo ___?
5. ___ hai caldo?

B. Can we spell? Provide the missing letters in the incomplete words.

1. Luisa ha ca_do.
2. Ho _isogno di mangiare [*to eat*].
3. Enrica ha sempre _agione.
4. Loro hanno _aura di volare [*to fly*].
5. La mamma ha paz_enza.

C. How do we express the following in Italian?

1. Say that you are nine years old.
2. Ask your friend Judy if she is thirsty.
3. Ask Jane and Paula if they are in a hurry.
4. Ask your rich friend, Ugo, if he needs an accountant.
5. Say that you feel warm but Carla feels cold.
6. Ask Giorgio if he is hungry.
7. State that we are right and they are wrong.
8. Say that you are afraid.
9. Ask Cristina and Diana if they feel like going to the movies [*andare al cinema*].
10. Say that your little brother, Pierino, is sleepy.
11. Say that your aunt needs an attorney.
12. Say that they are patient.

CHE COSA HAI?
[*What is wrong with you?*]

Ho mal di testa.
[*I have a headache.*]

Ho mal di denti.
[*I have a toothache.*]

Ho mal di schiena.
[*I have a backache.*]

Ho mal di stomaco.
[*I have a stomachache.*]

Ho mal di gola.
[*I have a sore throat.*]

Ho mal di piedi.
[*My feet hurt.*]

Ho fame.
[*I'm hungry.*]

Ho sete.
[*I'm thirsty.*]

Ho caldo.
[*I feel warm.*]

Ho freddo.
[*I feel cold.*]

You may notice that someone who is not feeling well and you want to be able to ask questions like:

Come stai? [*How are you?*]

You may get an answer like :

Male [*I feel badly.*] or **Non sto bene**. [*I'm not well.*]

You could respond with something like:

Che cosa hai? [*What is wrong with you?*]

or

Hai mal di testa? [*Do you have a headache?*]

Questions and negative statements

A. ***Do*** and ***does*** are NOT required to form questions in Italian.
Ex.: Giovanna e Paola hanno freddo?
Do Giovanna and Paola feel cold?

B. In Italian, a negative statement is expressed by placing the word ***non*** before the verb.
Ex.: No, **non** hanno freddo, hanno caldo.
No, they don't feel cold, they feel warm.

PROVIAMOCI

A. **Che cosa hanno?** - Using the drawings and the subjects as a guide, tell how the characters feel.

You

Michele

We

They

I

B. What a pain! - Working in groups of two or more, create exchanges using idioms with **avere**.

Exs.: Come stai?
Male!
Che cosa hai?
Ho mal di testa. E tu?
Io sto bene ma ho fame.

or

Che cosa hai? Hai mal di stomaco?
No, non ho mal di stomaco. Ho fame.

C. What is the problem of the day? - You have an acquaintance who thinks he can diagnose a person's ailments, troubles, character or life history, just by looking at him or her across a room. He is always wrong! When your friend makes a statement, correct him by telling what is really wrong.

Ex.: He: Carlo ha mal di denti. (head)
You: Carlo non ha mal di denti, ha mal di testa!

1. Renzo ha mal di testa. (throat)
2. Claudia ha mal di schiena. (feet)
3. Maria ha caldo. (cold)
4. Tu hai mal di piedi. (stomach)
5. Voi avete fame. (thirsty)
6. Noi abbiamo ragione. (torto)
7. Loro hanno pazienza. (fretta)
8. Tu e Luca avete sette anni. (otto)
9. Ho bisogno di un gelato (voglia)

PERFORMANCE ACTIVITIES

E ORA IN ITALIANO

Mrs. Romano stops into a neighborhood diner for coffee after her vacation. She greets the owner who is originally from Naples.

Sig.ra R.:	Buon giorno signor Posillipo. Come sta?
Sig. P.:	Non c'è male, e Lei?
Sig.ra R.:	Benissimo, grazie. E la signora dov'è?
Sig. P.:	È a casa. Non sta bene.

Sig.ra R.:	Mi dispiace [*I'm sorry*]. Che cosa ha?
Sig. P.:	Ha mal di gola e mal di testa e un brutto raffreddore[*bad cold*].
Sig.ra R.:	Forse [*maybe*] ha l'influenza?
Sig. P.:	È possibile. Ha caldo, ha freddo, sta male...
Sig.ra R.:	Ha bisogno del dottore.
Sig. P.:	Ha ragione, signora. Desidera? [*How can I help you?*]
Sig.ra R.:	Un cappuccino, per favore.
Sig. P.:	(a few moments later) Ecco, il cappuccino, signora.
Sig.ra R.:	Grazie.
Sig. P.:	Prego. [*You are welcome.*]

ASCOLTIAMO

Listen as your teacher reads aloud a series of statements or questions. After hearing each one, choose the most appropriate answer from the choices offered below.

1. a. Grazie. E tu? b. Benissimo, grazie. c. Va bene, grazie.
2. a. Buon giorno, signora. b. Grazie, signorina. c. Molto bene, grazie.
3. a. Ho pazienza. b. Ho mal di gola. c. Ho dieci anni.
4. a. No, ho sete. b. Sì, ho sete. c. Sì, ho freddo.
5. a. Sì, ho sonno. b. No, ho mal di testa. c. Sì ho fretta.

PARLIAMO

Have some fun! - Try the following situations as an oral translation exercise, or you can work on them with a partner and develop complete conversations. Don't be shy!

1. Massimo is taking an aspirin. What do you ask him? What does he answer?

2. Alberto is not participating in the football game. Ask your friend what is wrong with him. What does your friend answer?

3. You are not participating in class. Your teacher asks you what is wrong. What does the teacher say?. What do you answer?

4. As you are leaving school, you see your Italian teacher. How do you say good bye to him/her? And to your friend?

5. Miss Carli was sick yesterday. Greet her in the morning and ask how she feels.

6. State that you are right and Lucille is wrong.

7. Explain that Paul and Mary are not nine years old, they are ten years old.

8. State that you are not well. What does your friend ask you? What do you answer?

SCRIVIAMO

1. Write a short note to your friend. Say hello. Ask how s/he is. Tell how you feel. Write good bye and sign your name.

2. Carlo doesn't feel well. He has a sore throat and feels warm. He needs a doctor. Write a note to his girlfriend to inform her.

3. Your teacher has just dealt with a difficult student and has "kept his/her cool." What would you write to your pal across the isle from your desk?

ABOUT ITALY

The Origin of Titles

Renzo knows that Mr. Wright is a college teacher and asks Mrs. Romano about his father's profession. As John explains the American higher education system, Renzo is intrigued and a little envious of the idea of going away to college. He expects to go to the "liceo" and then to the University of Rome. Like most Italian students, he will continue to live with his parents.

Mrs. Romano tells John that Italian universities are more like graduate schools where one studies only the subjects related to the chosen field of studies. If you are a student in the *Facoltà di Medicina*, you do not study literature any more; if you are in the *Facoltà di Lettere e Filosofia*, no more math and sciences are required.

Italian and European universities started in the Middle Ages; some some of the oldest are those of *Bologna* (1158), *Padova* (1222) and *Napoli* (1224). Only men attended the university; that is why all titles are originally masculine, like *dottore, architetto* or *ingegnere*. Even wealthy women were supposed to stay home, do embroidering and play the harp. Now in

Italy there are many universities and they are attended by men and women. Equal professional opportunities are open to both sexes. There are also universities for foreigners like the famous one in *Perugia*.

Facoltà = (university) school, *filosofia* = philosophy,
lettere = arts and humanities, *liceo* =one of the Italian secondary schools

CULTURAL QUIZ BOWL

Quiz each other using questions like those below and others that you make up. Remember key question words such as: who, where, how, why, how many...

1. Which is the oldest university in Italy?
2. Who first attended Italian Universities?
3. Where could an American go to study the Italian language?

ASSISTENZA TURISTICA IN FRANCESE E INGLESE

Maria Claudia Vico

Corso Vanucci 80
06100 Perugia
Tel:075/36150

STUDIO MEDICO DENTISTICO

Dott. Fabio Foschi

Via S. Martino 75 Roma
Tel.(06) 647 1324

Dott. Prof. Arch. Luigi Nigro

Viale Carso 71 Roma
Tel. (06) 379 1588

CAPITOLO QUATTRO: LA FAMIGLIA
CHAPTER FOUR: THE FAMILY

FUNCTIONS

Identifying family
Family relationships

LANGUAGE

Definite articles (sing.)
Possessive adjectives (sing.)
Possessions with *di*
Singular, plural and invariable nouns
C'è, ci sono
Chiamarsi (1st, 2nd, 3rd persons)
Numbers to 50

ABOUT ITALY

The Italian Family

SITUATION

As John, Renzo and Mrs. Romano talk in the entrance hall, a great commotion from above descends the stairs in the form of an eight-year old boy being chased by a seventeen-year-old girl.

RENZO:	Ah, **ecco mio fratello** Robertino e **mia sorella** Laura.
JOHN:	Fratello...sorella. (*He points to Mrs. Romano.*) Sorella!
MRS. R.:	(*laughs*) Grazie, sei molto gentile John, ma io qui sono **la zia**. Come into the dining room and I'll explain.

In the dining room, Mrs. Romano takes a piece of paper and draws Renzo's family tree. As she does so, she explains the appropriate kinship term for each person as he or she relates to Renzo.

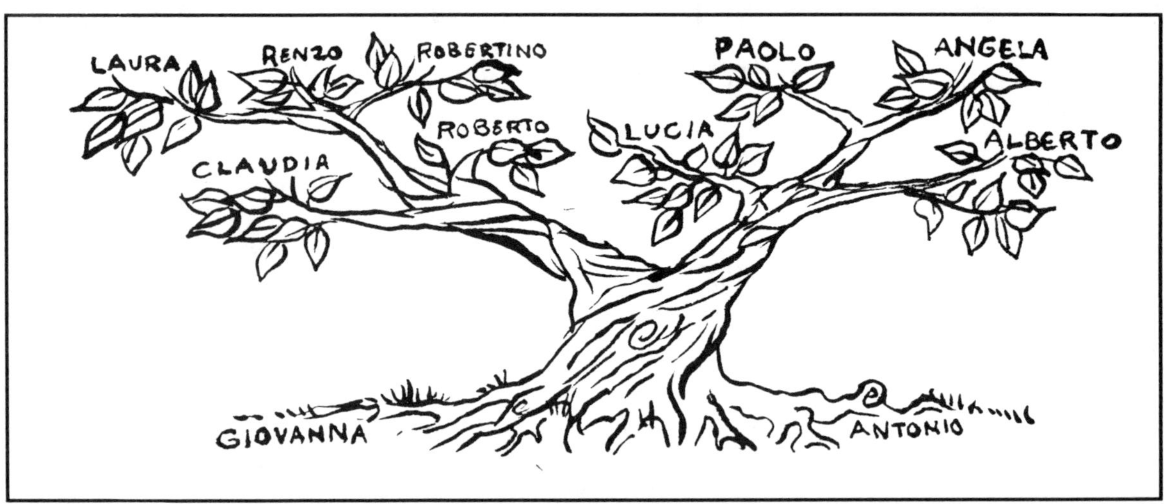

RENZO:	Sì, sì! Ecco la mia **famiglia**. Giovanna è mia **nonna** e **suo marito**, Antonio, è mio **nonno**. Mia nonna e mio nonno si chiamano Giovanna e Antonio Silvestri.
MRS. R:	Sì, e Claudia è **tua madre** e mio fratello Roberto, è **tuo padre**.
RENZO:	(*to John*) Tu hai fratelli?
JOHN:	Sì, I have...
MRS. R.:	Ho.
JOHN:	Just "Ho?"
MRS. R.:	Sì, "ho" va bene.
JOHN:	Ho un fratello e una sorella.

John draws his family tree for the others gathered around the table.
Capitolo quattro: La famiglia

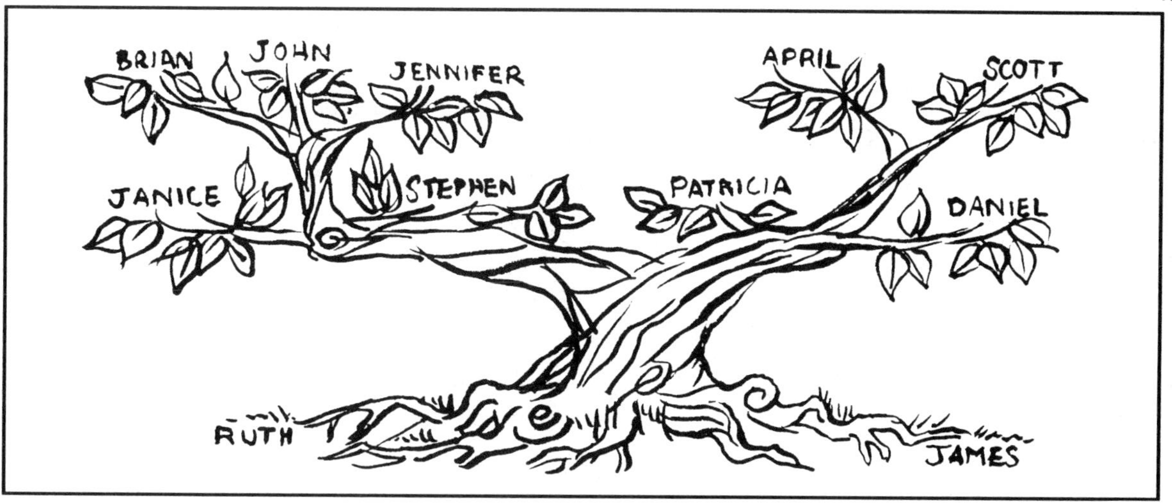

Renzo gets help to pronounce the names and English kinship terms, then the boys quiz each other.

RENZO: Come si chiama mia sorella?
JOHN: Tua sorella si chiama Laura. Who is Brian?
RENZO: Brian è tuo fratello. Oh, **scusa**. Brian is your brother.

Letizia e Claudio DeAngelis
con la piccola Paola

PARTECIPANO LA NASCITA
di
CARLO MARIA

Reggio Calabria, 17 maggio 1999

[announce the birth of]

PAROLE DA RICORDARE

VERBS

è	is
scusa	excuse me (familiar)
scusi	excuse me (polite)

ADJECTIVES

mio(m.)/**mia**(f.)	my
tuo(m.)/**tua**(f.)	your
suo(m.)/**sua**(f)	his,her

NOUNS

la famiglia	the family
i genitori	the parents
la madre	the mother
la mamma	the mother
il padre	the father
il papà	the father
il marito	the husband
la moglie	the wife
la figlia	the daughter
il figlio	the son
la sorella	the sister
il fratello	the brother
i parenti	the relatives
i nonni	the grandparents
la nonna	the grandmother
il nonno	the grandfather
la/il nipote	the grandchild (fem./masc)
la zia	the aunt
lo zio	the uncle
la cugina	the cousin (fem.)
il cugino	the cousin (masc)
la/il nipote	the niece/nephew

USEFUL EXPRESSIONS

c'è	there is
ci sono	there are
Chi è?	Who is?
ecco	here is, here are
mi chiamo...	My name is...
ti chiami...	Your name is...
sì	yes
si chiama...	His/her name is...
si chiamano...	Their names are...
ma	but
e	and
gentile	kind
con	with

OTHER USEFUL KINSHIP TERMS

la matrigna	the stepmother
il patrigno	the stepfather
la sorellastra	the stepsister/half-sister
il fratellastro	the stepbrother/half-brother
la suocera	the mother-in-law
il suocero	the father-in-law
la nuora	the daughter-in-law
il genero	the son-in-law

"È" vs, "E"

Though they may sound alike, "**è**" does NOT mean the same thing as "**e**". "**È**" means "is". "**E**" means "and". You can keep them straight in your mind if you remember that "is" has a dot flying over it like the accent in "**è**". "**E**" and "and" stand alone.

Possessive adjectives (singular)

Possessive adjectives agree in gender and in number with the **object** of possession, **not** with the possessor.

Renzo says: Laura è **mia** sorell**a**.
Laura says: Renzo è **mio** fratell**o**.
John says: Sì, Renzo è **suo** fratell**o**.

Here are a few possessive forms that you will need for the moment:

	masculine	feminine
my	**mio**	**mia**
your	**tuo**	**tua**
his/her	**suo**	**sua**

PROVIAMOCI

A. Let's talk about John and his family.

Ex.: Chi è James? È **suo** nonno.

1. Chi è April? È ... cugina.
2. Chi è Brian? È ... fratello.
3. Chi è Janice? È ...madre.
4. Chi è Daniel? È ... zio.
5. Chi è Ruth? È ... nonna.

B. Insert the Italian equivalent of each suggested adjective.

1. Andrea è (my) ... figlio.
2. Elena è (my) ... figlia.
3. Carlo è (your) ... nipote.
4. Caterina è (your) ...cugina.
5. Il signor Grigli è (his) ... nonno.
6. La signora Grigli è (his) ... nonna.

C. Chi è...? [Who is...?] You and a friend will draw a simple family tree with the names of your relatives. When they are complete you will exchange family trees and ask each other who is who in the family.

Ex. Student # 1 - Chi è Joann?
Student # 2 - Joann è mi**a** sorell**a**.

Student # 1 - Chi è Arthur?
Student # 2 - Arthur è mi**o** nonn**o**.

D. L'album di famiglia [*Family album*] You are sharing your family pictures with an Italian friend. Say:

1. Here is my brother, [name].
2. Here is my cousin, [girl's name].
3. Here are my brother, [name] and my sister [name].
4. Here are my father and my mother.
5. And here are my grandfather and my sister.
6. I have a brother and a sister.
7. Yes, here is my family.

E. Answer in complete Italian sentences.

1. Come si chiama tua zia?
2. Come si chiama tuo padre?
3. Come si chiamano i genitori di Renzo?
4. Come ti chiami tu?
5. Come si chiama il fratello di John?
6. Come si chiamano tuo cugino e tua cugina?

PROVERBI

L'anima e la mamma, chi la perde non la guadagna.
Tra moglie e marito non mettere il dito.
Un padre campa dieci figli, e dieci figli non campano un padre.

Definite articles (singular)

Let's consider three ways to say *"the"*

il, as in ***il*** padre di Renzo	for masculine singular nouns.
la, as in ***la*** madre di Renzo	for feminine singular nouns.
lo, as in ***lo*** zio di Renzo and **lo** studente d'italiano	for masculine singular nouns beginning with "**z**" or "**s**" followed by a consonant.

In special cases **la** and **lo** become **l'** before nouns beginning with a vowel as in:

l'armadio di Jennifer - or - **l'in**gegnere elettronico - or - **l'au**tomobile nuova [*new*]

PROVIAMOCI

A. Complete with the appropriate Italian equivalent for the definite article **the**.

1. ... sorella di John
2. ... zio di Robertino
3. ... fratello di Lucia
4. ... aranciata di Laura
5. ... automobile di Antonio

B. Give the missing article in each of the questions below, then supply the answer.

Ex.: Chi è **la** madre di Renzo? **La madre di Renzo è Claudia.**

1. Chi è ... nonno di Renzo?
2. Chi è ... cugina di Renzo?
3. Chi è ... zio di Renzo?
4. Chi è ... padre di Renzo?
5. Chi è ... sorella di Renzo?
6. Chi è ... nonna di Renzo?

PROVERBIO

L'abito non fa il monaco.

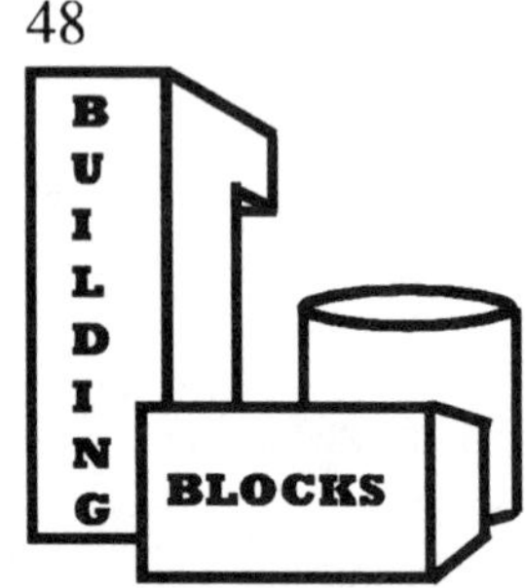

Possession with "DI"

There is no **-'s** in Italian. Possession is also expressed with **di** (of)

Ex.: John's mother = **la madre di John**

PROVIAMOCI

A. Give the Italian equivalent for each of the following.

1. Roberto's father
2. Laura's uncle
3. Paolo's grandmother
4. Renzo's cousin
5. Claudia's husband
6. Rossella's mother
7. Viviana's sister
8. Giorgio's aunt
9. Franco's brother
10. Maria's brother

B. Di chi è? [*Whose is it?*] Mrs. Wright has been cleaning all day. When Renzo arrives for a visit, she shows him all the things she has picked up around the house. Insert the missing definite article in each sentence.

Ex.: Questo è **il** libro di John.

1. Questa è ... giacca [*jacket*] di John.
2. Questo è ... cappello [*hat*] di mia figlia.
3. Questo è ... guanto da baseball di John.
4. Questa è ... aranciata di John.
5. Questa è ... penna di mio marito.
6. Questo è ... zaino di Brian.
7. Questa è ... automobilina di Jennifer.
8. Questo è ... poster di Brian.

C. La famiglia di Renzo.

a. I parenti - Working in pairs, tell how the people are related to Renzo or John by consulting their family trees.

Ex.: Student #1: **Chi è Alberto per Renzo?**
Student #2: **Alberto è suo zio.**

b. Come si chiama... (What's the name of...) Ask for the names of certain members of the boys' families.

Ex.: Student #1: **Come si chiama il padre di John?**
Student #2: **Si chiama Steven.**

D. Now ask your classmates for the names of the members of their families.

Ex.: Student #1: **Come si chiama tuo padre?**
Student #2: **Mio padre si chiama ... .**

... or you can try to keep your classmates on their toes with questions like:

Ex.: Student #1: **Chi è il padre di tuo padre?**
Student #2: **È mio nonno.**

Possessive adjectives with articles

With the exception of singular, unmodified, kinship terms, the possessive adjectives are preceded by a definite article.

Ex.: il libro di Angela = **il** suo libro but il padre di Angela = suo padre
la casa di John = **la** sua casa but la madre di John = sua madre

PROVIAMOCI

Mrs. Romano takes Renzo and Robertino to her attic to help clean. She finds all kinds of things that she gives to the boys.

Exs.: libro: *Questo è **il tuo** libro.* riga: *Questa è **la tua** riga.*

1. automobilina
2. zaino
3. poster
4. bandiera
5. fotografia
6. aeroplanino
7. penna
8. quaderno
9. modellino
10. matita

Which possessive adjectives do you find in this ad?

What does the ad promote?

OSTIA LIDO 3 CENTRO RESIDENZIALE

Prenota la tua villa o il tuo appartamento e
godi il mare con la tua famiglia
a pochi chilometri da Roma!

Ufficio Cantiere Ostia
Via Cavour 23 Tel. (06) 980 44 76

Singular, plural and invariable nouns

As we have learned in Chapter 2, all Italian nouns are either masculine or feminine. We can usually determine the gender of a noun from its ending.

-**o** = masculine singular	un libr**o**
-**a** = feminine singular	una scrivani**a**
-**e** = some are masculine,	un professor**e**
some are feminine	un'automobil**e**

Unlike English, where an "s" added to the end of a noun shows that it is plural, Italian nouns change their last letter. It really is an easy pattern:

Singular	**Plural**		
-o	**-i**	un libr**o**	due libr**i**
-a	**-e**	una scrivani**a**	due scrivani**e**
-e	**-i**	un professor**e**	due professor**i**
		un'automobil**e**	due automobil**i**

PROVIAMOCI

A. Look at the list of items in John's room. Change each noun to the plural.

Ex.: un letto - due lett**i**

1. una sedia
2. una lampada
3. una scrivania
4. una finestra
5. un tappeto
6. un'aranciata
7. uno stato
8. un armadio
9. uno zaino
10. un modellino
11. una porta
12. una sveglia
13. un televisore

Certain nouns are invariable because they are abbreviations, are taken from other languages, end in accented vowels or are only one syllable long.

abbreviations	un'auto (automobile)	due automobili
	un cinema (cinematografo)	due cinema
	una foto (fotografia)	due foto
	una moto (motocicletta)	due moto
foreign words	un comò (from French)	due comò
	un computer (from English)	due computer
	un poster (from English)	due poster
	uno snack bar (from English)	due snack bar
	uno stereo (from Greek)	due stereo
accented vowels	un caffè	due caffè
	una città	due città
	un'università	due università
single syllable	un re *[king]*	due re

A few nouns (of Greek origin) appear to be feminine but are really masculine.

un dramma	due dramm**i**
un panorama	due panoram**i**
un problema	due problem**i**
un programma	due programm**i**

B. Un inventario *[an inventory]* Tell how many of each items listed below you would find in your house.

Ex.: scrivania - Io ho **due scrivanie** a casa mia.

1. stereo
2. televisore
3. specchio
4. poster
5. zaino
6. modellino
7. foto
8. lampada

C'è, Ci sono

"There is" and "there are" are rendered in Italian with "**c'è**" and "**ci sono**."

C'è il cugino di Fausto a New York.	**There is** Fausto's cousin in New York.
Chi **c'è** in famiglia?	Who **is there** in the family?
Quante persone **ci sono**?	How many people **are there**?

PROVIAMOCI

A. Insert either **c'è** or **ci sono** as needed.

Nella famiglia di John ...

1. ... una mamma
2. ... due nonni
3. ... un papà
4. ... due zii
5. ... una cugina
6. ... due fratelli.

B. Che cosa c'è? ***[What is there?]*** Take a look at the following sketches and tell (in Italian) what is there.

Ex.: Ci sono due automobili.

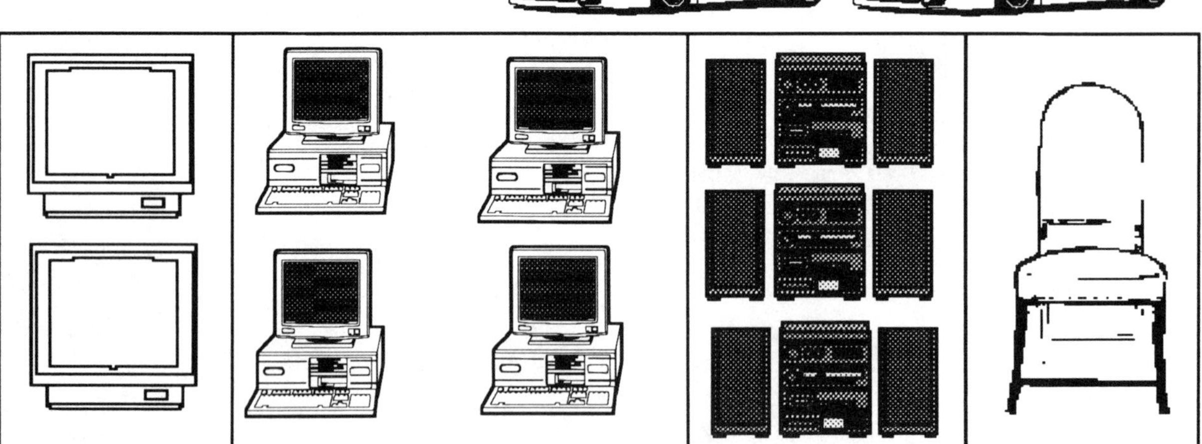

MORE NUMBERS

Here is some help for those of you who come from really large families!
Numbers from **undici** (11) to **cinquanta** (50)

undici	ventuno	trentuno	quarantuno
dodici	ventidue	trentadue	quarantadue
tredici	ventitré	trentatré	quarantatré
quattordici	ventiquattro	trentaquattro	quarantaquattro
quindici	venticinque	trentacinque	quarantacinque
sedici	ventisei	trentasei	quarantasei
diciassette	ventisette	trentasette	quarantasette
diciotto	ventotto	trentotto	quarantotto
diciannove	ventinove	trentanove	quarantanove
venti	trenta	quaranta	cinquanta

più (+) = plus **meno** (-) =minus
per (x) = times **diviso** (÷) = divided by
fa (=) = equals

PROVIAMOCI

A. Nella famiglia di John ci sono undici persone. Now, in Italian you state:

1. that in your family there are ... people.
2. that in your friend's family [use his/her name], there are ... people.
3. that in the Wright family there are five people.
4. that in the family of Cinderella [*Cenerentola*] there are four people.
5. that in Renzo's family there are twelve people.

B. Solve the following problems:

1. undici più quattordici fa ...
2. dodici per tre fa ...
3. quindici per due fa ...
4. diciotto diviso due fa ...
5. diciassette più ventitré fa ...
6. ventisette diviso nove fa ...
7. trentanove meno ventotto fa ...
8. ventiquattro più sedici fa ...

DO WE REMEMBER?

A. Vero o Falso [*True or False*] Tell if each of the following sentences is true. If a statement is false, correct it.

1. Il figlio di mio zio è mio cugino.
2. La madre di mio padre è mio nonno.
3. Il fratello di mia madre è mio zio.
4. Il marito di mia madre è mio nipote.
5. Mio nonno è il padre di mia madre.
6. La moglie di mio zio è mia zia.

B. Select the word that does not belong.

1. fratello, padre, Roberto, cugino, moglie, nonno.
2. Adamo, Massimo, Diana, Susanna, Teresa, sorella.
3. ho, sei, abbiamo, io, sono, avete, ha.
4. uno, lo, una, tuo, un, la, il
5. caldo, libro, sete, freddo, fame

PERFORMANCE ACTIVITIES

E ORA IN ITALIANO

One day while dusting the piano, Laura asks Mrs. Romano about the photos she displays there.

Laura:	Zia, chi è questo ragazzo?
Sig.ra R.:	È mio fratello, cioè [*that is*] tuo padre, a dieci anni.
Laura:	Ah, e questa signora chi è?
Sig.ra R.:	È mia madre e tua nonna.
Laura:	Ci sono altre [*other*] foto di famiglia?
Sig.ra R.:	Sì, sì, ecco una foto di tuo cugino Paolo a scuola, a sette anni.
Laura:	Quanti anni ha Paolo adesso [*now*]?
Sig.ra R.:	Oh, Paolo ha ventisette anni e Angela, mia figlia, ha ventitré anni.
Laura.:	Che interessante! Grazie, zia.

ASCOLTIAMO

Listen as your teacher reads aloud a series of statements or questions. After hearing each one, choose the most appropriate answer from the choices offered below.

	a.	b.	c.
1.	a. mio fratello	b. mio padre	c. mio cugino
2.	a. mio cugino	b. mio nonno	c. mia sorella
3.	a. mia sorella	b. mia madre	c. mia moglie
4.	a. mio padre	b. mio zio	c. mio fratello
5.	a. i parenti	b. i genitori	c. gli zii
6.	a. venti	b. ventinove	c. trenta
7.	a. diciotto	b. tredici	c. tre

LEGGIAMO

Mi chiamo Nicola. Sono di Bari Sono studente di scuola media e ho tredici anni. Ho due fratelli e una sorella. Mia sorella si chiama Romina. I miei fratelli si chiamano Antonio e Domenico. Mio padre e mia madre hanno un ristorante. Il ristorante si chiama "Alla Tavola d'Oro."

Answer the following questions about the note to the left.

1. Who wrote this note?
2. What school does he attend?
3. How old is he?
4. How many people are in his family?
5. What is the family business?

PARLIAMO

A. Create a family with your classmates. (Follow directions)

Teacher:	Facciamo una famiglia [*Let's make a family*]. Chi è il papà?
Student:	... è il papà.
Teacher:	Chi è la mamma?
Student:	... è la mamma.
Etc.	

** Each student in "the family" will make a sign on a full sheet of paper.

Ex.: Io sono il padre.

** When complete, each member holds up his/her sign and says aloud what s/he has written while showing the class. S/he then places his/her sign face down.

** Students "outside" the family must now try to recall exactly who is in the family and use the correct article.

Ex.: ... è il padre (*or* il papà).
... è la madre (*or* la mamma).

B. Things to do. Try using what you have learned to do the following:

1. ask a classmate the name of his/her mom, dad, grandfather etc.
2. see if you can remember who is who.
3. tell the names of your family members.
4. pick famous family. Tell who is who in that family.

SCRIVIAMO

A. In each of the following sketches use the clues so that you can provide the missing dialogue.

B. How would you say it? Write out each of the sentences below in good Italian.

1. My father's name is Alberto.
2. Gino is my mother's cousin.
3. I am Maria's brother.
4. Pia is Franco's sister.
5. Bruno is Viviana's boyfriend.
6. There are four cousins (male) in the [*in*] family.
7. My mother is 35 years old.
8. I have two brothers and three sisters.
9. There is a poster in the [*in*]bedroom.
10. We have two stereos.
11. There are 18 students in class.

G. Un sondaggio On the following page you will find a survey that you will use for the following activities.

1. Provide the requested information about yourself.

2. Interview a classmate and find out his/her information.
3. Gather classroom statistics.

Ex.: Dodici studenti hanno un fratello.
Undici studenti hanno una madre di trentacinque anni.

UN SONDAGGIO SULLA FAMIGLIA

I. Nome ____________________________ II. Numero di persone in famiglia _____________

III. Nome del padre ___________________ IV. Nome della madre _____________________
V. Età dei genitori: Padre _______ Madre ________

VI. Hai fratelli? Sì _____ No _____ Quanti? __________ — How many?
VII. Hai sorelle? Sì _____ No _____ Quante? __________
VIII. Nome e età — Age
Fratello(i) ____________ ___ ____________ ___
____________ ___ ____________ ___
Sorella(e) ____________ ___ ____________ ___
____________ ___ ____________ ___

IX. Indirizzo

Via _________________________________ Numero _________

CAP ______________ Città ___________________ — Zip code

X. Numero di telefono __________________________

ABOUT ITALY

THE ITALIAN FAMILY

The large Italian family, with several generations living under the same roof, is a thing of the past.

The majority of Italians live in cities or towns with a rather high concentration of traffic, stores, offices and dwellings. There are of course, residential sections, but one-family houses are less common. "Casa" in Italy means an apartment building and they come in all sizes and styles.

Although divorce is legal in Italy, the typical family includes parents and one or two children. Children go to school and, with few exceptions, the school day is over at 1:30 at the latest.

That means going home for lunch, and that makes life difficult for working mothers. Grandparents help when they can, although sometimes that means driving at rush hour or taking crowded buses to reach the grandchildren's house.

Young people must attend school until they are forteen years old, but most complete their secondary education enrolling in technical and professional institutes (about 60%) or in one of the different kinds of "liceo": classic, scientific or linguistic (about 34%).

Part-time jobs, as well as housing, are not easily available, that is why young people tend to live with their parents until they can afford their own "condo" or get married.

Italian youngsters look with interest at the life style of young Americans. They would like to share their freedom, but they appreciate the many advantages of living at home, where mother takes care of everything and father provides some spending money and, often, a moped.

WHAT DO YOU THINK?

1. How do Italian families compare with families in your country? Speak in terms of size, where they live, housing and school.
2. What do young Italians think about the American life style?
3. Is this information different from what you had previously thought about Italian families? Yes? No? Why?

Capitolo quattro: La famiglia

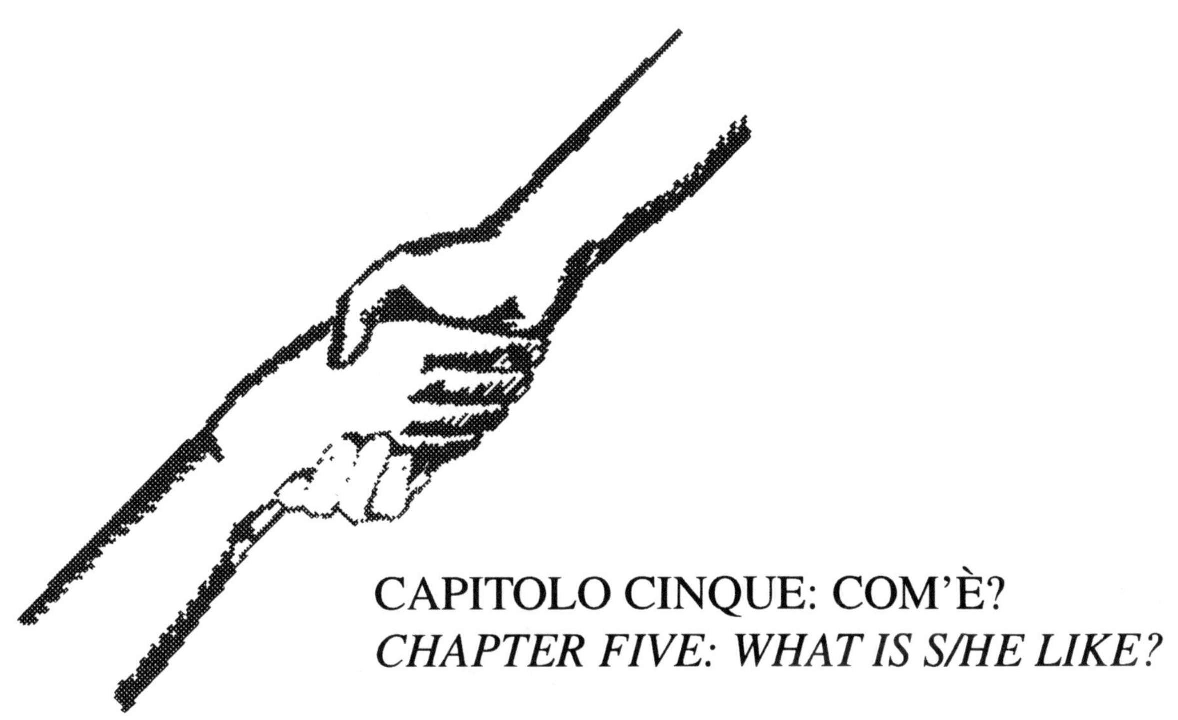

CAPITOLO CINQUE: COM'È?
CHAPTER FIVE: WHAT IS S/HE LIKE?

FUNCTIONS

Describing people and things

LANGUAGE

Qualifying adjectives:descriptive,
nationality and colors
Position of adjectives
The verb *essere*
Com'è? Come sono?
Plural definite articles

ABOUT ITALY

The legend of Rome

SITUATION

As the children and Mrs. Romano sit around the dining room table and continue their family game, John suddenly looks at Laura, blushes and says to Renzo:

JOHN: (*whispering*) Tua sorella è "pretty."
MRS. R.: Ooh, è "**carina!**" (*the children laugh*)
LAURA: È **carino** questo tuo amico!
JOHN: What did she say?
MRS. R.: She says that you are cute.
JOHN: No, I'm ugly.
MRS. R.: Tu sei "**brutto?**"
LAURA: No, non è **vero**! Loro sono **brutti!** (*She points to her brothers and they protest loudly*)
MRS. R.: Laura says: "It's not true. They are ugly!"
LAURA: Zia, **quanti** anni ha questo ragazzo?
MRS. R.: Ha quattordici anni.
LAURA: **Troppo giovane!**
MRS. R.: Sorry John, she says you are too young. (*to Laura*) Ma ha un fratello di diciassette anni.

PAROLE DA RICORDARE

NOUNS

l'amico/a	friend
la ragazza	girl
il ragazzo	boy
la studentessa	student (fem.)
lo studente	student (masc.)

ADJECTIVES

bello	beautiful, handsome
brutto	ugly
carino	pretty, cute
giovane	young
quanti	how many
vero	true, real

USEFUL EXPRESSIONS

Quanti anni ha?	How old is s/he?
È vero!	It's true!
Non è vero!	It's not true!

OTHERS

troppo	too, too much

PROVIAMOCI

How would you say that:

1. Laura is pretty
2. John is cute
3. he is not ugly
4. John is handsome
5. Laura is beautiful
6. you are young
7. you are thirteen years old
8. your cousin Lucy is fifteen years old
9. your uncle is forty years old
10. I am too young

Qualifying adjectives

When we say that someone is "cute, ugly, interesting etc.," we use adjectives. In Italian adjectives agree in gender and in number with the noun they modify. Take a look at the following:

1. John è carin**o**.
John is cute

John e Brian sono carin**i**.
John and Brian are cute.

Laura è carin**a**.
Laura is cute

Laura e Anna sono carin**e**.
Laura and Anna are cute

"**-o**" adjectives, like "carino," change as follows to reflect gender and number :

	Singular	Plural
Masculine	**-o**	**-i**
Feminine	**-a**	**-e**

2. Ecco un libro interessant**e**.
Here is an interesting book.

Ecco due libri interessant**i**.
Here are two interesting books.

Ecco una persona interessant**e**.
Here is an interesting person.

Ecco due persone interessant**i**.
Here are two interesting persons.

"**-e**" adjectives, like "interessante," change as follows to reflect gender and number:

	Singular	Plural
Masculine	**-e**	**-i**
Feminine	**-e**	**-i**

You may have noticed the same patterns that we have studied for nouns.

QUALIFYING ADJECTIVES

DESCRIPTIVE

intelligente	intelligent	**stupido**	stupid
buono	good	**cattivo**	bad
bello	beautiful	**brutto**	ugly
giovane	young	**vecchio**	old
nuovo	new		
grande	big	**piccolo**	little, small
ricco	rich	**povero**	poor
caldo	warm, hot	**freddo**	cold
facile	easy	**difficile**	difficult
lungo	long	**corto**	short (in length)
alto	tall, high	**basso**	short (in height)
grasso	fat	**magro**	skinny
simpatico	likeable, nice	**antipatico**	unpleasant
moderno	modern	**antico**	ancient
robusto	husky	**debole**	weak
biondo	blonde	**bruno**	dark

COLORS

rosso	red
arancione	orange
giallo	yellow
verde	green
azzurro	sky blue
blu*	dark blue
viola*	purple, violet
violetto	purple, violet
marrone*	brown
nero	black
bianco	white
grigio	gray
rosa*	pink

*= invariable

NATIONALITIES

americano	American
canadese	Canadian
cinese	Chinese
francese	French
giapponese	Japanese
inglese	English
irlandese	Irish
italiano	Italian
messicano	Mexican
olandese	Dutch
polacco	Polish
portoghese	Portuguese
russo	Russian
spagnolo	Spanish
svizzero	Swiss
tedesco	German

Nationalities are not capitalized in Italian.

Ex.: Monet è un artista **francese**, Michelangelo è un artista **italiano** e Georgia O'Keeffe è un'artista **americana**.

PROVIAMOCI

A. Come sono? [*How are they?*] Complete each sentence with an adjective that means the opposite of the one underlined.

1. Maria è una ragazza intelligente; suo fratello è ...
2. La Coca-cola è fredda; il caffè è ...
3. Il nonno è vecchio; John è ...
4. L'italiano è facile; il cinese è ...
5. La mia automobile è vecchia; l'automobile di Toni è ...
6. John è simpatico; Teresa è ...
7. La mia camera è grande; la camera di Marco è ...
8. Renzo è biondo; sua sorella è ...

B. Di che nazionalità sono? [*What nationality are they?*] Complete each statement with a suitable adjective of nationality.

1. Napoleone Bonaparte è ...
2. Shakespeare e Dickens sono autori ...
3. Pancho Villa è ...
4. Anastasia Romanov è ...
5. Sofia Loren e Marcello Mastroianni sono attori ...
6. Pablo Picasso è un artista ...
7. Abramo Lincoln è ...
8. Beethoven è un musicista ...
9. Godzilla è un mostro ...

C. Di che colore è? [*What color is it?*] Supply the appropriate colors.

1. La bandiera [*flag*] italiana è ...
2. Il cielo [*sky*] è ...
3. Il gesso è ...
4. L'elefante è ...
5. L'erba [*grass*] è ...

6. La banana è ...
7. L'arancia è ...
8. La bandiera americana è ...

How many nationalities do you recognize in the ad to the right? Do you know what an "au pair" is?

The verb "ESSERE" [*to be*]

1. We need the verb essere, "to be," when we want to describe people or things. Here it is in all its forms of the present tense:

io	**sono**	I am	noi	**siamo**	we are
tu	**sei**	you are	voi	**siete**	you are (plural)
lui/lei	**è**	he/she is	loro	**sono**	they are
Lei	**è**	you are (polite)	Loro	**sono**	you are (plural, polite)

Noi **siamo** studenti.
We are students.

Loro **sono** intelligenti.
They are intelligent.

2. "Essere" is also used to express "where one is from."

Io **sono** di Roma, e tu di dove **sei**?
I am from Rome, and where are you from?

Io *sono* di Chicago.
I am from Chicago

PROVIAMOCI

A. Complete with the correct form of the verb **essere**.

1. Robertino...il fratello di Renzo.
2. Noi ... italiani e loro ... giapponesi.
3. Tu di dove...?
4. Voi di dove ...?
5. Lei ... brava.
6. Chi ... il fratello di Laura?
7. Io non ... di New York.
8. ... di Milano tu e Giancarlo?
9. ... vero che Wang ... di Hong Kong?
10. Lui chi ... ?

B. Complete each of the following comparisons with an appropriate form of the verb **essere** and a descriptive adjective.

Ex.: Piera **è grassa**.
Enrica **è magra**.

Io ... ...
Tu ... ...

Il bambino ... ...
La nonna ... ...

Tu ...
Mario ... ...

Lui ... ...
Lei ... ...

Loro ... ...
Noi ... ...

C. Tell the nationalities of each of the following characters

D. Say where the following people are from and give their nationalities.

Ex.: Edward / Boston - **Edward è di Boston; è americano.**

1. Pablo / Madrid
2. Hans / Berlino
3. Pedro / Acapulco
4. Peter / Londra
5. Paolo / Milano
6. Joan / Ottawa
7. Wendy / Austin
8. Brigitte / Parigi
9. Ivan / Mosca
10. Woo / Pechino

E. Languages are masculine in gender. What language is spoken in each of the following countries?

Italia, Francia, Messico, Polonia, Germania, Austria, Brasile,
Olanda, Inghilterra, Svizzera, Grecia, Australia, Giappone

Ex.: L'italiano è parlato in Italia.

1. Lo spagnolo ...
2. Il tedesco ...
3. L'inglese ...
4. L'olandese ...
5. Il francese ...
6. Il polacco ...
7. Il giapponese ...
8. Il francese, l'italiano e il tedesco ...
9. Il portoghese ...
10. Il greco ...

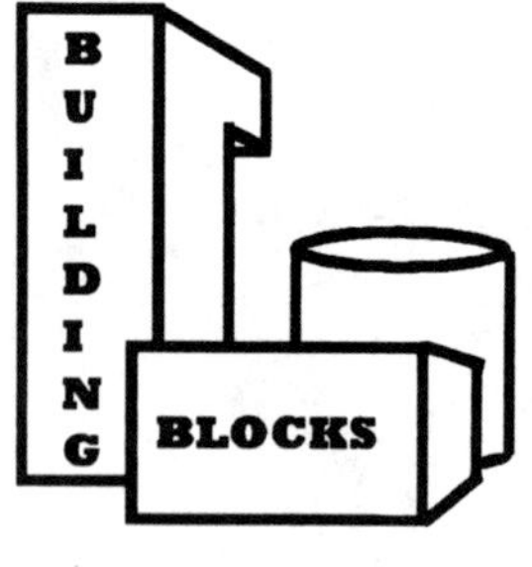

Placement of adjectives

Italian adjectives come after the noun they modify. However, some common adjectives, such as those listed below, tend to come before the noun.

bello	**brutto**
buono	**cattivo**
giovane	**vecchio**
nuovo	
grande	**piccolo**

una **piccola** scrivania (before noun)

una scrivania **enorme** (after noun)

PROVIAMOCI

A. Before or after the noun? Give the Italian equivalent of each expression.

1. a young English professor
2. a new american car
3. a beautiful Dutch girl
4. a difficult test
5. an old desk
6. a cold bedroom
7. a tall boy
8. a big house
9. a small poster
10. a Japanese friend

B. Make a list of five items that you own, describing them with an adjective.

Ex.: Ho un vecchio stereo.

Now compare your list with that of a classmate.

C. Com'è grande! [*How big it is!*] Renzo is impressed with the size of things in the United States. He is forever saying how big things are. For example, the first time he saw a Cadillac he said: "Com'è grande!" When he saw American shopping malls he said: "Come sono grandi!" Tell how Renzo would react upon seeing the following items.

1. An American supermarket
2. American coffee mugs
3. California superhighways
4. A B-1 bomber
5. Redwood trees
6. The Bronx Zoo
7. American farms
8. I grandi laghi [lakes]

D. Com'è bello! [*How beautiful it is!*] Laura is in "shopper's heaven" at the local mall. Mrs. Romano points out different items and Laura notes how beautful everything is.

Ex.: Com'**è** bell**o/a**! Come **sono** bell**i/e!**

What will she say when she sees:

1. il vestito [*dress/suit*]
2. le scarpe [*shoes*]
3. la camicetta [*blouse*]
4. le calze [*socks*]
5. la gonna [*skirt*]
6. i pantaloni [*pants*]
7. i guanti [*gloves*]
8. la giacca [*jacket*]

E. Hard to please. Robertino hates getting dressed in the morning. His mother asks him why he does not want to wear something and he answers that it is ugly. Following the example, form similar exchanges with a partner.

Ex.: questo cappello	Student #1	**Perché non porti questo cappello?** [Why don't you wear this hat?]
	Student #2	**Perché è brutto!**

1. questa camicia [*shirt*]
2. questi pantaloncini [*shorts*]
3. questa maglietta [*T-shirt*]
4. questo cappotto [*winter coat*]
5. queste scarpe [*shoes*]
6. questo pullover [*sweater*]
7. questi calzini [*men's socks*]
8. scarpe da ginnastica [*sneakers*]

Plural definite articles

When a noun becomes plural, the definite article "the" used with it must also change. Notice what happens to the articles you've learned:

singular		plural	
il	-	**i**	
lo	-	**gli**	
l'	-	**gli**	(m.)
l'	-	**le**	(f.)
la	-	**le**	

il fratello	-	**i** fratelli
lo zio	-	**gli** zii
l'amico	-	**gli** amici
l'amica	-	**le** amiche
la madre	-	**le** madri

Nouns ending in "**ca**" change to "**che**" in the plural, as in:

l'amic**a** > le amic**he**

PROVIAMOCI

A. Change the following expressions to the plural.

1. la buona aranciata.
2. lo studente intelligente
3. la vecchia casa
4. il brutto poster
5. la ragazza elegante
6. l'amico grasso
7. l'americano biondo
8. la signora francese
9. lo sport americano
10. lo zaino blu

B. Working in pairs, complete with the plural definite articles. You must choose from: **i**, **gli,** and **le.**

La famiglia di Renzo è italiana da molte [*many*] generazioni, ma ... amici di Renzo sono di nazionalità differenti. A scuola ci sono ragazzi italiani, ma anche francesi, inglesi, e tedeschi; sono ... "internazionali" cioè [*that is*], ... figli dei [*of the*] diplomatici stranieri [*foreign*] che lavorano [*work*] nella [*in the*] capitale. A Roma ... studentesse e ... studenti sono molto fortunati perché vivono [*live*] la storia attraverso [*through*] ... monumenti antichi e ... visite ai [*to the*] musei. Renzo e ... suoi amici amano [*love*] esplorare Roma antica e ... sue antichità [*antiquities*].

C. Change the following statements to the plural.

Ex.: Il fratello di Carlo è dottore.
I fratelli di Carlo sono dottori.

1. La cugina di Jennifer non è a casa.
2. L'amica di Paolo è simpatica.
3. Lo zio di Marco è di New York.
4. Lo studente è messicano.
5. Il bar italiano è elegante.
6. L'ingegnere americano è intelligente.

D. Complete the examples below with an indefinite article (**un, uno, una, un'**) in the first blank and a definite article (**il, lo, la, l'**) in the second.

1. È ... stereo giapponese. È ... stereo di John.
2. È ... vecchia fotografia. È ... fotografia di Ugo.
3. È ... computer Olivetti. È ... computer di Roberto.
4. È ... modellino carino. È ... modellino di Robertino
5. È ... amica simpatica. È ... amica di Jennifer.

"Di chi" *is used to express "whose?"*

Exs.: **Di chi** è l'automobilina? — **Whose** model car is it?
Di chi sono gli amici? — **Whose** friends are they?

PROVIAMOCI

A. With a classmate create short dialogues using the items listed below. Follow the examples:

Ex. in the singular: giacca / Giorgio
Di chi è la giacca? - È di Giorgio

Ex. in the plural: scarpe / Laura
Di chi sono le scarpe? - Sono di Laura

1. pullover / John
2. maglietta / Robertino
3. stivali / Roberto
4. zaino / Renzo
5. pantaloncini / Robertino
6. pantaloni / Brian
7. guanti / Laura
8. calze / Janice
9. gonna / Lucia
10. vestito / Papà

PERFORMANCE ACTIVITIES

E ORA IN ITALIANO

Laura is looking at a teen magazine and Mrs. Romano happens to look over her shoulder.

Sig.ra R.:	Che cos'è Laura?
Laura :	È una rivista per i giovani.
Sig.ra R.:	(*indicating a photograph*) Chi sono questi ragazzi?

Laura:	Sono musicisti molto popolari.
Sig.ra R.:	Mamma mia! Che cosa ha quel ragazzo sulla faccia [*on his face*]?
Laura:	È un tatuaggio.
Sig.ra R.:	Che brutto!
Laura:	No, è molto bello.
Sig.ra R.:	Perché un ragazzo bello come lui [*like him*] ha bisogno di un tatuaggio?
Laura:	Oh zia, molti musicisti famosi hanno tatuaggi.
Sig.ra R.:	Ah, sì? Non Luciano Pavarotti e certamente non i musicisti di questa famiglia!

ASCOLTIAMO

Listen as your teacher reads aloud a series of statements or questions. After hearing each one, choose the most appropriate answer from the choices offered below.

	a.	b.	c.
1.	a. francese	b. giapponese	c. cinese
2.	a. piccolo	b. grande	c. vecchio
3.	a. difficile	b. lungo	c. interessante
4.	a. nero	b. buono	c. caldo
5.	a. noiosa	b. corta	c. bassa
6.	a. verde	b. marrone	c. bianca
7.	a. giovane	b. grasso	c. bravo
8.	a. Roma	b. Milano	c. Venezia

LEGGIAMO

Read the passage below very carfully then determine if the statements that follow it are true [**vero**] or false [**falso**].

La famiglia di Renzo è italiana, gli amici di Renzo sono di nazionalità differenti. A scuola ci sono ragazzi italiani, inglesi, francesi e tedeschi. Roma è una città internazionale e molti stranieri vivono a Roma. Ci sono anche [*also*] molti turisti: americani, giapponesi, canadesi e inglesi. L'Italia è piccola ma di grande interesse turistico.

Vero? / Falso?

1. Renzo only has Italian classmates.
2. Rome is an international city.

3. Foreigners are not allowed to live within the city of Rome.
4. Italy is a large country.
5. Italy is a popular destination for Japanese tourists.

SCRIVIAMO

A. Describe three people in your family.

B. Write a short paragraph in your journal about a friend of yours.
- Give his/her name
- Tell what city or town he/she comes from and his/her nationality
- Describe him/her.
- Conclude by saying he/she is likeable.

PARLIAMO

There is a new Italian exchange student in your school who is visiting your class.

1. Say Hello to her. Then...
2. Ask for:
   a. her name
   b. how old she is
   c. the city she is from
3. Now give the following information about yourself:
   a. name
   b. age
   c. where you are from

ABOUT ITALY

THE LEGEND OF ROME

Renzo e zia Lucia tell John about the beginning of Rome as they studied it in Italian schools.

In Albalonga, where the town of Castelgandolfo now stands, lived a good king named Numitor with his daughter Rea Silva. They belonged to a prestigious family, the Gens Julia, descendent of the Greek hero Aeneas whose mother was the goddess Aphrodite, the Venus of the Romans. Numitor had a wicked brother, Amulius, who took his kingdom and forced Rea Silva to become a priestess of the goddess Vesta. In this way he was sure that no heirs

Rea Silva was young and beautiful, the god Mars fell in love with her and visited her in the temple where she was secluded. In due time twins were born, Romulus and Remus. Amulius was furious and ordered that Rea Silva and the children be killed. The servant in charge just could not kill the babies, so he put them in a basket and let it float with the current on the river Tiber. The basket traveled for a while and stopped among the reeds in a dry place. Romulus and Remus were hungry. They cried and cried, and thus called the attention of a she-wolf who came to feed them. Later a shepard found the children and took them home. They grew and became proud and strong young men.

One day, together with other friends, they decided to start a new settlement. They went on the hill called Palatinus and, according to the custom, decided to interpret the will of the gods by watching the way birds were flying. Unfortunately Romulus and Remus disagreed on the meaning of the flight pattern. To spite his brother, Remus jumped over the line marking the *pomerius*, that is, the large square that indicated the perimeter of the new city. That was a great insult. The two brothers got into a big fight and Remus was killed. Romulus then became the first king of the new city that was called Roma. It was the 21st of April of the year 753 before Christ.

The Forum was the center of political and religious life for the early Romans.

The Colosseum is the most famous monument from the proud days of ancient Rome. Begun in 72 A.D. and opened in 80 A.D., it could contain a crowd of 50,000 spectators.

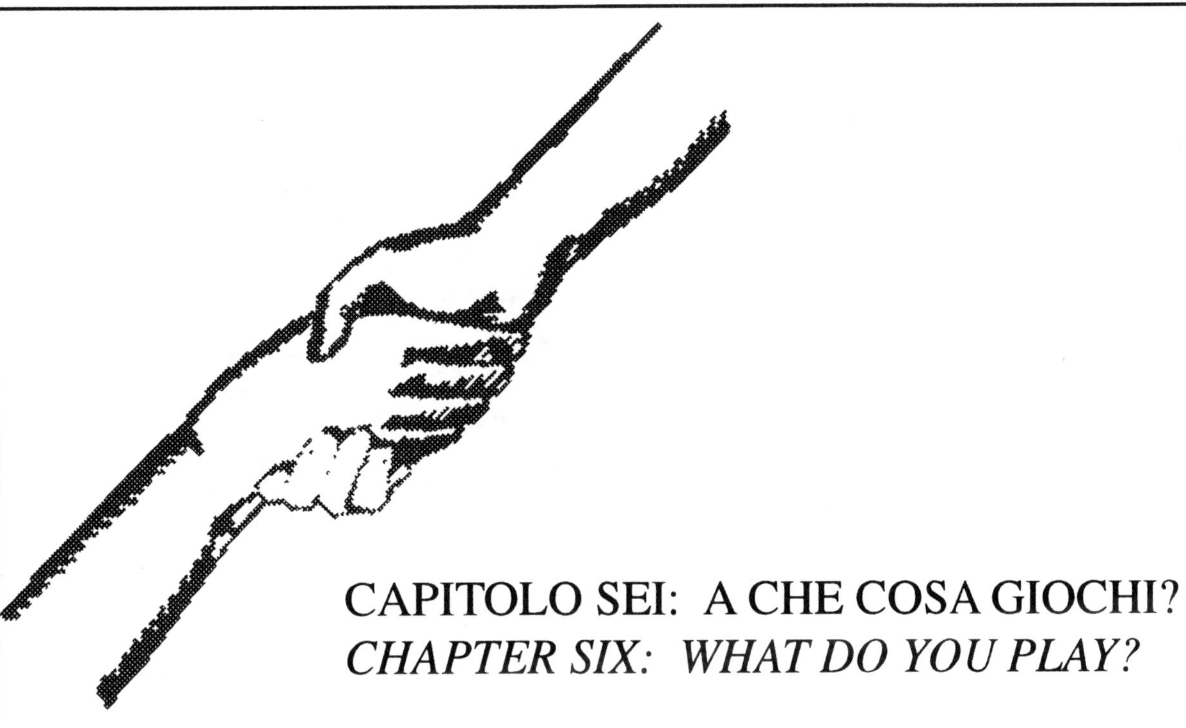

CAPITOLO SEI: A CHE COSA GIOCHI?
CHAPTER SIX: WHAT DO YOU PLAY?

FUNCTIONS

Requesting information
Describing
Telling time
Talking about leisure activities

LANGUAGE

Verbs in *"-are"* (singular)
Spelling changes
bene, male
Che ore sono?, A che ora...?
More numbers (51-100)
Ti piace giocare a...?

ABOUT ITALY

Il calcio

SITUATION

John explains to Mrs. Romano that he has a competition set up against Jeff Golden in "Hacky Sac." He tells her that he could use Renzo's help to win.

MRS. R.:	Renzo, John **ha bisogno di aiuto.**
RENZO:	**Perché?**
MRS. R.:	Ha una **partita**.
RENZO:	Che partita?
MRS. R.:	"Hacky sac."
RENZO:	**Cosa?**
JOHN:	It's like the game that you play with Laura e Robertino with the soccer ball, except that we use a small soft ball.
MRS. R.:	È come il **gioco** che **fai** con Laura e Robertino in **giardino**, ma **quando gioca** John, lui usa una pallina morbida.
RENZO:	Ah, non **giochi** con il pallone da calcio?
JOHN:	Giochi? Joke?
MRS. R.:	No, "giochi" means "you play." It comes from the verb "giocare," to play.
JOHN:	So the "**i**" means "you do something?"
MRS. R.:	Sì, **esatto**!
JOHN:	How do you say "I play?"
MRS. R.:	"**Gioco**," the "**o**" says "I do something."
JOHN:	(*to Renzo*) Io gioco bene, tu giochi bene, e Jeff gioca male. Don't worry!
MRS. R.:	**Non ti preoccupare**.
RENZO:	Va bene, noi siamo bravi.

Capitolo sei: A che cosa giochi?

MRS. R.: Renzo, **che ora è?**
RENZO: (*Renzo looks at his watch*) **Sono le cinque**.
MRS. R.: **Mamma mia! Com'è tardi**! (*she runs into the kitchen*)

PAROLE DA RICORDARE

NOUNS

l'aiuto	help
il giardino	garden
il gioco	game
la palla	ball
la pallina	small ball
il pallone	big ball
la partita	game, match

OTHERS

come	how, like
perché	why?, because
quando	when
tardi	late

VERBS

fai	you do
	you are doing
giocare a	to play

USEFUL EXPRESSIONS

Com'è tardi!	How late it is!
Esatto!	Exactly!
Non ti preoccupare!	Don't worry!
Mamma mia!	Oh, my goodness!
Che?	What?
Cosa?	What?
Che cosa?	What?

PROVIAMOCI

A. Caccia al tesoro [*Treasure hunt*] In the preceding "Situation" find:

1. two question words
2. an expression of agreement
3. an expression of alarm
4. an expression that relieves concern
5. sports related words
6. two expressions about telling time

PROVERBIO
Meglio tardi che mai.

B. Say it in Italian:

1. Mother needs your help.
2. He has a game.
3. What game?
4. I play well.
5. Do you play with a soccer ball?
6. No, I play with a small soft ball.
7. What time is it?
8. Oh, my goodness, it's six o'clock.
9. It is late.

Verbs ending in "-are"

The verb **giocare** [*to play*], is an example of a whole group of verbs in Italian. They all end in **-are** when in the infinitive. An infinitive is the name of the action expressed by a verb. It tells you of an action but doesn't tell you that anyone is actually doing it. To activate an infinitive you have to "conjugate" the verb. That is, to alter the form of the infinitive. In English you hardly notice conjugations:

to use	**to play**
I use	I play
you use	you play
he/she/it uses	he/she/it plays

The only change you see is the addition of an "**s**" in the third person. In Italian, on the other hand, the last three letters of the infinitive are dropped and here is what happens.

	usare	**giocare**
	us-are	gioc-are
io	us**o**	gioc**o**
tu	us**i**	gioc**hi**
lui/lei	us**a**	gioc**a**
Lei [you ,polite]	us**a**	gioc**a**

In Italian, as you can see, each person has different ending. The endings are "**o**," "**i**" and "**a**". The extra "**h**" you see above in **giochi** is used for sound purposes. The letter "**c**" followed by "**i**" or "**e**" makes a soft sound like "**ch**" in English. The extra "**h**" helps maintain the "**k**" sound. The same situation arises when there is a "**g**" before the verb ending. (see Chapter 1)

Here are some "**-are**" verbs that we will frequently use:

abitare (a, in)	to live	**nuotare**	to swim
aiutare	to help	**mandare**	to send
arrivare (a, in, da)	to arrive	**pagare**	to pay
ascoltare	to listen	**parlare (con,a)**	to speak, talk
cantare	to sing	**ritornare (a,in, da)**	to go back
comprare	to buy	**salutare**	to greet
desiderare	to desire	**studiare**	to study
festeggiare	to celebrate	**suonare**	to play (instrument)
giocare (a)	to play (sport/game)	**telefonare (a)**	to phone
guardare	to look at, watch	**tirare**	to throw, pull
imparare	to learn	**usare**	to use
incominciare	to start, begin	**viaggiare**	to travel

PROVIAMOCI

A. Each of the following English nouns reminds you of a verb in Italian. Can you guess what they are?

1. guard
2. pay
3. desire
4. commence
5. arrival
6. chanting
7. parlor

7. habitat
8. return
9. salutation
10. studio
11. user
12. festivity
14. telephone

B. Which verbs describe the following activities?

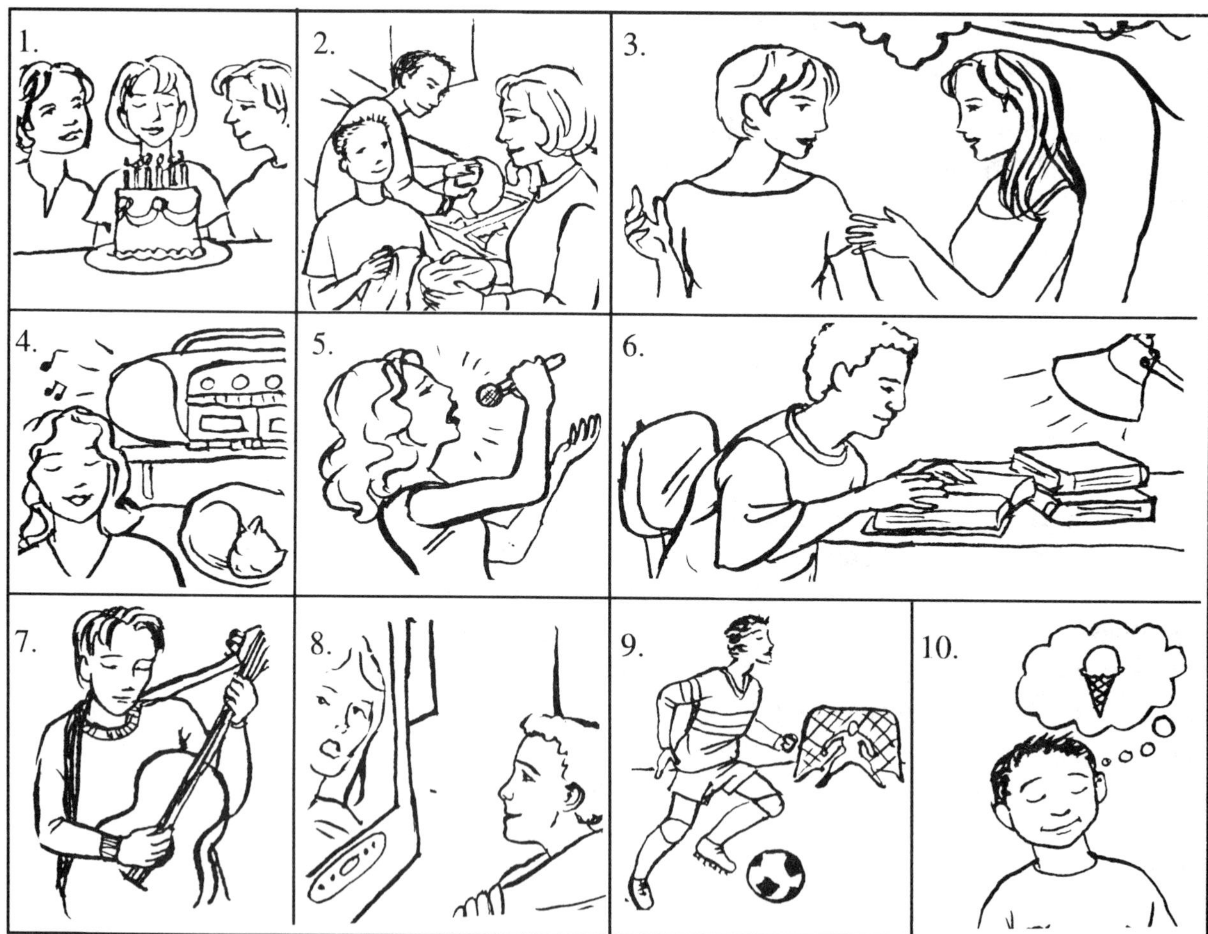

C. The sentences below are not quite complete. Read the sentences aloud supplying the correct ending for each verb.

1. Io abit ... a Siracusa.
2. Lui aiut ... la mamma in casa.
3. Tu non ascolt ... in classe.
4. Luciana cant ... bene.
5. Lei festeggi ... il compleanno.
6. Guard ... la televisione tu?
7. Io parl ... bene e lui parl ... male.
8. Mario non studi ....
9. Perché tu non salut ... il professore?
10. Pagh ... tu o pag ... io?
11. Tu dove abit ...?
12. A che cosa gioc ... John?

D. The sentences below require the correct conjugated form of the infinitive suggested. How would you complete each sentence?

Ex.: Carlo (guardare) la televisione. - **Carlo guarda la televisione.**

1. Il Papa [*Pope*] (abitare) in Vaticano.
2. Io (studiare) a casa.
3. Tu (desiderare) guardare il film.
4. Renzo (ritornare) in Italia a settembre.
5. La famiglia (abitare) a Roma.
6. Io (tirare) la palla a John.
7. Che cosa (cantare) tu?
8. Papà (pagare) per tutti [*everyone*]

E. The following sentences might be more clear if each had an appropriate subject. Can you provide the missing information?

Ex.: Studia con Laura. - **Renzo** studia con Laura. - or - **Lui** studia con Laura.

1. Nuoti in piscina?
2. Arrivo in bicicletta.
3. Usa il nuovo stereo.
4. Canta "Mamma."
5. Aiuto la nonna.
6. Parli francese in Canada.
7. Abita a 1600 Pennsylvania Avenue.
8. Canta "A modo mio" [*My Way*].

F. Group activity: Working in groups of three, complete the sentences for each cell in the grid. Take turns completing the cells, then compare your answers with those of another group. Finally, at the teacher's directions, say the answers aloud.

	io	tu	Renzo
Ex.: abitare (a, in)	a Pisa **Io abito a Pisa.**	a Napoli **Tu abiti a Napoli.**	in un appartamento **Renzo abita in un appartamento.**
1. aiutare	la mamma	gli amici	la zia
2. arrivare	a scuola	secondo	a Venezia
3. ascoltare	la radio	lo stereo	il professore
4. cantare	bene	male	una canzone [*song*]
5. festeggiare	la vittoria	il compleanno [*birthday*]	l'anniversario
6. desiderare	una Ferrari	una Maserati	un motorino [*moped*]
7. giocare	a baseball	a calcio	a Nintendo
8. guardare	la televisione	la partita	il film
9. usare	il telefono	il computer	la macchina [*car*]
10. parlare	italiano	spagnolo	inglese
11. suonare	il piano	il violino	la chitarra
12. salutare	gli amici	il nonno	la professoressa

G. Cosa fa Renzo? Cosa fai tu? [*What does Renzo do? What do you do?*]
Compare what you want to do to the things that Renzo does. When you do similar things use, **anche** [*also,too*], in your answer. When you do something differently, use **invece** [*instead, however*].

Ex.: Renzo gioca a calcio; **anch**'io gioco a calcio. - or - Io, **invece** gioco a baseball.

1. Renzo desidera un motorino; ...
2. Renzo parla italiano; ...
3. Renzo nuota bene; ...
4. Renzo abita in via dei Villini; ...
5. Renzo studia l'inglese; ...
6. Renzo guarda la TV; ...
7. Renzo ascolta una canzone di Zucchero; ...

H. Cosa fai? [*What do you do?/What are you doing?*] Using the sketch as a guide, tell what you do in each place.

1. In piscina ...
2. In biblioteca ...
3. In casa ...
4. Al parco ...
5. Alla cassa ...
6. Nel coro ...

I. Complete each sentence with the correct form of an appropriate verb. Get your ideas from the sketches.

Ex.: Io canto male.

1. Tu ... rapidamente [*fast*].

2. Gina ...

3. Tu ...alla cassa.

4. Lui ... la televisione.

5. Enrico ... i biglietti per il concerto.

6. Io ... a Nintendo.

7. Tu ... Gilda.

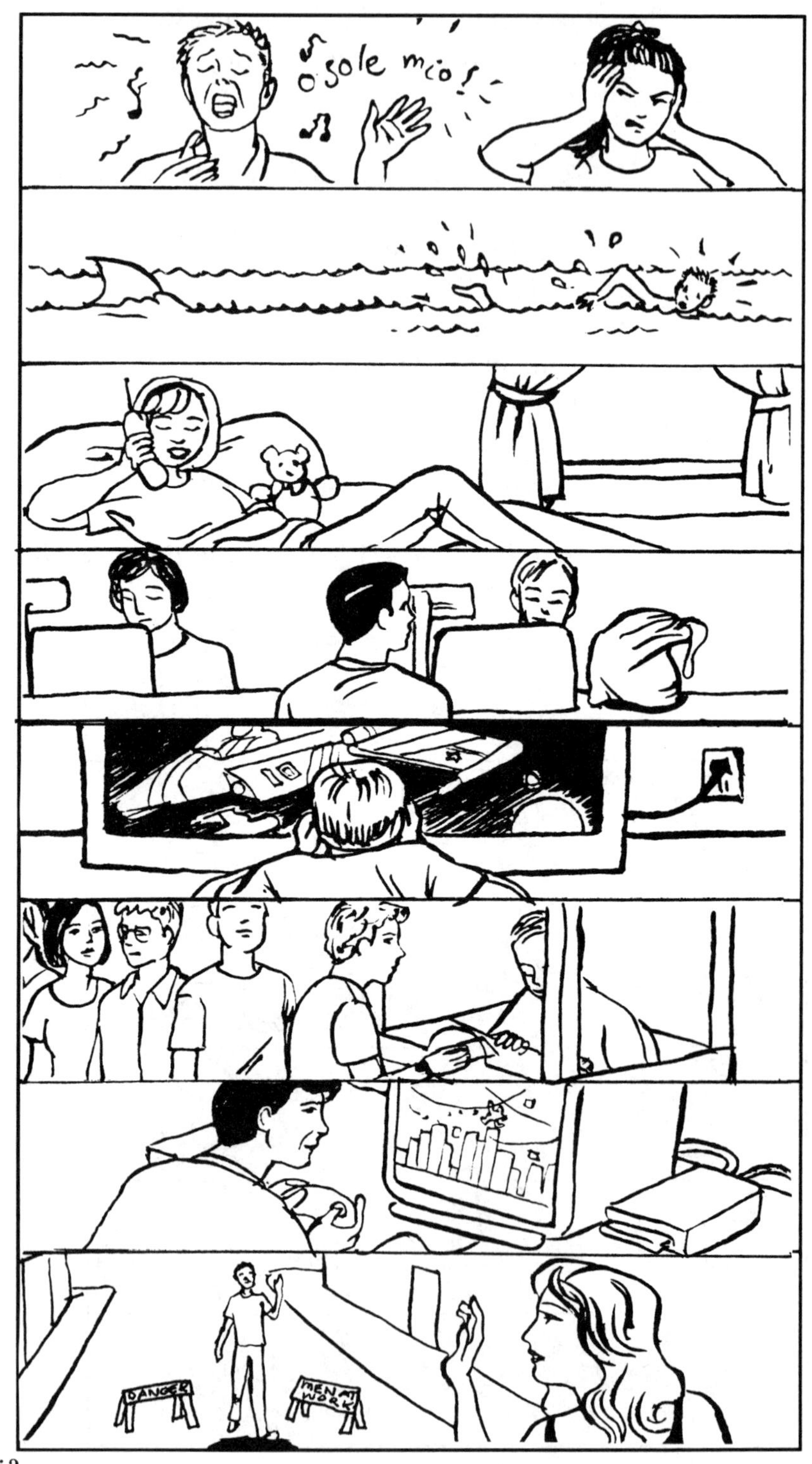

J. How do people do things? Each exchange below is based on a sketch. With a partner, determine which is the best way to complete each sentence, then practice the exchanges aloud.

Ex.: Student #1: Come canta Paolo; bene o male?
Student #2: Paolo canta bene.
Student #1: E Pierino?
Student #2: Pierino canta male

Student #1: Come ... tu?
Student #2: Io ... bene
Student #1: E Luisa?
Student #2: Luisa ... male.

Student #1: Come ... io?
Student #2: Tu ... bene.
Student #1: E Tommaso?
Student #2: Tommaso ... male.

Student #1: Come ... la palla Lia?
Student #2: Lia ... bene.
Student #1: E Rosanna?
Student #2: Rosanna ... male.

TELLING TIME

Do you remember how the conversation ended between Renzo and Mrs. Romano? Here is a reminder:

MRS. R.: Renzo, **che ora è?**
RENZO: (Renzo looks at his watch) **Sono le cinque.**
MRS. R.: Mamma mia! Com'è tardi!

There are two ways to ask "**What time is it?**" in Italian: **Che ora è?**

Che ore sono?

When one answers the question one says: **È** mezzogiorno [*noon*]

or **Sono le** (ore) dodici e dieci. [12:10 p.m.]

You may have already noticed that the answer is "**è**" if what follows is **singular** and "**sono**" if what follows is **plural**.

Here are some clocks to read:

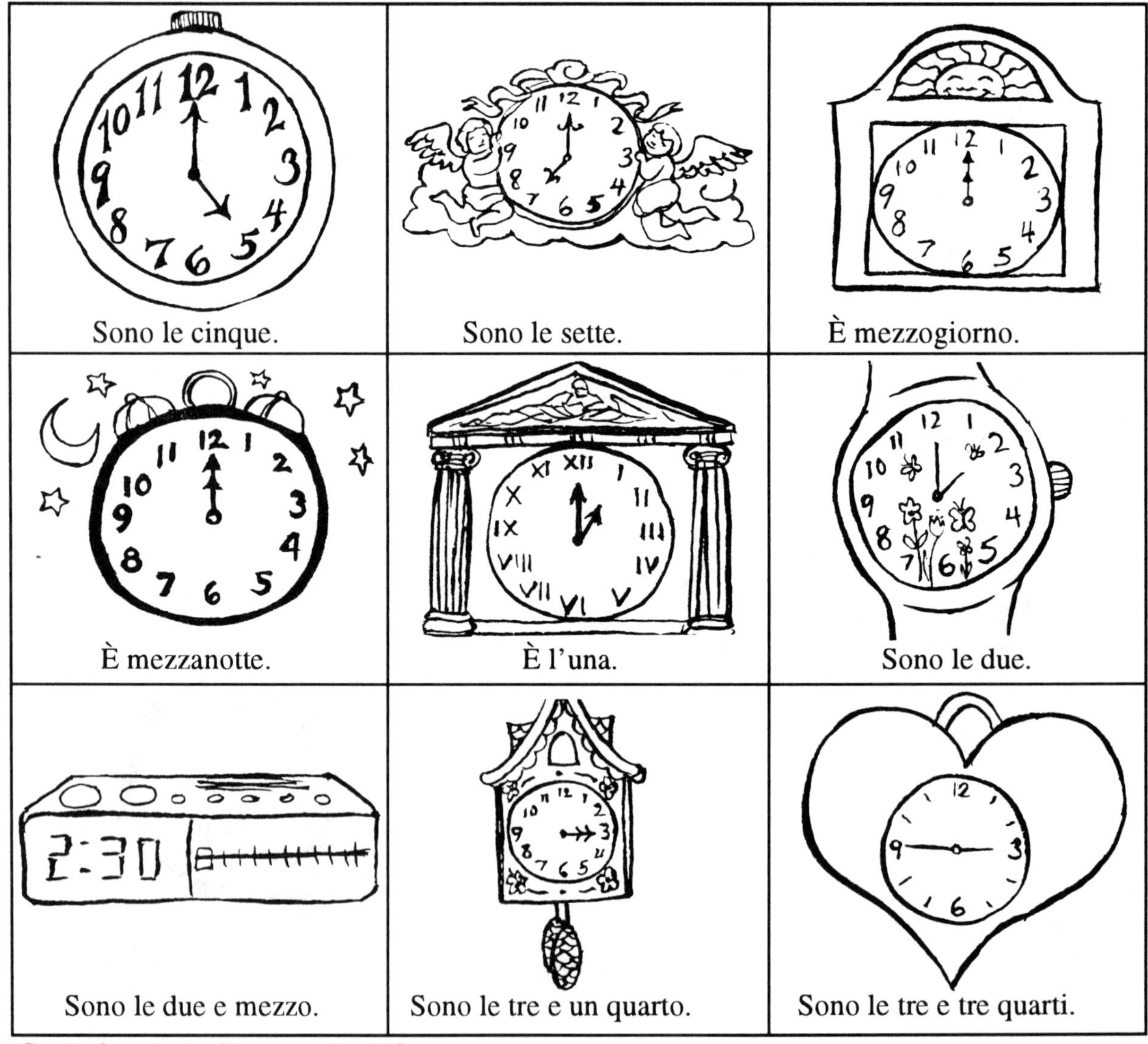

Sono le cinque. | Sono le sette. | È mezzogiorno.

È mezzanotte. | È l'una. | Sono le due.

Sono le due e mezzo. | Sono le tre e un quarto. | Sono le tre e tre quarti.

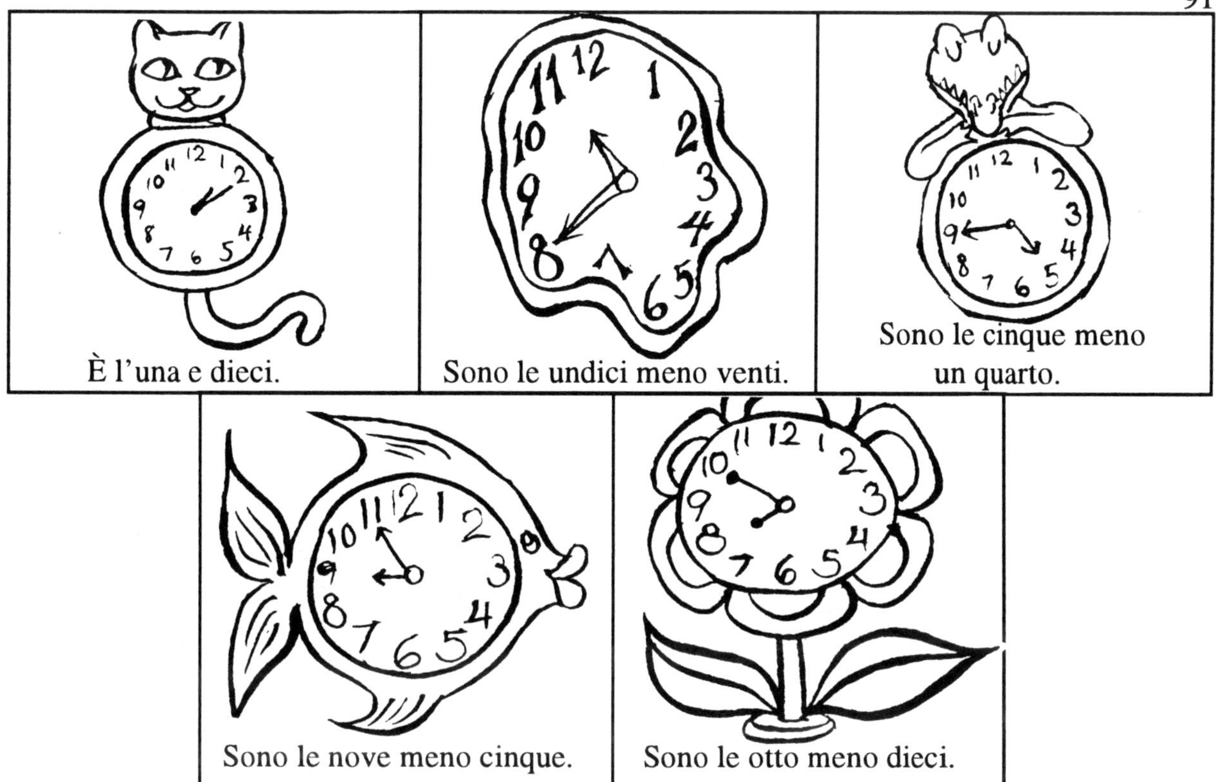

È l'una e dieci.

Sono le undici meno venti.

Sono le cinque meno un quarto.

Sono le nove meno cinque.

Sono le otto meno dieci.

As you have seen, instead of 15 minutes you can say "**un quarto**,"instead of 45 minutes you can say "**tre quarti**," and instead of saying 30 minutes you can say "**e mezzo**."

When the time is close to the next hour, you can say, "**meno venti**," "**meno un quarto**," "**meno cinque**," etc.

Italians do not use a.m. and p.m.. If necessary, to avoid ambiguity, they say, "**di mattina**" [*in the morning*], "**di pomeriggio**" [*in the afternoon*], "**di sera**" [*in the evening*], and "**di notte**" [*at night*].

PROVIAMOCI

A. Read the following aloud, then tell in English what time it is.

1. Sono le cinque e quaranta.
2. Sono le undici meno un quarto
3. È mezzanotte e mezzo.
4. Sono le nove meno dieci.
5. Sono le tre e trentacinque.
6. Sono le sette meno venti.
7. È l'una e trentacinque.
8. Sono le tre e quindici.
9. È mezzogiorno.
10. Sono le otto e mezzo.

B. Che ore sono? Say what time it is in Italian in all the way you can.

1. 12:00 (noon)
2. 9:30
3. 4:13
4. 8:15
5. 6:10
6. 5:40
7. 7:45
8. 10.50
9. 1:15
10. 2:40
11. 12:00 (midnight)
12. 3:05

C. Give the appropriate time in Italian.

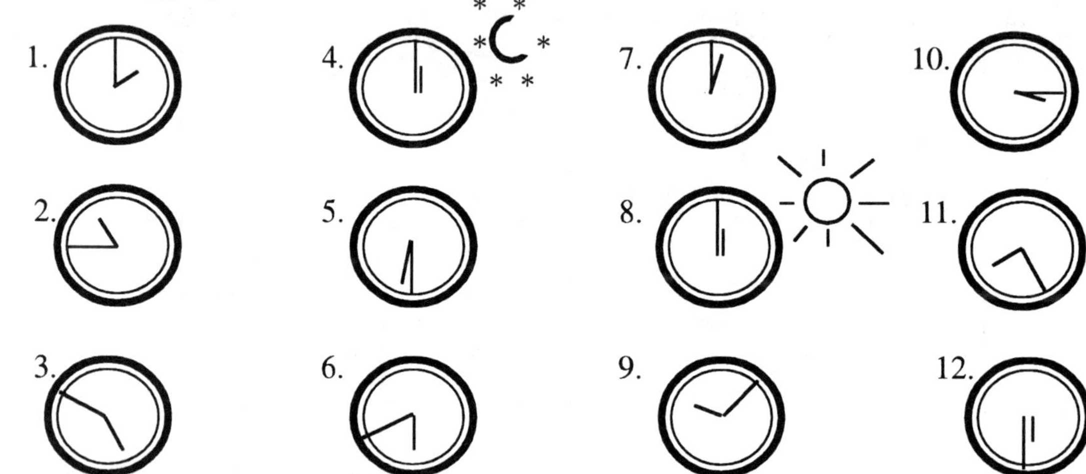

D. Dove sei? Pretend the schedule below is your daily school routine. Tell in English where you'll be at the times mentioned in the questions that follow.

Ex.: Dove sei alle [at] nove e trentacinque? **I'm in science!**

Time	Monday	Tuesday	Wednesday	Thursday	Friday
8:00	Homeroom	Homeroom	Homeroom	Homeroom	Homeroom
8:15	English	English	English	English	English
9:05	Science	Science	Science	Science	Science
9.55	Phys. Ed.	Study	Phys. Ed.	Study	Lab.
10:45	Social Studies	Soc. Stdys.	Soc. Stdys.	Soc. Stdys.	Soc. Stdys.
11:35	Lunch	Lunch	Lunch	Lunch	Lunch
12:25	Math	Math	Math	Math	Math
1:15	Italian	Italian	Italian	Italian	Italian
2:05	----------------Music (1st sem./Occupational Ed. 2nd sem.)--------------				
2:55	Activities	Acitvities	Activities	Activities	Activities

1. Dove sei alle dodici e quaranta?
2. Dove sei alle otto e mezzo?
3. Dove sei all'una e un quarto?
4. Dove sei alle due meno dieci?
5. Dove sei alle dieci e venticinque?

E. Dov'è Renzo? Here is Renzo's school schedule from Monday to Saturday. First, can you identify the subjects he takes?

Disegno	Geografia	Matematica	Scienze
Educazione fisica	Inglese	Musica	Storia
Educazione tecnica	Italiano	Religione	

"Ricreazione" is not a subject but a mid-morning break.

ORARIO DELLE LEZIONI

ORA	LUNEDÌ	MARTEDÌ	MERCOLEDÌ	GIOVEDÌ	VENERDÌ	SABATO
8,30	italiano	musica	disegno	inglese	italiano	matem.
9,25	storia	italiano	matem.	disegno	storia	ed. tec.
10,20	inglese	geografia	ed. tec.	matem.	geografia	italiano
11,15	ricreazione					
11,30	ed. tec.	ed. fisica	italiano	ed. tec.	inglese	storia
12,25	religione*	matem.	storia	ed. fisica	disegno	ed. civica

(* o attività alternativa)

Follow the example and give the appropriate information.

Ex.: It's Thursday - Sono le dieci e mezzo.
Renzo è a lezione di educazione fisica.

1. It's Monday. Sono le dodici e cinquanta.
2. It's Thursday. Sono le undici.
3. It's Wenesday. È l'una meno cinque.
4. It's Friday. Sono le dodici meno un quarto.
5. It's Tuesday. È mezzogiorno.
6. It's Saturday. Sono le nove e mezzo.

In Italy all official time schedules (trains, radio and television, theaters, stores etc.) use the 24-hour system (also known as military time).

Ex.: La partita di calcio Italia-Bulgaria è su [on] **RAIDUE** alle **venti e trenta** (8:30p.m.).

MERCOLEDÌ 20

RETEQUATTRO

9.40 La grande vallata
10.30 Aspettando il domani
11.20 Così gira il mondo
12.45 Ciao ciao
13.45 Sentieri - Sceneggiato
14.45 California - Sceneggiato
15.40 Una vita da vivere
16.30 La valle dei pini
18.30 General Hospital
19.30 Quincy - Telefilm
20.30 **Il sole nella stanza** - Film con Sandra Dee e Peter Fonda
23.30 Bunny Lake è scomparsa - Film con C. Lynley, L. Olivier
1.30 Ironside - Telefilm

ITALIA UNO

8.30 Strega per amore
9.30 Cannon - Telefilm
12.30 T.J. Hooker - Telefilm
11.30 Simon & Simon - Telefilm
12.30 T.J. Hooker
13.30 Magnum P.I. - Telefilm
14.15 Deejay Television
16.00 Bim bum bam - Disegni animati
18.00 Arnold - Tel.
18.30 A-Team - Telefilm
19.30 I Robinson - Telefilm
20.00 Evviva Palm Town Cartoni animati
20.30 **Domani mi sposo** - Film con J. Calà, I. Ferrari
22.20 Starsky e Hutch - Telefilm
23.20 Jonathan - Dimensione avventura
23.50 L'uomo da sei milioni di dollari - Telefilm
0.50 Wonder Woman - Telefilm

RAITRE

14.00 Rai Regione
14.30 Passaggi
15.30 Pattinaggio artistico
18.45 Derby
19.00 TG3
19.45 20 anni prima
20.30 **Sissi la giovane imperatrice** - Film con Romy Schneider
22.55 TV d'autore: Enzo Biagi
23.45 20 anni prima

CANALE 5

8.00 Fantasilandia
9.00 Una famiglia americana Telefilm
10.30 Casa mia - Gioco condotto da Lino Toffolo
12.00 I Jefferson - Telefilm
13.30 Cari genitori - Gioco condotto da E. Bonaccorti
14.15 Il gioco delle coppie - Gioco condotto da M. Predolin
15.00 Agenzia matrimoniale
15.30 Cerco e offro
17.00 Doppio slalom - Gioco
17.30 Babilonia - Gioco
18.00 OK! Il prezzo è giusto - Gioco condotto da Iva Zanicchi
19.45 Tra moglie e marito - Gioco condotto da Marco Columbro
20.25 **Il fiume dell'ira** - Film
22.30 Forum - Conduce Rita Dalla Chiesa
23.15 Maurizio Costanzo Show
0.45 Matalo - Film con Castel e Corrado Panni

F. Guida TV - Working with a partner and using the TV schedule excerpt above, identify the following shows and tell the channel on which they are broadcasted and at what time they start.

1. *The Price Is Right*
   a. Italian Title
   b. Channel
   c. Time
2. *One Life to Live*
   a. Italian Title
   b. Channel
   c. Time
3. *The Six Million Dollar Man*
   a. Italian Title
   b. Channel
   c. Time
4. *The Valley of the Pines*
   a. Italian Title
   b. Channel
   c. Time

4. *The Dating Game*
   a. Italian Title
   b. Channel
   c. Time
5. *As the World Turns*
   a. Italian Title
   b. Channel
   c. Time
6. *The Big Valley*
   a. Italian Title
   b. Channel
   c. Time
8. *An American Family (A TV movie)*
   a. Italian Title
   b. Channel
   c. Time

MORE NUMBERS

Da cinquantuno (51) a cento (100)

cinquantuno	cinquantasei	settanta
cinquantadue	cinquantasette	ottanta
cinquantatré	cinquantotto	novanta
cinquantaquattro	cinquantanove	cento
cinquantacinque	sessanta	

PROVIAMOCI

A.

Your List

1 book	*$12.25*
1 poster	*3.99*
*2 ice creams**	*2.50*
1 baseball glove	*24.00*
*1 sport coat**	*39.95*
3 pens	*1.75*
1 back pack	*17.65*
1 alarm clock	*8.55*
*1 down parka**	*89.00*

You have taken Renzo to the mall and you paid for everything. He is going to pay you back. Now tell him what you spent and for what. Use the list.

Ex.: Un libro: dodici e venticinque.

*Help: ice cream = il gelato
sport coat = la giacca
down parka = il piumino

B. a. Some Italian cities still have phone numbers with only six figures and they are often told in pairs. Here are some for you to read aloud.

Ex.: 32 • 83 • 75
trentadue, ottantatré, settantacinque

1. 82 • 79 • 15
2. 71 • 47 • 19
3. 67 • 59 • 76
4. 55 • 10 • 21
5. 39 • 88 • 93
6. 98 • 17 • 13

b. Bigger cities have seven digit phone numbers.
Read the following according to the model.

Ex.: 479 • 12 • 75
quattro, sette, nove, dodici, settantacinque

1. 551 • 82 • 20
2. 758 • 34 • 45
3. 637 • 69 • 58
4. 588 • 97 • 63
5. 765 • 77 • 66
6. 231 • 92 • 73

C. Answer the following questions in Italian.

Ex.: At what time do you get up? - **Alle sei e mezzo.**

1. When do you have breakfast?
2. When do you leave to go to school?
3. When do you have your first class?
4. At what time do you have your supper?
5. At what time do you watch your favorite show?

D. A che ora? [*At what time?*] - Answer the following questions in complete Italian sentences.

Ex.: A che ora arrivi a scuola? (7,15) - **Arrivo a scuola alle sette e un quarto.**

1. A che ora guardi la TV? (8,30)
2. A che ora nuoti in piscina? (10,15)
3. A che ora arriva l'autobus [*bus*]? (7,10)
4. A che ora ritorna dal lavoro [*from work*] papà? (4,45)
5. A che ora gioca a tennis la mamma? (2,20)

6. A che ora canti nel coro [*chorus*]? (9,35)
7. A che ora telefona tuo fratello a Jennifer? (8,00)

E. Andiamo a Roma! [*Let's go to Rome*]

DA/FROM NEW YORK - NYC - GMT-4
⊕ J.F.KENNEDY ITL. KM. 16 Δ 60'

		1234567	18.00	08.00G1	AZ 0611	PJYML	742
	15GIU	1234567	18.15	09.00G1	TW 0840	FCYBQ	747
16GIU		1234567	18.15	08.40G1	TW 0840	FCYBQ	747
		1234567	18.30	08.40G1	PA 0110	FCYBM	747
16GIU		1 3456	20.00	10.15G1	TW 0848	FCYBQ	767
16GIU	29LUG	123 6	21.00	11.00G1	AZ 0643	PJYML	742
30LUG		123 6	21.00	11.00G1	AZ 0609	PJYML	742

1. At what time does Flight AZ0611 leave from New York?
2. At what time does Flight AX0611 arrive in Rome?
3. Do you know what time it is where you live when it is 8:00 AM in Rome?

F. Write out the circled LOTTO numbers corresponding to each city.

1. BARI
2. CAGLIARI
3. FIRENZE
4. GENOVA
5. MILANO
6. NAPOLI
7. PALERMO
8. ROMA
9. TORINO
10. VENEZIA

LOTTO

Estrazioni di sabato 29-8-'99

BARI	31	84	**45**	37	57
CAGLIARI	30	79	42	74	**53**
FIRENZE	**38**	3	64	51	19
GENOVA	8	29	36	**19**	51
MILANO	56	**35**	63	16	15
NAPOLI	**51**	71	21	76	73
PALERMO	63	71	17	28	**40**
ROMA	51	54	80	**24**	15
TORINO	**31**	50	48	87	74
VENEZIA	55	15	35	11	**49**

PERFORMANCE ACTIVITIES

E ORA IN ITALIANO

It's breakfast and Mrs. Romano questions Renzo about his plans for the day.

Sig.ra R.:	Che programmi hai per oggi?
Renzo:	Accompagno John a scuola.
Sig.ra R.:	A scuola in agosto [*August*]?
Renzo:	Sì, John desidera vedere [*to see*] la partita di suo fratello.
Sig.ra R.:	Eh già, [*Oh, yeah*] i ragazzi incominciano presto[*early*] le partite di allenamento [*scrimmage*].
Renzo:	Ma la scuola ha un vero [*real*] campo da football?
Sig.ra R.:	Certo, c'è anche uno stadio.
Renzo:	Ma Brian paga per giocare?
Sig.ra R.:	Oh no, è un programma della scuola.
Renzo:	Io invece pago per giocare a minicalcio, a tennis, a pallacanestro.
Sig.ra R.:	Hai ragione. I ragazzi americani sono proprio [*really*] fortunati.

ASCOLTIAMO

Listen as your teacher reads aloud a series of questions. After each question, choose the most appropriate answer from the choices offered below.

1. a. alle quattro — b. Sono le quattro — c. Sì, sono le quattro.
2. a. la pallina — b. a calcio — c. John gioca bene.
3. a. al parco — b. nel coro — c. alla cassa
4. a. Canta bene — b. Canta male — c. Canta troppo.
5. a. Studio la storia — b. Studi la storia. — c. Studia la storia.

LEGGIAMO

Read the following passage, then answer the questions that follow based on the information you have read.

Di solito Renzo arriva presto a scuola e aspetta fuori [*outside*]con i compagni l'ora della prima [*first*] lezione. Qualche volta i ragazzi passano il tempo a giocare a "palletta" [to dribble with short kicks] con una palla da tennis o una lattina [*can*] di Coca Cola. Giocano anche le ragazze.

Renzo ha lezione dalle otto e mezzo alle undici e un quarto, quando c'è un breve periodo di ricreazione. Sono solo quindici minuti per andare in gabinetto [*restroom*] e fare uno spuntino [*snack*]. Alle undici e mezzo Renzo ritorna in classe.

La scuola finisce all'una e venti. Renzo ritorna a casa e mangia con la mamma, la nonna e i fratelli. Nel pomeriggio studia per due o tre ore, ma verso le cinque è libero [*free*]. Il martedì e il giovedì gioca con una squadra di calcio al circolo sportivo, il mercoledì ha lezione di chitarra. Tutta la famiglia è insieme [*together*] la sera, all'ora di cena [*supper*], alle otto e mezzo. Dopo cena Renzo spesso guarda la televisione o gioca a Nintendo. Alle undici va [*goes*] a letto.

Questions: Answer the following questions in English based on the information in the passage above.

1. How does Renzo pass the time at school before his first class?
2. What do Renzo and his friends commonly use instead of a soccer ball?
3. When does Renzo have his break from classes?
4. What does he do during the break?
5. At what time do classes resume after the break?
6. With whom does Renzo eat lunch?
7. How long does Renzo study on a typical afternoon?
8. What other afternoon activities does Renzo have?
9. At what time does the family eat supper?
10. What does Renzo do after supper?

PARLIAMO

A. Ask a friend in Italian for the following information and record your questions and answers.

Ex.: Do you sing well?
Question: **Tu canti bene?**
Answer: **No, io canto male.**

1. When do you arrive at school?
   Question: ...
   Answer: ...
2. At what time is the Italian class? [la lezione d'italiano]?
   Question: ...
   Answer: ...
3. Which [quale] radio station [stazione radio] do you listen to?
   Question: ...
   Answer: ...
4. Where do you play baseball?
   Question: ...
   Answer: ...
5. Who plays football in [a] San Francisco?
   Question: ...
   Answer: ...

B. Now share the information with your class.

Ex.: Il mio amico canta male (if a boy).
La mia amica canta male (if a girl).

SCRIVIAMO

A. In Italian, make a list of five activities you engage in on a typical day. Next to each activity write out the corresponding time in Italian.

Ex.: ascoltare la musica - alle otto di sera

C. Write a short note to your friend, Francesca. Tell her what you are doing Saturday. Include times.

ABOUT ITALY

IL CALCIO / *SOCCER*

The Italian national sport is soccer, which in Italy is called *calcio*. Many refer to it with the English name of football because it was in England, in 1863, that the game was played with rules similar to those of today. *Calcio* is the most popular sport. Kids of all ages have the irresistible urge to kick anything that comes close to their feet; if not a ball, it might be a pebble, an empty can or a piece of wrinkled paper lost on the street pavement.

Each Italian city has its soccer team (*la squadra di calcio*), Torino, Milano, Genova and Roma have two. They play each other every Sunday between September and June, and many Italians go to *lo stadio* or watch the game (*la partita*) on TV. The following Monday people discuss endlessly the performance of their favorite team. They read il *Corriere Dello Sport* and other sports newspapers and compare scores. Sometimes fans (*i tifosi*) disagree and end up in fist fights!

The best players of the various teams play in international games. They wear blue jerseys, which is why they are called *gli Azzurri*. Il *Campionato Mondiale* or simply *il Mondiale* is the international world championship.

Traditionally, soccer was played by men. In Firenze a very rough form of soccer is still played between teams of men from different sections of town. The teams play wearing traditional costumes from hundreds of years ago. Now, however, there are several women's teams all over Italy, and they are very good!

Italy has a sort of lottery called, "Totocalcio," played by millions of Italians. To win, one has to guess the results of Sunday's games.

ALPINISMO

■ IMBRAGATURA «GEKO»

Pensata per il free-climbing (pesa 335 g), è una cintura anatomica, morbida e resistent... prodotta con u... sistema di c... computerizza... strappo brevet... Camp (0341-89... Costa 116 mila li...

SUB

■ MASCHERA MARES

La maschera a sei lenti della Mares (0185-2011) è la prima subacquea a

permettere la visibilità di lato e in basso. Così si può tenere tutto sotto controllo senza interrompere la nuotata. È di silicone e vetr... mperato. Costa

PATTINAGGIO IN LINEA

■ AIR WARP NIKE

Gli Air Warp della Nike (t... 929911) hanno l'ammort... nell'avampiede e nel tall... che assorbono le vibraz... anche a terreni irregol... mila lire. N... già stati ... di pai... E i r... son... per ce... tre a...

■ LA SCARPA DEI MONDIALI

La Diadora (tel. 0423-6581), in occasione d... Mondiali, ha messo sul mercato una linea di ... calcio con i colori delle squadre. Il modello r... quello dell'Olanda, che sarà calzato durant... da Seedorf. I tacchetti sono... e la soletta è antisho... proteggere le ar... Un paio...

TENNIS

■ BLACKBURNE DS 97

Le racchette a doppia incordatura distribuiscono meglio l'impatto con la palla anche nelle zone periferiche. Questa della Blackburne (importata da Scaglia Sport, tel. 02-581731) è il modello Ds 97 e costa 637 mila lire. In Italia i praticanti del tennis sono 2,2 milioni, di cui il 43 per cento saltuari.

CAPITOLO SETTE: IL TEMPO LIBERO
CHAPTER SEVEN: LEISURE TIME

FUNCTIONS

Exchanging information (about games and activities)
Dates, weather and seasons

LANGUAGE

Verbs in "*-are*" (plural)
The calendar: days of the week, months, seasons, weather
Che tempo fa?

ABOUT ITALY

Renzo's leisure time

SITUATION

As the boys help Mrs. Romano in the yard they talk about the match.

RENZO:	Dov'è la casa di John? (*John indicates the direction*) È **lontana**? (*Renzo waves his hand to indicate far away*)
JOHN:	No, è ... uh ...(*Frustated, John indicates with a motion that the house is nearby*)
RENZO:	Allora è **vicina**.
JOHN:	Sì, molto vicina, cinque minuti. (*pleased with himself*) A Roma, a che cosa **giocate** tu e ...
RENZO:	Gli **amici**? Beh, **giochiamo a calcio, a minicalcio, a pallacanestro, a tennis. Andiamo in bicicletta o in motorino**.
JOHN:	Motorino? (*pretends to be revving up a motorbike*) Oh, motorcycle!
RENZO:	No, non la motocicletta, più piccolo.
JOHN:	A moped?
RENZO:	Sì, moped. **Poi** andiamo a nuotare **al mare**.(*Renzo imitates swimming*)
JOHN:	I get it, swim. In the sea? (*undulates arms like a wave*)
RENZO:	Sì, nel mare, andiamo spesso alla **spiaggia** di Maccarese vicino a Roma. Ma andiamo anche in **piscina**. (*pointing to his aunt's swimming pool*)
JOHN:	Mrs. Romano, can you ask him what he does in the winter?
MRS. R.:	Cosa fai d'**inverno**?
RENZO:	**Mi piace** andare in montagna a **sciare**. **Ti piace** sciare?
JOHN:	You ski? Cool!

MRS. R.: Ragazzi, perché restate qui a parlare? Fa caldo oggi! Andate in piscina.
JOHN: Va bene, vado a casa **a prendere**[*to get*] il costume da bagno.
RENZO: **D'accordo**. A più tardi.

PAROLE DA RICORDARE

NOUNS

gli amici	friends
la bicicletta	bicycle
il calcio	soccer
l'inverno	winter
il mare	sea
il minicalcio	mini-soccer
la montagna	mountain
la motocicletta	motorcycle
il motorino	moped
la pallacanestro	basketball
la piscina	swimming pool
la spiaggia	beach
il tennis	tennis

OTHERS

allora	then, so
beh	well
lontano (da)	far [from](adv.)
più	more
poi	then
vicino (a)	near [to](adv.)
molto	very (adv.)
oggi	today
moltissimo	very much

VERBS

andiamo	we go/are going (andare)
giocate	you play, (plural)
giochiamo	we play/are playing
prendere	to get/ take
restare	to stay
sciare	to ski
vado	I go/am going (andare)
sai	you know

ADJECTIVES

lontano (da)	far; far away from
vicino (a)	near
molto	much; a great deal

USEFUL EXPRESSIONS

vado a sciare	I go skiing
andiamo a sciare	we go sking
più piccolo	smaller
Cosa fai?	What do you do?
D'accordo	Agreed!
mi piace	I like
ti piace (?)	you like; (do you like?)

PROVERBIO

Lontano dagli occhi, lontano dal cuore

PROVIAMOCI

Puoi dire... ? [*Can you say... ?*]

1. your father has a motorcycle.
2. you and your sister play basketball.
3. you and your cousin go to swim in [a] swimming pool.
4. Paul and Mary don't have a moped.
5. Jeff's house is nearby.
6. you and your friend have a bicycle.
7. "Do you play soccer at school?"
8. we go skiing in the winter.
9. "Are we playing basketball today?"
10. John's house is not far away.

Verbs ending in "-are" plural forms

Did you notice the verb **giocare** with an ending you haven't seen before? The new ending is "**-iamo**". "**-Iamo**" says that "we" are doing whatever activity the verb represents. "**-Iamo**" is the first of three plural forms of **-are** verbs conjugated in the present tense.

Here are the verbs, **usare** and **giocar**e conjugated in all their forms in the present tense.

Usare [*to use*]

io	us**o**	I use	noi	us**iamo**	we use
tu	us**i**	you (sing.) use	voi	us**ate**	you (pl.) use
lui	us**a**	he uses	loro	us**ano**	they use
lei	us**a**	she uses			
Lei	us**a**	you (polite) use	Loro	us**ano**	you (pol., pl.) use

Giocare [*to play*]

io	gioc**o**	I play	noi	gioch**iamo**	we play
tu	gioch**i**	you (sing.) play	voi	gioc**ate**	you (pl.) play
lui	gioc**a**	he plays	loro	gioc**ano**	they play
lei	gioc**a**	she plays			
Lei	gioc**a**	you (polite)	Loro	gioc**ano**	you (pol., pl.) play

Remember that subject pronouns are not always used in Italian. They really aren't necessary because the verb endings tell you who is performing the action. Of course, where confusion may arise, the subject pronouns are used.

Ex.: Jeff e Anna abitano in città. **Lui** abita vicino a John ma [*but*] **lei** abita lontano.

You couldn't eliminate the pronouns above because you wouldn't know who lives close by and who lives far away. When John speaks to Renzo (in the dialogue), the whole conversation is about Jeff so the subject pronoun, "**lui**" is unnecessary.

Below you will find more frequently used **-are** verbs:

aspettare	to wait for	**insegnare**	to teach
ballare	to dance	**lavorare**	to work
cercare	to look for, try	**mangiare**	to eat
chiamare	to call	**portare**	to carry, bring, wear
comprare	to buy	**restare**	to stay
domandare	to ask	**tagliare**	to cut
entrare in	to enter	**trovare**	to find
frequentare	to attend	**visitare**	to visit

PROVIAMOCI

A. Create complete sentences using the verb **giocare**. Follow the model.

Exs.: **Tu ... a Nintendo**?
Tu **giochi** a Nintendo?
Io non **gioco** a Nintendo.

1. Lui ... a pallacanestro
2. Loro ... a calcio
3. Io e Laura ... a pallone
4. Voi ... a football con gli amici
5. I ragazzi ... al parco.
6. Lei ... a tennis con John
7. Noi ... a Hacky Sac con Jeff e Roger
8. Tu ... a baseball in America?
9. Gli amici di Renzo ... anche a pallacanestro.
10. I ragazzi Silvestri ... a tombola [*BINGO*].

B. Complete the following sentences with the correct verb ending.

1. Noi and ... in piscina alle undici.
2. Voi aspett ... l'autobus vicino alla scuola.
3. Loro chiam ... i fratelli.
4. Caterina ed io compr ... i libri di storia.
5. Tu e Franco entr ... in classe insieme.
6. Renzo e sua sorella frequent ... le scuole italiane.
7. Tu, che cosa impar ...in questa classe?
8. Chi insegn ... il corso di francese?
9. Lui che cosa port ... alla nonna per il suo compleanno?
10. Perché i ragazzi non mangi ... gli spinaci?

C. Put the verb in parentheses in the proper form.

Io mi (chiamare) ... Paolo Costa. (Frequentare) ... la scuola media [*middle school*] "Dante Alighieri." La mattina (arrivare) ... a scuola alle otto e dieci. Oggi la prima lezione, matematica, (incominciare) ... alle otto e venti. La professoressa Rossi (insegnare) ... matematica da trent'anni. Lei (cercare) ... di insegnare bene a tutti i ragazzi però [*but*] loro (studiare) ... poco [*little*]. Io e il mio amico Franco (imparare) ... molto perché (ascoltare) ... attentamente. Voi (ascoltare) ... il professore?

NOTA CULTURALE

Dante Alighieri, from Florence, is considered by many as the father of the Italian language.

C. Working in groups of three, practice creating sentences in each cell of the grid below. Take turns completing the cells, making sure group members switch columns. In so doing each group member will get an opportunity to create sentences for different kinds of subjects.

	Papà ed io	**Tu e Luigi**	**Gli zii**
Ex. aspettare	l'autobus ***Aspettiamo l'autobus.***	la mamma ***Aspettate la mamma.***	il treno ***Aspettano il treno.***
1. lavorare	in giardino	al ristorante	in ufficio
2. mandare	una lettera	un pacco [package]	un telegramma
3. tornare	a casa	dal supermercato	dall'America
4. trovare	un dollaro	una pallina	un appartamento
5. usare	la moto	la bicicletta	il computer
6. visitare	lo zoo	il museo	l'acquario
7. salutare	i parenti	gli amici	la signora Romano
8. entrare	in casa	in macchina	in camera
9. imparare	l'italiano	la matematica	l'Internet
10. telefonare	in Italia	a Roma	a Maria

Can you tell what each sentence created in the exercise above means in English?

D. Un'intervista [*An interview*]

1. Now that you know how to use some common verbs, you can really start to converse. Complete the following questions and answers, then try them out with classmates.

English version	Italian version
Q: What's your name? (literally: "What do you call yourself?)	Q: Come ti (chiamare) ...?
A: My name is ___ (name). (literally: "I call myself ___.")	A: Mi (chiamare) ...______.
Q: Where do you live?	Q: Dove (abitare) ...?
A: I live on ___(fill in a name) street, number ___(fill in).	A: (Abitare) ...in via ___, numero ___.
Q: What school do you attend?	Q: Che scuola (frequentare) ...?
A: I attend ___(fill in the name).	A: (Frequentare) ... ___.
Q: What do you study?	Q: Che cosa (studiare) ...?
A: I study ____ (list subjects).	A: (Studiare) ... ___.

2. Surely you'll want to know other things about your partner. Using the pictures as a guide, ask him/her if he/she does the suggested activity. Your partner should then answer your question.

Ex.

Ex.: **Q:** (Tu) Suoni la chitarra?
A: No, non suono la chitarra.

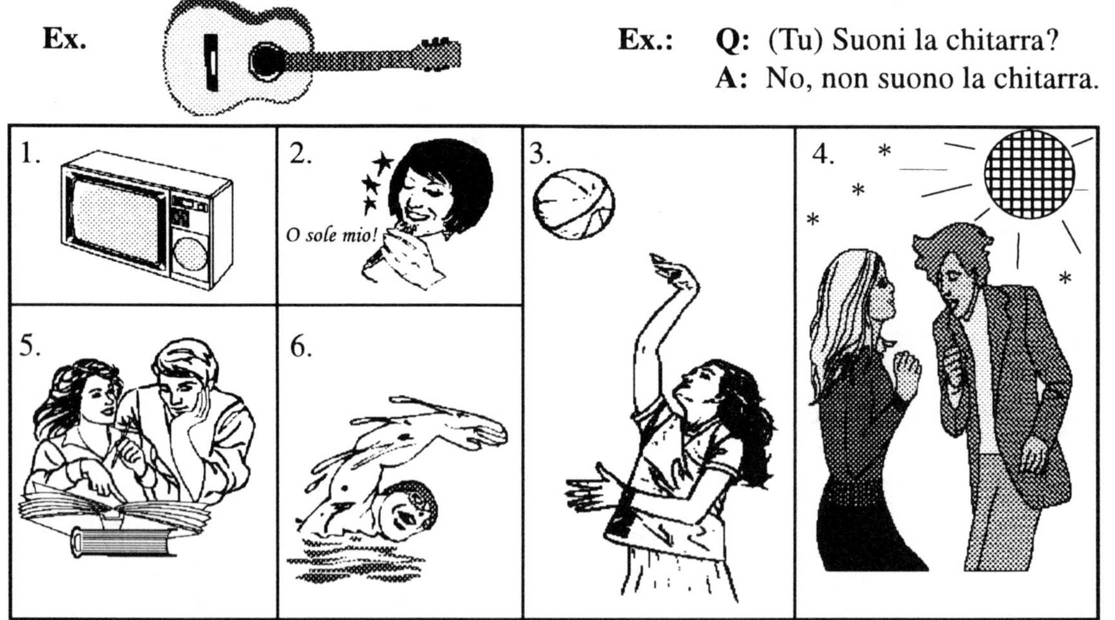

3. A similar conversation to that in exercise 2 can take place with more than one person. The question in the example will become:

Q: (Voi) Suonate la chitarra?

and the answer would be:

A: (Noi) Non suoniamo la chitarra.

Using the same suggestions in exercise 2, now carry on your interview with more than one person.

E. Family Friends: A few weeks before coming to the United States, Renzo's mom had invited a woman that she worked with, and her family, to dinner. The woman has two daughters. Using the English below and the sketches of the situation as a guide, determine what the characters are saying in Italian.

Which school do you attend?
We attend Giulio Cesare.
What do you study?
We study English, History, Math, Science, Latin and Italian.
Why don't we listen to CD's?
Let's listen to Zucchero.
I have CD's of Eros Ramazzotti, Claudio Baglioni, Lucio Dalla e Gianna Nannini.
What beautiful music!
We always listen to Eros Ramazzotti!

I MESI DELL'ANNO

THE MONTHS OF THE YEAR

All months are masculine.

gennaio	**febbraio**	**marzo**	**aprile**	**maggio**	**giugno**
luglio	**agosto**	**settembre**	**ottobre**	**novembre**	**dicembre**

I GIORNI DELLA SETTIMANA

THE DAYS OF THE WEEK

Days are masculine, with the exception of "domenica" (la domenica).

lunedì **martedì** **mercoledì** **giovedì**

venerdì **sabato** **domenica**

1. In Italy, Monday is the first day of the week.

2. Here is how Italians ask and answer about the date:

Che giorno è oggi? [*What day is today?*]
Quanti ne abbiamo? [*What is the date?*]
Qual'è la data di oggi? [*What is the date today?*]

È domenica. [*It is Sunday.*]
Ne abbiamo 10 (dieci). [*It is the tenth.*]
Oggi è il 10 (dieci) aprile. [*Today is the tenth of April.*]

3. When a number begins with a vowel, an apostrophe is used:

Oggi è **l'**8 (otto) giugno. Oggi è **l'**11 (undici) ottobre

4. For the first day of the month the ordinal number is used.

Oggi è il **1° (primo)** maggio. Today is the first of May.

5. You certainly have noticed that the days and months are not capitalizes in Italian.
Remember also that:
a) "On" + day is **not** translated in Italian.
b) When something happens on a certain day every week, Italian uses an article.

Lunedì ho un appuntamento. **On** Monday I have an appointment. (Just on the coming Monday)

La domenica canto nel coro. **On** Sundays I sing in the choir.

PAROLE UTILI CON LE DATE

USEFUL WORDS WITH DATES

la data	date	**di mattina**	in the morning
oggi	today	**di pomeriggio**	in the afternoon
domani	tomorrow	**di sera**	in the evening
dopodomani	day after tomorrow	**di notte**	at night
ieri	yesterday		

PROVIAMOCI

A. Renzo's sister, Laura, teaches John a jazzy little rap that helps to remember the months of the year. Can you reproduce it?

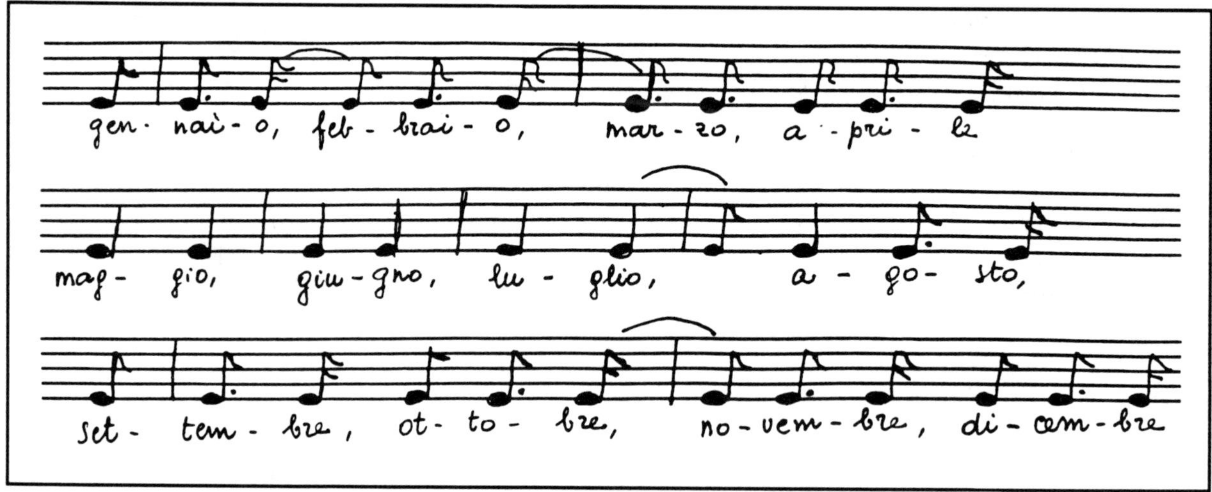

B. Express the following dates in Italian.

1. May 10
2. July 6
3. January 25
4. June 2
5. Tuesday, March 30
6. Sunday, September 1
7. Wednesday, November 15
8. Monday, August 5
9. Thursday, December 9
10. Saturday, April 6

C. Ask your partner for the following dates then exchange roles. Follow the model.

Ex.: 16/12 **Q.: Qual'è la data di oggi?**
A.: Oggi è il sedici dicembre.

1. 25/8 2. 12/3 3. 4/7 4. 7/115. 30/1 6. 16/10

D. When were you born? Now go around the classroom and ask your classmates when they were born and listen to their answers.

You say: **Quando sei nato/a?** [*When were you born?*]
He/she says: **Sono nato/a il cinque agosto.** [*I was born on August 5th.*]

E. Give the following important dates in Italian.

1. New Year's Day
2. St. Patrick's Day
3. Columbus Day
2. Valentine's Day
5. Lincoln's Birthday
6. Washington's Birthday
7. Independence Day
8. Your birthday
9. Christmas Day

F. With the help of Mrs. Romano, John has put together a schedule for his family. Help him explain his family activities to Renzo.

LUGLIO						
Lunedì, 17	Martedì,18	Mercoledì,19	Giovedì, 20	Venerdì, 21	Sabato, 22	Domenica, 23
tagliare l'erba	*lavare la macchina*	*andare in piscina* *guardare la sorellina*	*suonare nella banda*	*aiutare la nonna*	*giocare a baseball*	*andare in chiesa*

Lunedì io ... l'erba. Martedì mio fratello ... la macchina ed io ... la sorellina. Mercoledì mio cugino ed io ... in piscina. Giovedì mio fratello e mia cugina ... nella banda comunale [*town band*]. Venerdì mia madre e mia zia ... la nonna in casa. Sabato io ... a baseball nel parco. Domenica noi ... in chiesa.

G. Working in pairs, ask and answer the following questions in Italian. Let student #1 ask and student #2 answer, then switch roles. Record your conversation in writing.

1. What day is today?
2. What is today's date?
3. What do you do [*Cosa fai*] on Mondays?
4. What do you do on Sundays?
5. Do you study on Friday evenings?
6. What are you doing [*Cosa fai*] on Saturday?
7. What do you watch on Wednesday evening?
8. Do you watch the games on Monday?
9. Who is playing football on Monday evening?

LE STAGIONI DELL'ANNO

THE SEASONS OF THE YEAR

La primavera - spring
L'estate - summer
L'autunno - autumn
L'inverno - winter

piantare giocare a baseball

nuotare tagliare l'erba

giocare a football rastrellare le foglie

sciare pattinare

Cosa fai in ogni stagione? [*What do you do in each season?*]

PROVIAMOCI

A. Complete each with an appropriate verb form.

Ex.: D'inverno io **pattino** sul ghiaccio [*ice-skate*].

1. D'estate loro ... l'erba.
2. D'inverno noi ... sul ghiaccio.
3. In primavera tu ... a baseball.
4. In autunno lui ... le foglie.
5. D'estate John ... in piscina.

B. Che cosa fai? [*What do you do?*]

1. D'inverno io ...
2. In primavera io ...
3. In autunno io ...
4. D'estate io ...

CHE TEMPO FA?

WHAT IS THE WEATHER DOING?

Fa bello. [*It is nice out.*]
È una bella giornata.
[*It is a beautiful day.*]

Fa brutto. [*It is bad.*]
È una brutta giornata.
[*It is an ugly day.*]

Piove. [*It is raining.*]

Fa freddo [*It is cold.*]   Fa caldo. [*It is hot (warm)*]   Fa fresco. [*It is cool.*]

Tira vento [*It is windy.*]   Nevica. [*It is snowing.*]   È sereno. [*It is clear.*]

È nuvoloso. [*It is cloudy.*]   C'è il sole. [*It is sunny.*]   C'è nebbia. [*It is foggy.*]

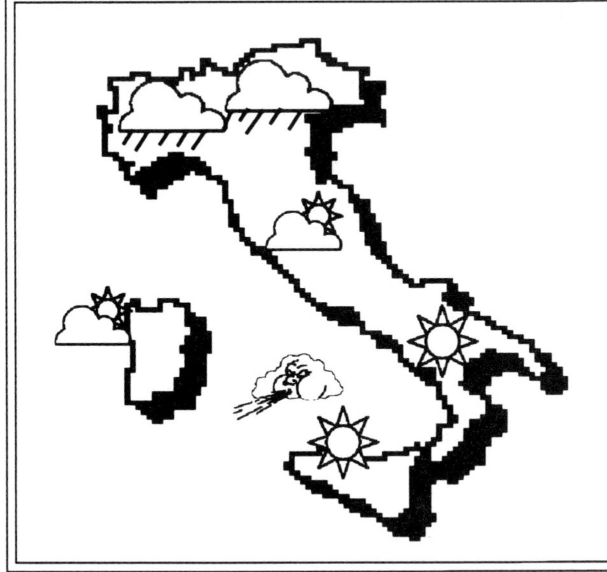

PREVISIONI DEL TEMPO

A nord molto nuvoloso
con piogge intermittenti.

Nelle zone centrali parzialmente
nuvoloso e caldo.

Sereno a sud con temperature
in aumento.

Vento nelle isole con mare mosso.

PROVIAMOCI

A. Fill in the missing information on the chart.

Mese	Tempo	Attività
A gennaio	fa freddo	e gioco a tennis.
A maggio		
A luglio		e vado in piscina.
A ottobre	fa fresco	
A dicembre		e vado a sciare.

B. Che tempo fa oggi nella tua città? [*What's the weather today in your town?*] Describe the weather in your town in Italian.

C. Secondo voi [*In your opinion*] che tempo fa in queste città? Take turns with a partner asking and responding with your opinions on the weather in the following cities. Record your answers in writing. You can research this information on the Internet.

1. Orlando, Florida
2. Denver, Colorado
3. Sydney, Australia
4. Moscow, Russia
5. Tokyo, Japan
6. San Francisco, California
7. Montreal, Quebec
8. Edinburg, Scotland
9. Rome, Italy
10. Capetown, South Africa

D. Describe the weather in Italian using the clues below.

1. John's father leaves home with an umbrella.
2. Mrs. Wright tells John to wear his boots.
3. Don't forget your swimsuit!
4. Put the latch on the shutter!
5. You need sunglasses today!
6. The airport must be closed.
7. The Jones are going to the beach today.
8. The visibility on the road is drastically diminished.
9. It is the perfect night to be gazing at stars!

PERFORMANCE ACTIVITIES

E ORA IN ITALIANO

Renzo talks about his vacation plans with his classmate, Isa.

Isa:	E allora [*so*], dove passi l'estate quest'anno?
Renzo:	Vado in America da mia zia.
Isa:	Che bello! Resti sempre a casa sua? Dove abita?
Renzo:	Mia zia abita a Rochester e porta la mia famiglia a New York e alle cascate del Niagara.
Isa:	Ma non andate al mare?
Renzo:	No, andiamo al lago e inoltre [*furthermore*] la zia ha una bella piscina.
Isa:	Allora fa sempre caldo a Rochester?
Renzo:	Oh no, d'inverno fa molto freddo e c'è tanta neve.
Isa:	E tua zia ha una piscina? Che strano!

Read the following article and then answer the questions below.

Italia sulle Alpi:

È già tempo di sci.

Grazie alla forte nevicata del 16 novembre, c'è già molta neve sulle piste di Cortina e di altre zone alpine. Le previsioni del tempo per la prossima settimana indicano cielo sereno e temperature moderate. Gli entusiasti dello sci avranno le condizioni favorevoli per passare una settimana bianca sulla neve.

Which areas have been affected most by recent snows?
What weather is predicted for the week?
Who will benefit most from this weather?

ASCOLTIAMO

Listen as your teacher reads aloud a setting in English followed by a passage in Italian which will be read twice; then choose the most appropriate response to the question based on the passage you have just heard.

1. Che giorno è domani?

   a. il primo dicembre　b. il primo gennaio　c. il primo febbraio

2. In quale mese i ragazzi italiani hanno vacanze lunghe?

   a. a gennaio　b. a dicembre　c. a febbraio

3. Dove vanno spesso [*often go*] d'estate i ragazzi Silvestri?

   a. in montagna　b. al mare　c. a casa degli zii

4. Come sono le sere di primavera a Napoli?

   a. fredde　b. fresche　c. calde

5. Che tempo fa a Perugia?

   a. È una bella giornata.　b. Nevica.　c. È molto nuvoloso.

PARLIAMO

A. Che cosa fai ...? Interview a classmate and record his/her answers.

1. sabato mattina?
2. venerdì mattina?
3. domenica pomeriggio?
4. domani sera?
5. oggi pomeriggio?
6. dopodomani?
7. stasera?
8. sabato sera?

B. Now share the information with your class. Begin by saying:

Lui/lei sabato mattina ...
Venerdì sera ...
etc.

C. Ask your classmates what activities they do during the summer. Choose from the following:

Ex.: Pattinare [*skate*] al parco - (You say): **Pattinate al parco?**
(They say): **Sì, pattiniamo al parco.**

1. Giocare a calcio
2. Guardare un video
3. Visitare lo zoo
4. Ascoltare le cassette
5. Festeggiare la festa dell'Indipendenza
6. Invitare gli amici a un picnic
7. Mangiare un bel gelato
8. Tagliare l'erba

D. Una piccola poesia [*A little poem*] - Memorize the following poem and recite it in class.

Trenta giorni ha novembre
con april, giugno e settembre;
di ventotto ce n'è uno,
tutti gli altri ne han trentuno

Remember "Row, Row, Row Your Boat?" The above poem can be recited as a "round." Let the first group begin the poem, as soon as it completes the first line, the second group starts the first line, and so on ...

E. Working with yout partner, ask whether or not he/she likes the following activities. Record the responses and then switch roles. Follow the model below.

Ex.: Ti piace giocare a Nintendo? Sì, mi piace (molto/moltissimo).
No, non mi piace (affatto [*at all]*).

1. parlare al telefono
2. fare le spese [*go shopping*]
3. guardare la tivù
4. leggere [*to read*] libri
5. viaggiare [*to travel*]
6. festeggiare il Natale
7. nuotare nel mare
8. suonare la chitarra
9. andare al cinema
10. studiare la matematica
11. giocare a tennis
12. imparare l'italiano
13. lavorare
14. sciare con gli amici
15. ascoltare la musica rock
16. tagliare l'erba

Can you add other activities to this list?

SCRIVIAMO

1. Describe today's weather and write down some of the activities you will do.

2. Make a list of a few activities you do in each season.

3. In a short paragraph talk about your typical summer.

4. You and a friend are spending some time together this week. In a short paragraph write about the things you will do together.

5. **Saluti da Taormina!** Taormina is a beautiful seaside resort in Sicily. Visitors can swim in the sea, listen to concerts and watch shows under the stars at the fabulous Teatro romano [Roman theater], eat in lovely restaurants and even go skiing on the slopes of nearby Mt. Etna! Write a short postcard message to a friend from Taormina.
   - Tell where you are.
   - Tell what the weather is.
   - Tell what you do every day [ogni giorno].

ABOUT ITALY

RENZO'S LEISURE TIME

Renzo is having a great time in the United States and is enjoying John's company very much. In the summer, he usually spends a month at the beach and, often, a couple of weeks in the mountains. His parents strongly believe that it is important for the children's health to be away from Rome at least a few weeks every year. Renzo thinks that they are right; especially now that he compares life in a big city with the clean air, the open spaces and the conveniences of American suburban life.

When school is in session, Renzo does not have much free time. It is true that classes are over around one o'clock, but there is homework to do every day. Renzo's teachers are demanding and his parents expect him to get good grades. He tries to do at least part of his homework right after lunch so that he might have a few hours for himself in the late afternoon. If he has money, he can go to a movie with his friends, (the first show is at 4:00) or, with a little planning, they can play *minicalcio*, a reduced form of soccer, played on the area of a tennis court. It is very popular among teenagers. The rental of the field is affordable when shared by ten players, and the smaller space required is more easily available in the city.

Twice a week Renzo goes to the swimming pool. He is a good athlete and his coach has high hopes for him. Renzo likes swimming and sometimes he dreams of representing Italy as an athlete of CONI (Comitato Olimpico Nazionale Italiano). In winter, he sometimes goes skiing, but only Sundays are available and the ski slopes are far from Rome. It takes a few hours to reach them.

The highlight of the school year is the cultural trip: a whole week spent in some interesting places in Italy or abroad. Renzo and his friends have studied Venice "in the field." They hope to go to Paris and London soon.

At home, 8:30 is supper time and Renzo must be in. He is too young to go out again; besides, he usually has more studying to do. He can console himself with a computer game, listen to music or join the family in the living room and watch TV. Of course, he can't wait to be a little older, own a moped and have more freedom. Life is hard!

CLASS ACTIVITY

List similarities and differences in how young people in Italy and in the United States spend their free time.

The beaches of the Tyrrhenian sea are perfect for Renzo to enjoy long summer days.

The high peaks of the Apennine Mountains provide slopes where the Silvestri family can ski.

Renzo likes taking trips with his school friends to interesting places like the "Queen of the Adriatic," Venice!

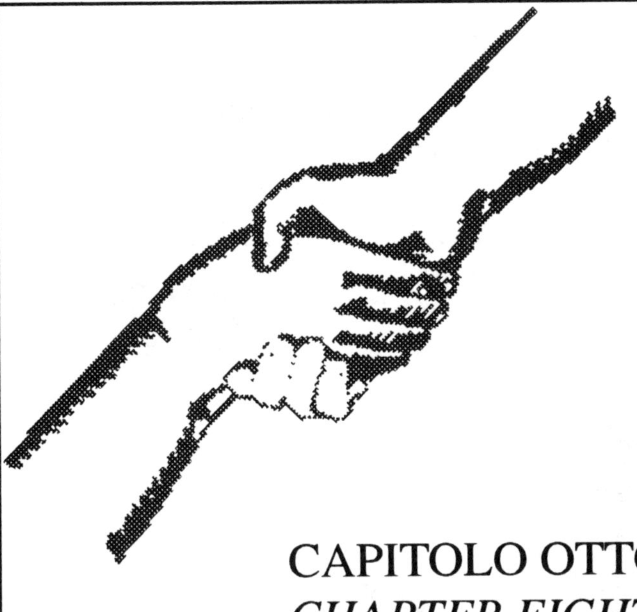

CAPITOLO OTTO: LA GRANDE PARTITA
CHAPTER EIGHT: THE BIG GAME

FUNCTIONS

Providing and obtaining information
Encouraging a course of action
Describing
Commenting on personal traits
Making comparisons
Expressing opinions

LANGUAGE

Verbs in "*-ere*"
Da quanto tempo ... ?
More descriptive adjectives
Più and *meno*
Mi piace, mi piacciono

ABOUT ITALY
Laura as a student of the "*liceo*"

SITUATION

As John and Renzo approach Jeff's house, they can see Jeff and Roger Adams practicing on the street in front of the house. Jeff is big for his age and a bit husky. Roger is small and thin.

RENZO:	Chi è Jeff; **quello** grande e grosso o quello più piccolo?
JOHN:	Quello grande.
RENZO:	Quanti anni ha?
JOHN:	Quattordici.
RENZO:	Mamma mia! Com'è grande!
JEFF:	(*noticing the boys approaching*) Hey, Wright, who is that little guy?
RENZO:	Che dice? Che dice?
JOHN:	Dice che sei molto piccolo.
RENZO:	**Ma** che **tipo**, non mi **conosce** e **già m'insulta**! Certo non è gentile!
JOHN:	Conosce? "Nosce ... nose ... knows!" Yeah, he doesn't know you and he's already insulting you. Non ti preoccupare, noi siamo bravi!
RENZO:	(*to himself*) Sì, ma è importante vincere. (*aloud*) Su, andiamo! Perché perdiamo tempo e non incominciamo a giocare?
JOHN:	Hai ragione!
JEFF:	(*winking at Roger*) Yeah, and the losers treat the winners to sundaes.
RENZO:	No, not Sunday, noi giochiamo adesso! (*John laughs*)

(Despite his size and cockiness, Jeff is no match for the smaller, more agile, Renzo. He does

not know that Italian kids play street soccer with anything handy, from soda cans to wadded paper, and they start at an early age. Renzo is a fast learner and he and John win.)

RENZO: (*smiling*) Mi piace giocare a "Hackey sac!" E sono sicuro che a Jeff e Roger non piace perdere. (*gives John a "high five."*)

PAROLE DA RICORDARE

ADJECTIVES

importante	important
gentile	kind, nice
grosso	big, huge, husky
superiore	superior

PRONOUNS

quello	that, that one
mi	me

OTHERS

adesso	now
già	already
spesso	often

USEFUL EXPRESSIONS

Andiamo!	Let's go!
Che tipo!	What a (funny) guy!
Mi piace	I like
perdere tempo	to waste time
Su!	Come on!

VERBS

conoscere	to know (person, place)
insultare	to insult
perdere	to lose
sa (sapere)	he knows (facts, how to)
vincere	to win

PROVIAMOCI

A. Vero o falso? [*True or False*] Read the following statements and correct those that are false.

1. Renzo è piccolo.
2. Anche Jeff è piccolo.
3. Jeff ha sedici anni.
4. A Renzo piace giocare a Hackey Sac.
5. Jeff insulta Renzo
6. John è amico di Renzo.
7. Renzo non vuole [wants] giocare.

B. Can you complete the sentences?

1. Jeff ha ... anni.
2. Anche Renzo ha ... anni ma lui è ....
3. I ragazzi vogliono [*want*] giocare ... Hackey Sac.

4. Jeff non ... Renzo e già lo insulta.
5. ... dice Jeff?
6. Jeff dice che Renzo è molto ....
7. A Jeff non ... perdere.

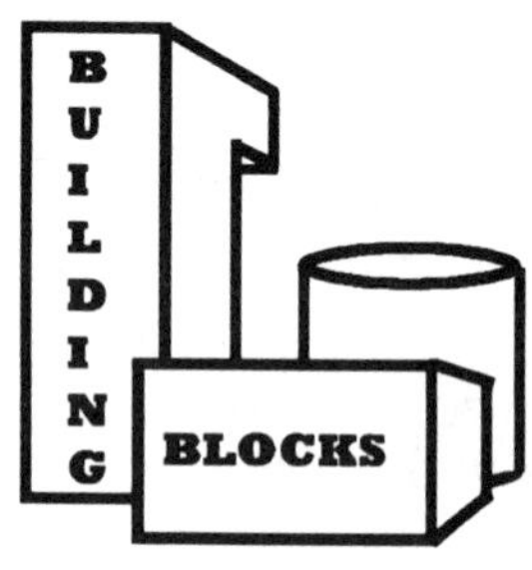

Verbs ending in "-ere"

Conoscere is an example of the second kind of verbs that exists in Italian. Many of the changes that occur when you conjugate an "**-ere**" verbs are the same kind as the "**-are**" verbs that you already know.

Portare (to carry, bring or wear)		**Conoscere** (to know [somebody or someplace])	
io	port**o**	io	conosc**o**
tu	port**i**	tu	conosc**i**
lui/lei/Lei	port**a**	lui/lei/Lei	conosc**e**
noi	port**iamo**	noi	conosc**iamo**
voi	port**ate**	voi	conosc**ete**
loro/Loro	port**ano**	loro/Loro	conosc**ono**

Some common "**-ere**" verbs are:

chiedere	to ask	**promettere**	to promise
chiudere	to close	**ricevere**	to receive
correre	to run	**ripetere**	to repeat
credere (in, a)	to believe	**rispondere (a)**	to answer
decidere	to decide	**scrivere**	to write
discutere	to discuss	**spendere**	to spend (money)
leggere	to read	**vedere**	to see
mettere	to put, place	**vendere**	to sell
perdere	to lose, miss, waste	**vincere**	to win
prendere	to take, get, have (food or drink)	**vivere**	to live

PROVIAMOCI

A guessing game: Make a list of the Italian verbs which are related to the English words given below. Compare your list to that of one of your classmates.

1. creed	8. discussion	15. promise
2. repetition	9. arrival	16. desire
3. return	10. telephone	17. visit
4. entrance	11. lector	18. use
5. receipt	12. scripture	19. pay
6. feast	13. study	20. labor
7. decision	14. frequent	21. courier

Now look how "**-ere**" verbs appear in the conversation between Renzo and John after their match.

Renzo:	**Da quanto tempo conosci** Jeff?
John:	How long have I known him? Ah ..., **Conosco Jeff da cinque anni.**
Renzo:	Jeff perde spesso a "Hacky Sac?"
John:	Perde?
Renzo:	(*gives the thumbs down signal with a questioning look*)
John:	Loses? No, non perde spesso. (*Demonstrates opposite with the thumbs up.*)
Renzo:	Ah, vince? Adesso capisco perché non sa perdere.
John:	Crede di essere superiore.
Renzo:	Non è molto simpatico.

Amico and **simpatico** have irregular plurals.

amico > amici　　　　simpatico > simpatici

PROVIAMOCI

A. Everybody thinks (believes) that s/he is special. Tell what these people think of themselves and if you agree (don't forget to make the adjectives agree with the nouns.)

Exs.: Luisa/bello - **Luisa crede di essere bella ed [*and*] è vero.**

Tu/carino - **Tu credi di essere carino ma [*but*] non è vero.**

1. Marco / intelligente
2. I ragazzi / magro
3. Gina / alto
4. Roberto / gentile
5. Jeff / superiore
6. Le sorelle / simpatico
7. Noi due / timido [*shy*]
8. Voi / basso
9. Carlo e Pina / superiore
10. Robertino / carino

Ed is used instead of **e** when a vowel follows.

B. What is the correct ending?

1. Io viv ... con [*with*] la mia famiglia.
2. Tu vinc ... spesso [*often*] al lotto?
3. Lui non vend ... il motorino [*moped*].
4. Quanto spend ... voi al supermercato?
5. Noi scriv ... spesso ai [*to the*] nonni.
6. Loro perchè non rispond ... in classe?
7. Il professore ripet ... la domanda [*the question*]
8. Maria e Francesca ricev ... lettere dagli [*from*] amici italiani.
9. Tu che cosa promett ... alla [*to*] mamma?
10. Io legg ... un libro di Stephen King.
11. Gina prend ... la pizza.
12. Papà perd ... spesso l'autobus
13. Tu e Alfredo legg ... il giornale.
14. Il papà e la mamma di Renzo discut ... molto di politica.
15. Io non cred ... agli U.F.O.
16. Io e Gianni corr ... dieci chilometri [*about six miles*].
17. Lei conosc ... l'amico del [*of the*] professore?
18. Il negozio [*store*] chiud ... alle otto.

C. Can you supply the missing verbs in the cells of the following grid ?

	promettere	ricevere	leggere
Tu	prometti		
Loro		ricevono	
Tina			
Io			leggo
Voi			

D. Playing with verbs

a. Complete each sentence with the appropriate form of the verb provided.

1. Lui (chiedere) informazioni al vigile [*policeman*].
2. Io non (conoscere) un buon ristorante italiano in centro [*downtown*].
3. Lei non (credere) a Babbo Natale.
4. Voi (decidere) di andare a un picnic oggi.
5. Loro (discutere) di sport con gli amici.
6. Noi ripetiamo la parola [*word*] difficile.
7. Tu ed Enrico (rispondere) sempre [*always*] in italiano.
8. Tu (vedere) i compagni a scuola.
9. I nonni (vivere) in Italia.

b. Tell what the sentences in the prevoius exercise mean in English.

c. Using the sketch as your cue, complete each of the following sentences with an appropriate verb in the correct form.

1. Noi ... la porta perché tira vento.

2. Tu ... la mattina?

3. Io e Giovanni ... il giornale [*newspaper*].

4. Io ... un vaso di fiori sul tavolo [*on the table*]

5. Il signor Banfi ... l'autobus [*bus*].

6. Tu ... una lettera da [*from*] Luciana.

7. Marco ... una lettera alla [*to*] nonna.

8. Loro ... soldi [*money*].

9. Lui ... la frutta al mercato [*fruit at the market*].

10. Tiger Woods ... sempre.

d. Answer the following questions based on the picture on the following page.

1. Chi ascolta?	Rocco ...
2. Chi legge?	Rita ed io ...
3. Chi risponde?	Gina ...
4. Chi riceve "A"?	Io ...
5. Chi parla?	Tu e Pia ...
6. Chi ripete?	Ada ...

7. Chi scrive? Carlo
8. Chi perde tempo? Tu e Pia ...

e. Write down what goes on in your Italian class. Compare your observations with those of a friend.

Da quanto tempo ...?
How long ...?

Do you remember the conversation between Renzo and John?

RENZO: **Da quanto tempo** conosci Jeff?
[***How long*** *have you known Jeff?*]

JOHN: Conosco Jeff **da** cinque anni.
[*I have known Jeff* ***for*** *five years.*]

PROVIAMOCI

A. Give the English quivalent for each of the following:

1. Conosco Lorenzo da cinque anni.
2. Gli atleti corrono da trenta minuti.
3. Ripetiamo questa canzone [*song*] da una settimana.
4. Da quanto tempo scrivi in italiano?
5. Da quanto tempo abitate in questa casa?
6. Da quanto tempo non ricevi notizie [*news*] dal tuo amico?

B. Using the information provided, tell how long these people have been doing each activity.

Ex.: Tu e Gina / vivere in città / anno
Tu e Gina vivete in città da un anno.

1. Renzo / leggere / cinque minuti
2. Tu / scrivere / dieci minuti
3. Voi / correre / mezz'ora
4. Io / prendere le vitamine / un anno
5. Papà / leggere questo libro / una settimana.
6. Noi / discutere / venti minuti.

C. Ask your partner how long s/he has been doing the following activities. Then report your findings to the class. Follow the examples.

Ex.: Giocare a calcio

(you ask)	***Maria, da quanto tempo giochi a calcio?***
(partner says)	*Gioco a calcio da sei anni.*
(you report)	*Ragazzi, Maria gioca a calcio da sei anni.*

1. studiare l'italiano
2. abitare a questa città [*city*]
3. frequentare questa scuola
4. aspettare la fine [*the end*] della lezione
5. conoscere il professore / la professoressa d'italiano
6. prendere l'autobus da solo [*by yourself*]
7. scrivere in italiano

D. Now try the same exercise (C), but address your questions to more than one person at the same time.

Ex.: Giocare a calcio

(you ask)	***Da quanto tempo giocate a calcio?***
(they answer)	**Giochiamo a calcio da sei anni.**
(you report)	***Ragazzi, loro* giocano a calcio *da sei anni.***

Comparing things and people

You have already learned some common adjectives for describing people and other things (Chapter 5). Suppose you have the problem of distinguishing between two people or things that share the same characteristic. In English we use the words **more** or **less** or add the suffix "**-er.**"

Mario is intelligent. Max is more intelligent. Mario is less intelligent than Max.

In Italian, the word "**più**" corresponds to the word "more", and the word"**meno**" corresponds to "less". The English, "than", is expressed in Italian with "**di**".

Mario è intelligente. Massimo è **più** intelligente. Mario è meno intelligente di Massimo.

PROVIAMOCI

A. Who's who and what's what? Based on the following pictures, answer the questions using the suggested adjectives.

Ex. Chi è Jeff?
grande
È il ragazzo più grande.

Chi è Rosanna? alto

Chi è la signora Romano? bello

Quale [which] cane è Benjie? piccolo

Qual è la casa di Renzo? elegante | Qual è il libro di Dante? grosso | Chi è Edoardo? intelligente

B. How much do you know? Answer the following questions in Italian. Follow the example.

Ex.: Quale [*Which*] città è più grande? Roma o New York?
È più grande New York.

1. Quale oceano è più grande? L'Atlantico o il Pacifico?
2. Quale stato è più piccolo? Il Rhode Island o il Maryland?
3. Quale macchina è meno costosa? La Fiat o la Ferrari?
4. Quale attore è meno alto? Mel Gibson o Michael J. Fox?
5. Quale paese [*country*] è più caldo? Il Canadà o l'Australia?

VOCABULARY EXPANSION

In Chapter 3 you learned a few words that denote parts of the body; they are:

il dente	tooth	**lo stomaco**	stomach
il piede	foot	**la testa**	head
la schiena	back		

Here are a few more words. Some are given in the plural form as it is more frequently used. (You will study more about the human body in the second volume of Amici , p. 170)

i capelli	hair	**le spalle**	shoulders
gli occhi	eyes	**le braccia**	arms
la bocca	mouth	**le mani**	hands
il naso	nose	**le gambe**	legs
le orecchie	ears		

At this point you may want to describe what people look like. Some useful suggestions are given below:

capelli	**biondi** [*blond*], **castani** [*brown*], **ricci** [*curly*], **lisci** [*straight*]
occhi	**azzurri, verdi, neri, castani**
spalle	**larghe** [*broad*], **strette** [*narrow*]
braccia, gambe	**lunghe** [*long*], **corte** [*short*], **forti** [*strong*], **deboli** [*weak*], **muscolose**[*muscular*], **magre** [*thin*]

Adjectives in Italian must reflect the gender and the number of the noun they describe, so:

John è magr**o**. I ragazzi sono magr**i**.
Laura è magr**a**. Le ragazze sono magr**e**.

PROVIAMOCI

A. Renzo and Jeff These two boys are very different from each other. Create sentences that compare the two. How many differences can you find?

Ex.: **Jeff è alto ma Renzo è basso.**

B. Laura e Daria Laura has a best friend back in Rome. Despite their similar interests, the girls are very different physically. Using the same procedure you just used in the exercise above, write about the differences you see in the two girls.

C. Using a magazine, describe some of the newsmakers you see in the photographs to your partner.

D. Creepy Collages Create unusual looking characters by cutting out and pasting together different body parts of people you find in magazines. Pieces don't have to match; the creepier, the better! Describe your creation in Italian to the class.

VOCABULARY EXPANSION

Now that you know how to describe and compare some basic physical characteristics of people, you might want to know how to describe some character traits. Here is a list of some common adjectives:

gentile	kind	**sgarbato**	rude
spensierato	carefree	**serio**	serious
generoso	generous	**avaro**	stingy
calmo	calm	**nervoso**	nervous
energico	energetic	**pigro**	lazy
forte	strong	**debole**	weak
timido	shy	**sfacciato**	insolent
prepotente	bossy	**docile**	docile

A. Describe each of the following characters with at least two adjectives.

Snow White	Hercules	Jack (of beanstalk fame)
Cinderella	Rumpelstiltskin	Beauty and the Beast
Paul Bunyan	Red Riding Hood	Goldilocks
Thumbelina	Rip Van Winkle	The Little Mermaid

B. Compare the following people for their character traits.

Ex. Jeff/John/simpatico - **Jeff è meno simpatico di John.**
John è più simpatico di Jeff.

1. Renzo/Roger/gentile
2. Babbo Natale [*Santa*] /Scrooge/generoso
3. La Piccola Fiammiferaia [*Little Match Girl*] /Cenerentola/povero
4. Lo zio Marco/papà/nervoso
5. Davide/Golia/forte

C. Answer each question in a complete sentence.

1. Chi è più alto, Michael Jordan o Michael Jackson?
2. Chi è più timido, il coniglio [*rabbit*] o il leone?
3. Chi è meno forte, Arnold Schwarzenegger o Joe Pesci?
4. Chi è più sgarbato, Oscar o Kermit?
5. Chi è meno grasso, Drew Carey o Michael J. Fox?
6. Chi è più veloce [*fast*], il cavallo [*horse*]o la pecora [*sheep*]?

D. Now make your own comparison using ***più di*** or ***meno di*** and the adjectives that you have just studied. Produce at least five sentences.

Mi piace, mi piacciono

At the end of the game Renzo says: "*Mi piace giocare a 'Hacky Sac!'*" ***Piace*** comes from the verb, ***piacere***. Italians use the verb "***piacere***" when they like something or someone.

If you like someone or something, you say "***Mi piace,***"; if not, you say: "***Non mi piace***". If you like a group of people or things, you say "***Mi piacciono***"; if not, you say: "***Non mi piacciono***".

PROVIAMOCI

A. Complete each sentence with ***piace*** or ***piacciono***.

1. Mi ... i ragazzi biondi/le ragazze bionde.
2. Non mi ... ballare.
3. Mi ... le vacanze [*vacations*].
4. Non mi ... studiare.
5. Mi ... studiare.
6. Non mi ... i ragazzi/le ragazze prepotenti.
7. Mi ... vincere, non mi ... perdere.
8. Mi ... i compagni gentili.
9. Mi ... mangiare, ma non mi ... preparare il pranzo [*dinner*].

B. Say whether you like or don't like the following:

1. la musica classica
2. Mel Gibson
3. i broccoli
4. Dave Matthews Band
5. Disney World
6. gli spaghetti
7. le Bahamas
8. i San Francisco 49'ers
9. Whoopi Goldberg
10. Princess Amidala
11. i cannoli siciliani
12. il calcio

C. Complete with an appropriate adjective.

1. Mi piace la musica...
2. Mi piacciono le persone ...
3. Non mi piace il tempo ...
4. Mi piacciono i ragazzi/ le ragazze ...
5. Non mi piace il dottore ...
6. Mi piacciono i mesi ...
7. Non mi piacciono le macchine ...
8. Mi piace il professore ...

D. Working in pairs, ask a classmate if s/he likes the following.
Use: "**Ti piace...?**" or "**Ti piacciono ...?**"
The answer will be: "**Sì, mi piace.../mi piacciono...**"
or " **No, non mi piace.../non mi piacciono...**"

1. andare a scuola
2. l'italiano
3. le macchine sportive
4. le canzoni di Celine Dion
5. l'inverno
7. i film di "Star Trek"
8. lavorare in giardino
9. giocare a tennis
10. i CD di Andrea Boccelli
11. le riviste sportive
12. lo sci acquatico [*water skiing*]

E. Now switch roles.

DO WE REMEMBER?

Do we remember the question words?

chi?	who?	Chi sei?
che, che cosa? cosa?	what? what kind?	Che dice? Che libro legge?
dove?	where?	Dove sei?
come?	how?	Come giochi a "Hacky Sac?"
quando?	when?	Quando guardi la TV?
quanto/a	how much?	Quanto costa?
quanti/e?	how many?	Quanti fratelli hai?
perché	why?	Perché studi l'italiano?
quale/quali?	which (one/ones)?	Quali automobili preferisci?

A. Now working with your partner, use as many question words as possible to complete the dialog below.

Renzo: ... abita Jeff?
John: Abita qui vicino.

Renzo:	... anni ha?
John:	Ha quattordici anni.
Renzo:	Vedo due ragazzi. ... è Jeff?
John:	Jeff è il ragazzo più grande.
Renzo:	Mamma mia! ... mangia?
John:	Prende molte vitamine!
Renzo:	... gioca Jeff, bene o male?
John:	Oh, Jeff gioca molto bene.
Renzo:	... perde sempre?
John:	Io perdo sempre.
Renzo:	Ma ... perdi tu?
John:	Perché sono piccolo.
Renzo:	... pesa [*weigh*] Jeff?
John:	Pesa settantacinque chili [*168 lbs*].
Renzo:	Non ti preoccupare, noi due pesiamo di più.

B. With your partner act out the previous exchanges.

C. Find out if your partner likes the following.

Ex. leggere - You: ***Ti piace leggere?***
Partner: ***Sì, mi piace leggere./ No, non mi piace leggere.***

1. guardare la TV
2. scrivere lettere
3. le persone sgarbate
4. i ragazzi calmi
5. il gelato italiano
6. giocare a pallacanestro
7. discutere di sport con gli amici
8. leggere romanzi [*novels*]
9. i nonni generosi
10. vincere sempre

D. Write out the Italian equivalent of the following sentences.

1. Jeff is bigger than John.
2. Renzo is a likeable boy.

3. Renzo attends middle school and Robertino attends elementary school.
4. Jeff always loses.
5. I like Italian, but i don't like homework [*i compiti*]
6. I always play soccer; I like it very much.
7. Do you like to read a book by [*di*] Stephen King?

E. What would you say?

1. You have found a brand new pen on your desk and ask your partner whose it is.
2. You express your opinion about "spaghetti al pesto" after you have sampled it.
3. You suggest that you and Renzo play now, not later.
4. You state that you have been playing tennis for five years.
5. You say to your friend that you don't like to spend money.
6. You tell your new neighbor that you know a Chinese restaurant.
7. You state that Firenze is smaller than Milano.

PERFORMANCE ACTIVITIES

E ORA IN ITALIANO

Laura is looking at a clothing catalogue with Mrs. Wright and Mrs. Romano.

Laura:	Zia, guarda com'è bello questo vestito azzurro. Mi piace molto. Va bene anche per la festa della scuola.
Sig.ra R.:	Ma è molto corto ...
Laura:	È un vestito d'estate, zia, e le mie gambe non sono brutte.
Sig.ra R.:	Hai ragione, Laura, però quest'anno le ragazze portano i vestiti lunghi
Laura:	È vero, ma non mi piacciono. E poi ho bisogno di un vestito per andare al mare. Mi piace prendere il sole sulle [*on the*] gambe, e anche sulle spalle e sulle braccia.
Sig.ra W.:	Sono d'accordo con Laura, Lucia. Qui fa caldo d'estate; è vero che Laura usa molto i pantaloncini, ma un vestito è più elegante.
Sig.ra R.:	Voi due avete sempre ragione.
Laura:	(to Mrs. W.) Grazie, signora.

ASCOLTIAMO

Listen as your teacher reads aloud a setting in English followed by a passage in Italian which will be read twice; then choose the most appropriate response to the question based on the passage you have just heard.

1. Why isn't John very surprised?
   a. He knows Jeff very well.
   b. He is very confident in Renzo's help.
   c. He knows that Renzo is smaller than Jeff.

2. What does Renzo like?
   a. to eat ice cream
   b. to play and win
   c. to be a good athlete

3. Where did soccer originate?
   a. in Asia
   b. in America
   c. in Europe

LEGGIAMO

Three people saw a bank robbery. Each of the three gave a description of the suspect to the police. Pretend you are the police sketch artist and draw the suspect according to each of the decriptions below.

#1 È un uomo alto e magro. Ha lunghi capelli castani, un grande naso e grandi orecchie. I denti sono molto brutti.

#2 È una vecchia signora, bassa e robusta. Ha i piedi piccoli e le mani grandi. I capelli sono bianchi e ricci. Ha la bocca grande e rossa.

#3 È un bel giovane. Ha capelli biondi e corti. Il naso è piccolo e la bocca è larga. È molto muscoloso ma ha le gambe un po' corte.

#4 È una signorina di sedici anni. Ha lunghi capelli ricci e occhi azzurri. È un tipo atletico con le braccia e le gambe muscolose ma è anche molto seria.

PARLIAMO

A. Ask your partner the following questions. Record his/her answers, then exchange roles.

1. Chi risponde più spesso in classe?
2. Discuti di sport o di cinema con gli amici?
3. Credi di essere intelligente?
4. Leggi libri o giornali?
5. Cosa prendi quando hai mal di testa?
6. Conosci il francese?
7. Chi vedi a scuola?
8. Corri quando suona il telefono?

B. Gino, an exchange student from Italy, is interviewing you. Let a classmate take the part of Gino. When you are finished with the questions, exchange roles. The responses must be in complete sentences.

1. Come ti chiami?
2. Quanti anni hai?
3. Dove e con chi abiti?
4. Che scuola frequenti?
5. Come vai a scuola la mattina? Prendi l'autobus?
6. A che ora arrivi a scuola?
7. Quali materie studi?
8. Studi molto? Quante ore studi la sera?
9. Ti piace studiare?

C. Working with your partner, create a conversation using the suggestion below.

Your Italian friend is visiting from Italy and spending the entire summer at your house. You are discussing some activities you might do over the weekend.

SCRIVIAMO

A. Making lists.

1. List four activities that you like to do and four that you don't like to do after school.
2. List four characteristics of your ideal sweetheart.

B. Write a note to Gino, the Italian exchange student, telling him where you live, how long you have been living there. Also tell him that your house is far from the school and in the morning you need to take the bus.

ABOUT ITALY

LAURA AS A STUDENT OF THE LICEO

Laura has different interests from her little brother. She has been studying piano and flute for several years, and she likes to think that some day she will be a famous performer. Practicing takes up a lot of her time, and she has to study too. In the fall she will attend the second year of the Liceo Classico. It was not really her choice. You see, once Italian students finish middle school they have fulfilled their required education. Theoretically, they could go to work, but very few do so. Instead , they choose to continue school according to their interests or their parents' wishes.

At the age of fourteen, Laura had many educational options to choose from. She loves music and she wanted to go to the conservatory, but mom and dad expected her to go to the liceo classico,to get a good general education. The liceo is a very challenging school and Laura does not like all the subjects. They are: Italian, Latin and Greek languages and literatures, history, physical education and religion or some alternative course. She also studies philosophy, mathematics, physics, sciences and art history. In addition, Laura has private music lessons. At the end of next year she will have to take comprehensive examinations to obtain her diploma [la maturità classica].

Laura thinks that she does not have enough free time. She would like to go to the movies and to the disco more often, to "hang out" with her friends in the afternoon and go window shopping downtown at the boutiques of famous designers.

Traditionally, young people in Italy do not work, not even when school is not in session. In the summer Laura has only her music to practice. She likes to go on vacation with her family. Every summer she makes new friends and devotes time to her hobby: a beautiful collection of unusual rings. The problem is that time flies and September always arrives too soon.

Ti piace andare alla spiaggia?

Ti piacciono le macchine italiane?

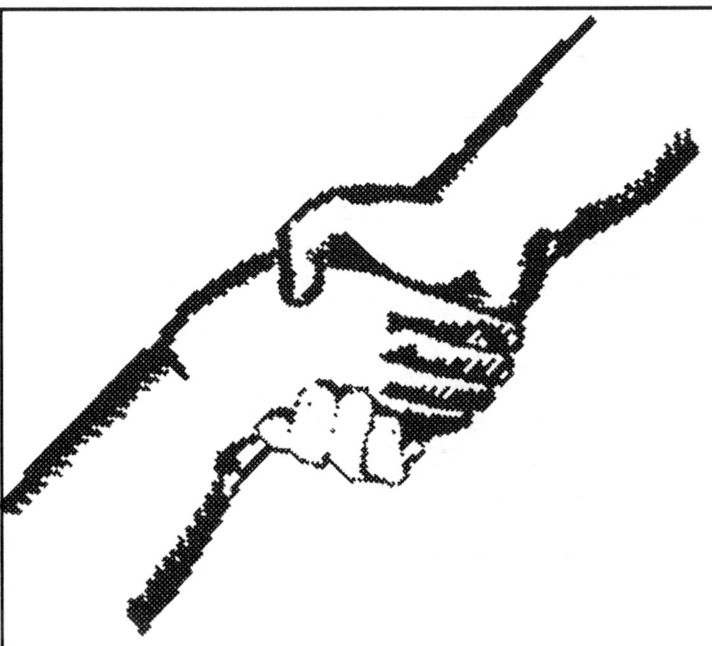

CAPITOLO NOVE: CHE COSA PRENDI?
CHAPTER NINE: WHAT ARE YOU HAVING?

FUNCTIONS

Introductions
Polite exchanges
Asking for advice
Encouraging decisions
Asking about taste and preferences

LANGUAGE

Verbs in "*-ire*"
Direct object pronouns (*lo, la, li, le*)

ABOUT ITALY

Bars and Restaurants in Italy

SITUATION

Happy at last to have won a game against Jeff Golden, John wastes no time in claiming his reward.

JOHN: Now we celebrate our victory.
RENZO: Sì, ora **celebriamo**, no, **festeggiamo** la vittoria. Ma come?
JOHN: Sundaes at "Posillipo's!"
RENZO: No, not Sunday; now!
JOHN: (*giggles*) Renzo, "Sundae" è un **tipo** di **gelato**.
RENZO: Ma io non ho **soldi**.
JOHN: Non ti preoccupare. Pagano Jeff and Roger.
RENZO: Allora andiamo.

The boys make their way to "Posillipo's", a small sandwich shop and café in the neighborhood, run by Mr. and Mrs. Posillipo.

MR. P.: What will you have today boys?
JEFF: Four sundaes, please.
MR. P.: (*teasing*) All for you? You are going to get a little "**pancia**" there.
RENZO: (*to John*) Ma lui parla italiano?
MR. P.: Certo sono di Napoli!
RENZO: Ed io sono di Roma
JOHN: Signor Posillipo, **le presento** il mio amico Renzo, il nipote della signora Romano. Renzo, il signor Posillipo.
RENZO: **Piacere**.
MR. P.: **Piacere mio**. Sei qui in America da molto tempo?
RENZO: Da due settimane. **Parto** per l'Italia il due settembre.

MR. P.: (*as Mrs. Posillipo enters from the back room*) Ah, ecco mia moglie.
RENZO: Piacere di conoscer**La**, signora.
MRS. P.: **Molto lieta**.
JOHN: Renzo è il nipote della [of] signora Romano. È di Roma.
MRS. P.: Ora **capisco** perché parlate italiano. (to Renzo) Come sta la zia? Non la vedo da due settimane.

You are probably very pleased with yourself because you can now understand most of the Italian in the conversation that you have just read and heard. Just like John, you are making great progress.

PAROLE DA RICORDARE

NOUNS

il cioccolato	chocolate
il gelato	ice cream
il nipote	grandchild/nephew
la pancia	belly
i soldi	money
il tipo	kind, type

VERBS

capisco	I understand
copre	covers
festeggiare	to celebrate (a private event)
partire	to leave for a trip, a voyage
presentare	to introduce

USEFUL EXPRESSIONS

Piacere	Pleased to meet you
Piacere mio	The pleasure is mine
Piacere di conoscerLa (form.)	Pleased to meet you
Molto lieto/a, lieti/e	Delighted
Le presento (formal)	Let me introduce
Ti presento (familiar)	Let me introduce
Vi presento (plural familiar)	Let me introduce
Lo prendo anch'io.	I'll have it too.

OTHERS

anche	also
certo	of course
certamente	certainly
liquido	liquid
mentre	while
Dai, su!	Come on!

Remember: "***nipote***" can mean several things.

il/la nipote	grandchild/nephew or niece
i/le nipoti	grandchildren/nephews or nieces

PROVIAMOCI

A. Answer the following questions according to the dialog.

1. Che cos'è il "sundae"?
2. Ha soldi Renzo?
3. Chi paga il gelato?
4. Di dov'è il signor Posillipo?
5. Da quanto tempo è in America Renzo?
6. Quando parte per l'Italia?

B. **Introductions**. You have met Luisa, an exchange student from Venice.

a. You invite her to your Italian class and introduce her

1. to Mrs. Angeli, your teacher
   You say ...
   Luisa says ...
   Mrs. Angeli says ...
2. to Marvin, your friend
   You say ...
   Luisa says ...
   Marvin says ....
3. to Alice and Bee, the class "stars"
   You say ...
   Luisa says ...
   Alice and Bee say ...

b. In groups of three or four continue the role playing.

Verbs ending in "-ire"

In the previous "situation" you were introduced to the last kind of regular verbs in Italian, those that end in "**-ire**"

There are two types of "**-ire**" verbs; those like **partire** (to depart) and those like **capire** (to understand).

partire		capire	
io	part**o**	io	cap**isco**
tu	part**i**	tu	cap**isci**
lui/lei/Lei	part**e**	lui/lei/Lei	cap**isce**
noi	part**iamo**	noi	cap**iamo**
voi	part**ite**	voi	cap**ite**
loro/Loro	part**ono**	loro/Loro	cap**iscono**

Verbs like **partire**

aprire	to open
coprire	to cover
dormire	to sleep
offrire	to offer
seguire	to follow
sentire	to hear
servire	to serve

Verbs like **capire**

finire	to finish
preferire	to prefer
pulire	to clean
spedire	to send
suggerire	to suggest

Now see how often these new verbs occur in the following situation.

Mentre il signor Posillipo prepara i "sundaes" , sua moglie **pulisce** il tavolo, poi lo **copre** con una tovaglia [*tablecloth*]. Il signor Posillipo domanda ai ragazzi che "topping" **preferiscono**.

JOHN: Fudge.
RENZO: (*puzzled*) Signora, lei che cosa **preferisce**?
MRS. P.: Io **preferisco** il "fudge". È un tipo di cioccolato liquido.
RENZO: Allora [*then*] lo prendo anch'io. [*I'll take it too*]

PROVIAMOCI

A. Give the Italian verbs that mean the oppposite of the following. (The numbers in parentheses indicate the chapters where you learned the required verbs.)

1. partire (9) ... (6).
2. comprare (7) ...(8).

3. aprire (9) ... (8).
4. perdere (8) ... (8).
5. cercare (7).
6. mandare (7) ...(8).
7. domandare (7) ... (8).
8. incominciare (7) ... (9)

B. Complete with the correct verb ending.

1. John apr ... la porta del caffè Posillipo.
2. I genitori di Renzo part ... per l'Italia alla fine di agosto.
3. La signora Posillipo copr ... il tavolo con una bella tovaglia.
4. Tu dorm ... sempre in classe?
5. Tu e John offr ... il gelato agli amici?
6. Noi segu ... in macchina gli amici di John.
7. A che ora fin ... di studiare loro?
8. Io non cap ... sempre il professore quando parla.
9. Anch'io prefer ... il gelato al cioccolato.
10. Il sabato papà pul ... la macchina.
11. Marco e Gianni sent ... suonare il telefono e non rispondono.

C. Complete each sentence with he correct form of the verb.

1. Gli amici di John (preferire) ... l'aranciata.
2. La professoressa (suggerire) ... di studiare di più.
3. Io e Laura (pulire) ... la camera ogni [*every*] settimana.
4. Tu (sentire) ... suonare il telefono?
5. Voi che cosa (servire) ... a tavola?
6. A chi (spedire) ... il pacco [*package*] la zia?
7. Noi (preferire) ... gli spinaci alle [*to*] zucchine.
8. Robertino, perché non (finire) ... di scrivere la lettera alla [*to*] nonna?
9. Giorgio (aprire) ... le finestre perché fa caldo.
10. Laura (suggerire) ... a Renzo di aiutare la zia in cucina [*kitchen*].
11. Quante ore (dormire) ... tu la notte?
12. La mamma (offrire) ... il gelato agli amici.
13. Io (preferire) ... giocare a Nintendo.
14. Loro (suggerire) ... di prendere un gelato al cioccolato.

PROVERBIO
Chi di spada ferisce di spada perisce.

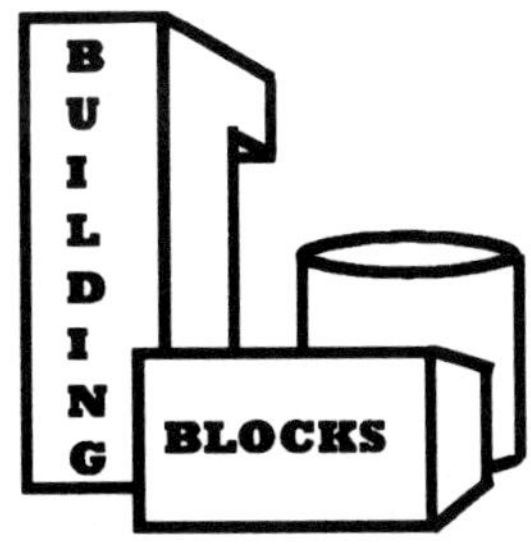

Direct Object Pronouns

Do you remember Mrs. Posillipo talking about Mrs. Romano?

Non **la** vedo da due settimane.

la is an example of a direct object pronoun.

lo	him, it	**li**	them
la	her, it	**le**	them

In Italian these pronouns are placed before the conjugated verb and agree in number and gender with the nouns they replace, so:

Io conosco **Renzo**. = Io **lo** conosco. Io conosco **Laura**. = Io **la** conosco.

Io conosco **gli** zii . = Io **li** conosco. Io conosco **le** zie. = Io **le** conosco.

PROVIAMOCI

A. Working with your partner, ask her/him the following questions. Your partner needs to answer each question using a direct object pronoun (**lo, la, li, le**). Exchange roles. Follow the example.

Ex. Jim, ascolti **le canzoni** di Celine Dion?

Sì, **le** ascolto or No, non **le** ascolto

1. Studi l'italiano ogni sera?
2. Prendi i libri in biblioteca?
3. Compri spesso le patatine [*potato chips*] al supermercato?
4. Mangi spesso il pesce fritto [*fried fish*]?
5. Pulisci sempre la tua camera?

6. Capisci gli studenti di scambio quando parlano inglese?
7. Preferisci il burro [*butter*] invece dell' [*instead of*] olio?
8. Ascolti sempre la tua migliore [*best*] amica?
9. Incontri le tue amiche la sera?

B. Complete each exchange with an appropriate direct object pronouns.

1. RENZO: Conosce il padre di Renzo?
   MR. P.: Sì, ... conosco da molto tempo.

2. RENZO: Inviti spesso [*often*] gli amici a prendere il gelato?
   JEFF: No, non ... invito spesso.

3. MR. P.: Vedi spesso le cugine di John?
   RENZO: No, non ... vedo affatto [*at all*]; non ... conosco.

4. MRS. P.: Renzo, guardi la TV americana?
   Renzo: Sì, ... guardo spesso ma non ... capisco.

Buon appetito!

[*Enjoy your meal!*]

Traditionally, Italian families gathered around the dinner table for lunch (**pranzo**) and dinner (**cena**). **Il pranzo** (around 1:00 p. m.) used to be the main meal and consisted of "pasta" or rice, meat or fish, vegetables, and fruit. **La cena** (around 8:00 p. m.) often included a soup, eggs or cheese or canned tuna or leftovers from lunch, vegetables and fruit. But now, in families where both parents work, lunch is more American style. People will either eat at a snack bar, bring lunch from home, or leave it in the fridge for the children when they come home from school. **Il pranzo** is reserved for Sundays and holidays and **la cena** may be the main meal of the day, provided that mother has time to cook.

APPARECCHIAMO LA TAVOLA

[Let's set the table]

il piatto	plate	**il cucchiaio**	spoon
il piatto fondo	bowl	**il bicchiere**	glass
la forchetta	fork	**il tovagliolo**	napkin
il coltello	knife		

PAROLE DA RICORDARE

Here is a reference table with some essential words referring to food.

il cibo	food
il pane	bread
l'antipasto	"antipasto"
la pasta	"pasta"
la minestra	soup
il pesce	fish
arrosto	roasted
fritto	fried
alla griglia	grilled
bollito	boiled
in umido	stewed
la verdura	vegetable
i broccoli	broccoli
i fagiolini	string beans
l'insalata	salad
la patata	potato
il pomodoro	tomato
gli spinaci	spinach
l'uovo (pl. **le uova**)	egg
il formaggio	cheese
il prosciutto	ham
l'olio	oil
il sale	salt
il pepe	pepper
lo zucchero	sugar
il dessert	dessert
il dolce	cake
Exs.: il Saint Honoré	
lo zuccotto	
il panettone	
la torta	cake
il gelato	ice cream
la macedonia di frutta	fruit cocktail

Proverbio: ***A tavola non s'invecchia***

la carne	meat
il manzo	beef
il maiale	pork
il vitello	veal
la bistecca	steak
il pollo	chicken
la frutta	fruit
l'albicocca	apricot
l'arancia	orange
la banana	banana
la fragola	strawberry
la mela	apple
la pera	pear
la pesca	peach
l'uva	grapes
la colazione	breakfast
il caffè	coffee
il latte	milk
il burro	butter
i fiocchi di granoturco	corn flakes
la cioccolata calda	hot cocoa
i biscotti	cookies
la marmellata	jam
il pranzo	lunch
la cena	supper
la merenda	snack
il panino	sandwich(in a roll)
il tramezzino	sandwich
la pizzetta	small pizza
le bevande	drinks
l'acqua	water
l'acqua minerale	mineral water
la birra	beer
il vino	wine
la bibita	soft drink

CULTURAL NOTE

Italian meals tend to be very balanced. Typically, a big meal begins with an **antipasto** (*appetizer*), followed by a **primo piatto** (*first course*)of a pasta, rice or soup dish. The second course consists of a **pietanza** (*main dish*) of meat, poultry or fish with **contorni** (*side dishes*) of vegetables. Italians don't consume as many sweets as Americans and usually conclude their meals with fresh fruit.

PROVIAMOCI

A. Answer the following questions.

1. Mangi spesso la pasta?
2. Preferisci il pesce o la carne?
3. Quale verdura non ti piace?
4. A casa tua mangiate spesso le patate?
5. Dove compra il gelato la mamma?
6. Che cosa prendi a colazione?
7. Ti piacciono le uova fritte?
8. Preferisci la frutta o il dolce?
9. Mangi mai [*ever*] il formaggio?
10. Gli italiani mangiano tanta frutta. E tu?

B. Complete with an appropriate word.

1. La mamma prepara la ... per il compleanno [*birthday*] di John.
2. Renzo prende una ... fredda perché ha sete.
3. Come pietanza, o secondo piatto, mi piace ...
4. Per dessert va bene una ... ?
5. La mattina, a colazione, io prendo ...

C. What do you like? Working in pairs, ask each other whether or not you like the following.

Ex.: Ti piacciono gli spinaci? **Ti piace la frutta?**

1. la pasta
2. le fragole
3. il pollo arrosto
4. il pesce fritto
5. i broccoli
6. il pesce
7. i fagioli
8. la minestra
9. le arance
10. l'insalata
11. le patate
12. la bistecca

D. Interviewing peers. Ask your classmates what they eat for breakfast, lunch or dinner. Then state what you eat. Follow the examples below.

Che cosa prendi a colazione?	Io prendo soltanto [only] il caffè. E tu? Io prendo il latte con [with] i fiocchi di granturco.
Cosa preferisci a pranzo?	Il pollo fritto con l'insalata.
Cosa ti piace a cena?	Pasta, carne e verdura.

DO WE REMEMBER?

A. Answer the following personal questions using lo, la, li, le in your responses.

Ex. Chi prepara **la cena** a casa tua? > **La** prepara Papà.

1. Chi frequenta la scuola media nella tua famiglia?
2. Chi legge il giornale la sera?
3. Chi guarda le notizie [*news*] in televisione dopo [*after*] cena?
4. Chi compra i fiori [*flowers*] per il compleanno della mamma?
5. Chi lava i piatti [*dishes*]?
6. Chi porta fuori [*out*] il cane [*dog*]?
7. Chi prepara le lasagne?

B. Complete the following exchanges:

1. Renzo:	John, quante ore (dormire) ... la notte?
John:	... otto ore.
2. Sig.ra Romano:	Renzo, John, (preferire) ... l'aranciata, o il gelato?
Renzo e John:	... l'aranciata.
3. Sig.ra Wright:	John, quando (pulire) ... la tua camera?
John:	La ... sabato.
4. Renzo:	Zia, a che ora (aprire) ... la banca?
Sig.ra Romano:	... alle otto e mezzo.

C. Perform the following tasks.

1. Tell your aunt that you are opening the door because the bedroom is hot.
2. Say that Patrizia is sleeping because she is tired [*stanca*].
3. State that you do clean your bedroom!
4. Say that you like chicken but that your parents prefer fish.
5. Ask your brother if he prefers fruit salad or cake.
6. Ask John if he always understands Renzo.

D. Now complete the following story by writing the correct form of the verbs in the blanks

Oggi (essere) ... una bella giornata di agosto e la famiglia Romano (decidere) ... di andare a fare un picnic in campagna [*country*]. Fa caldo e c'è molto sole. Quando loro (arrivare) ..., i ragazzi (essere) ... molto allegri [*cheerful*] e contenti [*happy*] di passare il tempo a giocare a frisbee, a pallavolo, a calcio e a bocce. La signora Romano (mettere) ... una coperta [*blanket*] sull'erba e (preparare) ... i panini e molte altre cose da mangiare. Renzo (giocare) ... a bocce con lo zio mentre [*while*] Robertino (correre) ... dietro [*after*] le farfalle [*butterflies*] . Laura (preferire) ... leggere un libro e aiutare la zia. Tu come (passare) ... il tempo d'estate? Io (lavorare) ... durante le vacanze.

PERFORMANCE ACTIVITIES

E ORA, IN ITALIANO

Before their trip to the States, the Silvestri family had dinner at the Roman restaurant, "Il Caminetto".

Sig. S.:	Allora siamo pronti per ordinare? Cameriere!
Cam.:	Prego, signori? Cosa prendono per primo?
Sig.ra S.:	I ragazzi prendono gli spaghetti al pomodoro, e per me penne all'arrabbiata. E tu, Alberto?
Sig. S.:	Io preferisco un piatto di ravioli "alla Caminetto" .
Cam.:	E da bere?
Sig.R.:	Acqua minerale per tutti.
Cam.	Va bene.

The first course is very good. When they are almost finished, the waiter is ready to take orders for the main course and change plates.

Cam.:	Cosa desiderano per secondo?
Sig.ra S.:	Per i ragazzi una bistecca di vitello e contorno d'insalata mista. Io prendo il pesce alla griglia con contorno di patatine al burro.
Cam.:	E Lei, signore?
Sig. S.:	Arrosto di maiale e fagiolini in insalata.
Cam.:	Va bene.

After all that food the family does not need dessert. (Mr. Silvestri is happy; the bill is going to be stiff!)

CULTURAL INFORMATION

In Italian restaurants people do not order the whole dinner at the beginning as in North America. Meals do not come pre-packaged with fixed side dishes; customers can pick and choose from the menu that remains on the table to the end.

ASCOLTIAMO

Listen as your teacher reads aloud a setting in English followed by a passage in Italian which will be read twice; then choose the most appropriate response to the question based on the passage you have just heard.

1. What is this announcement about?
   a. the opening of new family restaurant
   b. a restaurant closing for vacation
   c. a restaurant going out of business

2. Why isn't Giovanni having coffee?
   a. He does not like it very much.
   b. He prefers coffee and milk.
   c. It does not let him sleep at night.

3. Which item do both girls order?
   a. spaghetti b. tortellini c. salad

4. What does your friend prefer doing?
   a. to skip lunch.
   b. to eat at a restaurant near the hotel
   c. to try the food at the hotel's restaurant.

LEGGIAMO

Answer the following questions based on the information in the recipe below.

INGREDIENTI	
Spaghetti	400 g
Burro	50 g
Parmigiano grattugiato	30 g
Salsa besciamella preparata con:	
Latte	500 g
Burro	50 g
Farina	50 g
Sale	
Noce moscata	

SPAGHETTI CON LA BESCIAMELLA

Cuocere gli spaghetti "al dente" (circa 9 minuti) in acqua e sale. Condire con burro e parmigiano grattugiato. Aggiungere la salsa besciamella e mescolare bene.

farina = flour
sale = salt
noce moscata = nutmeg

1. What is the main ingredient in this dish?
2. Would Italians have this as a primo or secondo?
3. If each portion calls for 80gr. of pasta, how many people does the recipe serve?
4. List four other ingredients.
5. Match these verbs in the recipe with their English equivalent:

1. aggiungere	a. mix
2. condire	b. grate
3. cuocere	c. add
4. grattugiare	d. sauce
5. burro	e. cook
6. salsa	f. season
7. mescolare	h. butter

PARLIAMO

A. You are in a restaurant in Firenze with a group of friends and are ready to order a meal. The waiter comes to take your orders. After ordering the first course, discuss with your friends what each of you will have for the rest of the meal.

Ristorante Agnello

Menu

Antipasti	
Prosciutto con carciofini	9.000
Prosciutto e melone	10.000
Antipasto "Agnello"	10.000
Salmone affumicato Scozia	10.000
Primi	
Fettucine pomodoro e basilico	10.000
Tortellini al ragù bolognese	10.000
Spaghetti alla carbonara	10.000
Penne all'arrabbiata	10.000
Risotto con pistilli di zafferano	10.000
Secondi	
Scaloppina di vitello al Trebbiano	12.000
Tagliata di manzo con rucola	20.000
Pollo alla cacciatora	10.000
Agnello alla griglia	15.000
Agnello all'orientale	15.000
Filetto di sogliola al vino	12.000
Contorni	
Contorni di stagione	3.500
Insalata verde	3.000
Insalata mista	3.500
Dessert	
Frutta di stagione	3.000
Macedonia di frutta fresca	3.500
Coppa di gelato	6.000
Tartufo	6.000
Tiramisù	6.000
Bevande	
Acqua minerale San Pellegrino	2.000
Vino Rosso / Bianco della casa	5.000
Bibite	3.500

B. You are telling your friend about the new Italian restaurant where you ate the other day. He/she wants to know where it is, the house specialties, what dishes you recommend there, and so on.

C. You and your friend are discussing where to eat tonight. You suggest going to a Chinese restaurant, but your friend does not care to go there. Discuss other possibilities.

SCRIVIAMO

A. You are planning a formal dinner for your grandparents anniversary. Prepare a special menu that includes appetizer, first and second dishes, vegetables, beverages and dessert.

B. Prepare a shopping list of the ingredients you will need to buy at the supermarket.

C. Write a short invitation to a friend to eat at your house. Tell when and what you will be eating.

ABOUT ITALY

THE ITALIAN BAR

"Bar", "Baretti", and "Caffè" are very popular in Italy: they are everywhere. The Italian bar is a lively place, with people coming and going all the time. The espresso machine stands on the long counter where most customers are served. In order to be served at the counter you need to pay at the cash register first and then give the "scontrino" [*receipt*] to the "barista" [*bartender*]. People go to the bar in the morning for coffee or "cappuccino" and sometimes, a "cornetto" [*croissant*]. At lunch time many stop by for an "aperitivo" [*before dinner drink*], a "pizzetta" or some other appetizing snack displayed on the counter. They are available all day, along with ice cream and pastries.

Behind the counter, there is a mirrored wall with shelves of liqueurs and other alcoholic beverages. There is no drinking age in Italy. Theoretically anyone can order a whiskey, although no responsible bartender would serve it to a child. Young people like to sit together in a bar in the afternoon and have an ice cream or a drink. They can have a beer if they want to, but many go for an American soda. Since alcohol is not forbidden and wine is part of everyday meals, not many young people indulge in it. On the other hand, they smoke a lot. Every culture has its sins.

Some bars are very fashionable, like Doney's on Via Veneto in Rome. It is a place to go to watch people strolling by and to be seen. Many an aspiring movie star has sat there in the hope of being noticed by a famous director.

At resorts, at the beach or in the mountains, as well as in little towns, bars and cafés are meeting places. People go there knowing that somebody they know will show up to share some conversation.

ITALIAN RESTAURANTS

In Italy there is something for everyone who likes to eat. One can find everything from very fine restaurants to popular fast-food outlets just like the ones you are used to at home. In Italy elegant dining establishments are called *ristoranti*. A restaurant with a more "homey" atmosphere is called a *trattoria*. A *tavola calda* is a place where people can dine cafeteria style. A *rosticceria* is where the main attractions are tasty grilled or barbecued dishes but offer many other choices and even take-out. Of course one can find *pizzerie* everywhere, but beware; many Italians consider a pizza an evening meal so pizze aren't always made all day long.

Italians have many alternatives for dining out; from elegant restaurants to fast foods. Tasty take-out dishes are available at the local *rosticceria*.

Capitolo nove: Che cosa prendi?

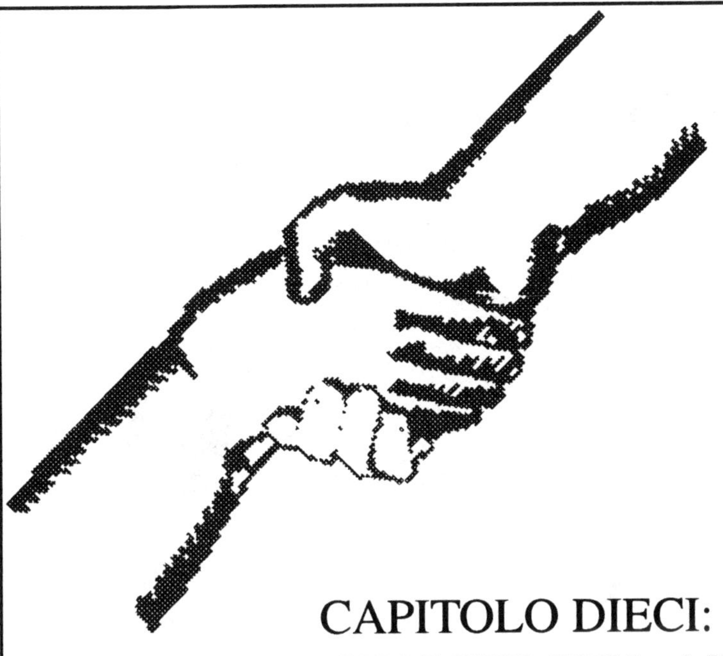

CAPITOLO DIECI: MUSICA, RAGAZZI!
CHAPTER TEN: MUSIC, KIDS!

FUNCTIONS

Locating things
How to get to places
Expressing ownership

LANGUAGE

Simple prepositions
The verb *andare*
Means of transportation
Possessive adjectives (pl.)

ABOUT ITALY

Music and the Silvestri Family

SITUATION

The sundaes were great, now it is time to head home. As Renzo and John approach the Romano house, they hear the sound of a piano.

JOHN:	Che bella **musica**!
RENZO:	È mia sorella che suona una **canzone** per la zia.
JOHN:	La riconosco. Mio padre la canta **nella** [*in the*] **doccia**. È una vecchia canzone di Elvis.
RENZO:	Oh, è più vecchia **ancora**. Si chiama "O sole mio", ed è una famosa canzone napoletana.
JOHN:	Suoni anche tu il **piano**?
RENZO:	No, io suono la chitarra.
JOHN:	Anch'io suono la **chitarra**.
RENZO:	Perché non vai a casa, prendi la chitarra, torni qui e **facciamo** un trio con Laura?
JOHN:	Sì, va bene.

(*In no time John is at the Romano's with his guitar. When Laura sees him she switches from a piece by Chopin to something much more familiar.*)

JOHN:	Hey, that was "number one" last month.
LAURA:	Noi conosciamo tutte le **vostre** canzoni in Italia. Le ascoltiamo alla radio. Andiamo pazzi per la musica americana!
MRS. R.:	Sei **sorpreso**?

Capitolo dieci: Musica, ragazzi!

JOHN: Il **mondo** è così piccolo!

(*Mrs. Romano suggests that the "trio" work up a program of music for the next evening, as she has invited the entire Wright family to dinner and Renzo's mom will be arriving from her business trip.*)

PAROLE DA RICORDARE

NOUNS

la canzone	song
la chitarra	guitar
la doccia	shower
il mondo	world
la musica	music
il piano	piano
la radio	radio
il trio	trio

OTHERS

ancora	still, yet
nella	in the

ADJECTIVES

napoletano	Neapolitan
sorpreso	surprised
tutte	all (fem., pl.)
vostre	your (fem. pl.)

VERBS

facciamo	we make/do we are making/ doing
vai	you go/are going

USEFUL EXPRESSIONS

Andiamo pazzi per... We are crazy about , we go crazy for...

PROVIAMOCI

A. True-False: Correct the false statements.

1. Laura suona una canzone italiana.
2. Il papà di John conosce questa canzone.
3. John e Renzo suonano la chitarra.
4. Laura suona anche la chitarra.
5. Renzo e Laura ascoltano le canzoni americane alla radio.

B. Complete each sentence with a word from the list below.

chiama	musica	chitarra	suona
radio	canzone	piano	trio

1. Il signor Wright canta una ... napoletana.
2. La canzone si ... "O sole mio".
3. La sorella di Renzo suona il ...
4. Renzo suona la ...
5. Anche John ... la chitarra.
6. Tutti e tre formano un ...
7. Laura ascolta le canzoni americane alla ...
8. Gli Italiani vanno [*they go*] pazzi per la ... americana.

Simple prepositions

So far in his study of Italian, John has seen a number of prepositions. These little words are used to indicate the relationship of one word to another in a sentence.

a	to, at, in	**in**	in, at	**per**	for, in order to, through
di	of, - 's	**su**	on, over	**tra/fra**	between, among and also "in" when referring to time
da	from, by	**con**	with		

A. Often Italian prepositions are used like their English equivalent.

Io compro un dolce **per** [*for*] Laura.
Renzo passa [*spends*] l'estate **con** [*with*] la zia.
L'università **di** [*of*] Roma è grandissima.
Il Caffé Posillipo è **tra** [*between*] la banca e l'ospedale.
Scrivo una lettera **a** [*to*] Giovanna.
Papà ritorna **da** [*from*] Los Angeles domani.
Renzo e Laura abitano **in** [*in*] Italia.

B. Sometimes the use of particular prepositions does not correspond exactly to the English equivalent.

Renzo vive **a** Roma	Renzo lives in Rome.
Di dove sei?	Where are you from?
Io studio l'italiano **da** un anno.	I have been studying Italian for a year.
La Famiglia Silvestri abita **in** via ...	The Silvestri family lives on ... street.
Il modellino è **di** Robertino.	It is Robertino's model.
Il treno arriva **tra** venti minuti.	The train arrives in twenty minutes.
John va a scuola **in** macchina.	John goes to school by car.
Gli studenti vanno **in** Italia.	The students go to Italy.
Il Colosseo è **a** Roma.	The Colosseum is in Rome

PROVIAMOCI

A. Provide an appropriate preposition following the given clue.

a. Easy! Here you need prepositions that have the same meaning in English.

1. Il cane è (between) ... il piano e la finestra.
2. Renzo è (in) ... camera sua.
3. La gente [*people*] mangia (in order to) ... vivere.
4. Compriamo un dolce (for) ... il nonno.
5. Mi piace andare in discoteca (with) ... i miei [*my*] amici.
6. (At) ... che ora vai a letto?
7. Il treno arriva (from) ... Chicago e va (to) ... Boston.

b. Be careful! Here the English equivalent does not work. Consult the examples in the "Building Blocks" section above.

1. Frank è (in) ... Boston.
2. Anna studia francese (for) ... tre anni.
3. L'amico ('s) ... Renzo abita (on) ... via Nomentana.
4. Dov'è l'aeroplanino ('s) ... Robertino?
5. I nostri (our) amici italiani abitano (in) ... Firenze.
6. La lezione (of) ... italiano è interessante.
7. Il professore vive in America (for) ... molto tempo [*time*].
8. Luciana arriva a scuola alle otto (by) ... bicicletta.

B. How many prepositions can you spot in this ad?

a.

ItalViaggi

vi offre viaggi in località vicine e lontane.
L'offerta speciale di giugno è una splendida
gita a

SIRACUSA

3 giorni e 2 notti
con guida che parla inglese

Viaggiate nel conforto di
un autopullman ariacondizionato.

Partenze ogni martedì e venerdì
a partire dal 2 giugno
per sole Lit. 750.000

Corso Vittorio Emanuele 251 Napoli
Tel. (081) 5764782
Fax: (081) 576 5313

b. Provide the following information:

1. name of the travel agency
2. destination of the trip
3. means of transportation
4. departure days
5. cost of the trip
6. What makes this trip attractive to tourists?

C. Create sentences using each of the following verbs or expressions. Make sure to include a preposition.

1. abitare
2. arrivare
3. scrivere
4. rispondere
5. prendere il libro
6. vivere ... Italia

7. ricevere	9. studiare la lezione	11. suonare la chitarra
8. essere	10. comprare un regalo [*gift*]	12. passare l'estate

The verb ANDARE *[to go]*

You have already seen the verbs **andare** in various forms (vado, andiamo, etc.). You may have noticed that it doesn't change like other **-are** verbs you have studied. There are several commonly-used verbs that do not follow the regular pattern of conjugation. We will learn them as they come up.

io	**vado**	I go	noi	**andiamo**	we go
tu	**vai**	you go	voi	**andate**	you (plural) go
lui	**va**	he goes	loro	**vanno**	they go
lei	**va**	she goes			
Lei	**va**	you (polite) go	Loro	**vanno**	you (pol. pl.) go

PROVIAMOCI

A. Complete with the correct form of **andare**.

1. Io ... a scuola ogni giorno.
2. Loro ... in piscina perché fa caldo.
3. Dove ... tu e Laura?
4. Io e Laura ... a Firenze.
5. Lui dove ... oggi?
6. La famiglia Wright ... in Italia per un anno.
7. Chi non ... a scuola oggi?
8. Il signor Romano e sua moglie non ... a Toronto.
9. Tu dove ... quando sei stanco [*tired*]?
10. Claudia non ... a ballare perché ha mal di testa.

B. When Renzo was small he used to like to go to Fiumicino, near Rome, where the international airport , "Leonardo da Vinci". is located. He was amazed at the many destinations of the passengers awaiting departure. Not being particularly shy, he would ask people where they were going.

Ex.: To a gentleman in a turban: Dove **va**? (India)
Gentleman: **Vado** in India.

Take the part of the travelers and answer according to the clues given.

1. To a lady dressed in a black robe:	Dove va?	(Iran)
2. To a black man in a colorful kaftan:	Dove va?	(Kenya)
3. To two tall blonde girls:	Dove andate?	(Danimarca)
4. To two men in imposing uniforms:	Dove vanno Loro?	(Libia)
5. To a little Asian girl:	Dove vai?	(Giappone)

C. You may have noticed in exercise B. that Renzo sometimes used the formal [*Lei*] way of asking questions. Now switch roles. You take the part of Renzo. Here are the people you talk to and their answers:

1. A man wearing a cowboy hat:	Vado in Texas.
2. Two boys in long white robes:	Andiamo in Marocco.
3. A black lady in a long colorful turban:	Vado in Etiopia.
4. A little girl in a sari:	Vado in India.
5. Two bearded men in burnooses:	Andiamo in Arabia Saudita.

COME ANDIAMO.....?

When mentioning a means of transportation, Italian uses "**in**" where English uses "**by**".

Ex.: Vanno in macchina. [*They go **by** car.*]

To walk = **andare a piedi**
To go horseback riding = **andare a cavallo**

andare in macchina

andare in aereo

andare in autobus

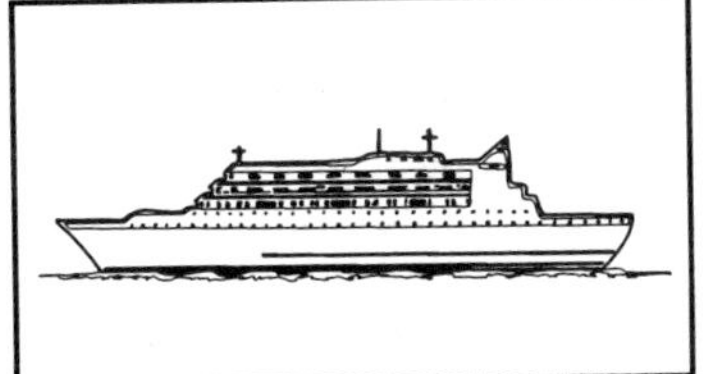

andare in nave

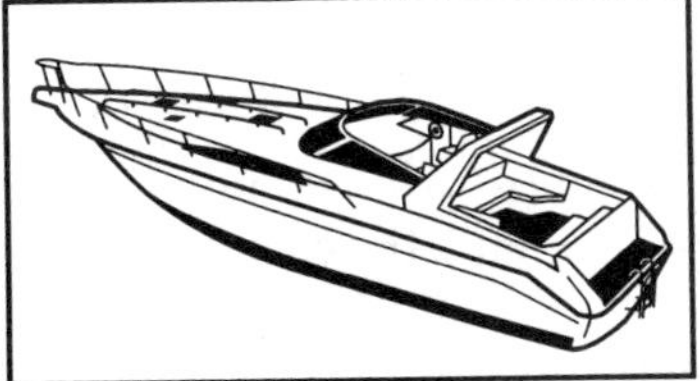

andare in barca

andare in tassì

andare in moto

andare in treno

andare in bicicletta

PROVIAMOCI

A. Come ci [*there*] va Laura? Say how Laura goes to the following places.

Ex.: in America: **Laura va in America in aereo**.

1. in discoteca
2. a scuola
3. a Napoli
4. al parco
5. in piscina
6. all'aeroporto
7. in crociera [*cruise*]
8. al supermercato
9. al cinema

B. Come ci vanno? How do the following people reach their destination?

1. John va a scuola ...
2. I signori Silvestri ritornano in Italia ...
3. Io vado da Bologna a Firenze ...
4. Noi andiamo al parco ...
5. La signora Romano va al supermercato ...
6. Giovanni va al Liceo Giulio Cesare a ...
7. Loro vanno in Sardegna ...

C. Come ci vai tu? How do you reach the following places?

Ex.: la scuola: **In autobus!**

1. il cinema
2. il supermercato
3. lo stadio
4. la Florida
5. le Galapagos
6. l'Argentina
7. il centro commerciale [*shopping center*]
8. la sala dei videogiochi [*arcade*]
9. McDonald's
10. i grandi magazzini [*department stores*]

D. Complete each sentence with the correct form of the verb **andare** and a means of transportation. Check your answers with those of your classmates to see how many of you think alike.

1. Mio padre ... in ufficio in ...
2. Noi ... a scuola in ...
3. Voi ... in chiesa [*church*] a ... o in ...?
4. La mamma ... in banca [*bank*] in ...
5. Io e Carlo non ... a New York in aereo, ... in ...
6. Brian ... a lavorare dopo scuola in ...
7. Tu come ... a Boston? In macchina o in ...?
8. Domani noi ... a pescare [*fishing*] in ...

More about expressing possession

In Chapter 4 you learned the use of possessive adjectives with singular, unmodified kinship terms:

Laura è mi**a** sorell**a**
Renzo è mi**o** fratell**o**.

You also learned that **in all other cases** possessives adjectives are preceded by an article:

Il libro di Angela	=	**Il** suo libro
La casa di John	=	**La** sua casa
Un amico di Lucia	=	**Un** suo amico

But someone may own more than one book or have more than one friend. Here is what you need.

	masc. sing.	fem. sing.	masc. pl.	fem. pl.
my	il **mio** libro	la **mia** amica	i **miei** libri	le **mie** amiche
your	il **tuo** libro	la **tua** amica	i **tuoi** libri	le **tue** amiche
his/her	il **suo** libro	la **sua** amica	i **suoi** libri	le **sue** amiche
your (polite)	il **Suo** libro	la **Sua** amica	i **Suoi** libri	le **Sue** amiche

Remember that you need the article when you talk about more than one relative or when the kinship term is modified:

My uncles = **I** miei zii   My old uncle = **Il** mio vecchio zio

PROVIAMOCI

A. Complete each of the following with an appropriate possessive.

1. Dov'è (your) macchina?
2. (My) cara [*dear*] nonna è in Italia.
3. (Your) appartamento è vecchio.
4. (Her) amica parla italiano.
5. (My) professori sono bravi.
6. (Your) genitori arrivano oggi?
7. (My) dischi [*records*] sono vecchi.
8. (Her) cugini sono intelligenti.
9. (My) foto sono a colori.
10. Questa non è (your) penna.

B. Change the following singular expressions into the plural.

Exs.: il mio motorino - **i miei motorini**
la sua giacca - **le sue giacche**

1. la mia motocicletta
2. sua nipote*
3. la tua bicicletta
4. il suo specchio
5. il tuo gelato
6. il mio libro
7. mia sorella*
8. tua zia*

* Don't forget the article

Possessive adjectives; plural forms

Of course, something can belong to more than one person at the same time. For example, you might say: "Our house is on Jefferson Avenue." In such cases you need to know the plural forms of the possessive in Italian. They are:

	masc. sing.	fem. sing.	masc. pl.	fem. pl.
our	il **nostro** libro	la **nostra** amica	i **nostri** libri	le **nostre** amiche
your (pl.)	il **vostro** libro	la **vostra** amica	i **vostri** libri	le **vostre** amiche
their	il **loro** libro	la **loro** amici	i **loro** libri	le **loro** amiche
your (pol., pl.)*	il **Loro** libro	la **Loro** amica	i **Loro** libri	le **Loro** amiche

* Today, the formal plural form of the possessive is used rarely. "Vostro" is appropriate in most cases. "Loro" is used only in cases of extreme formality.

With the table above, we can now construct the sentence we chose at the beginning of this explanation:

Our house is on Jefferson Avenue. = **La nostra casa è in via Jefferson.**

PROVIAMOCI

A. John and Renzo constantly exchange information about their families. Complete the following conversation with appropriate possessive forms. Refer to the tables above.

John: (**Our**) casa è in una piccola città [*city*] in America.
Renzo: (**Our**) appartamento è in una grande città in Italia.
John: (**Our**) amici lavorano all' [*at the*] università.
Renzo: (**My**) genitori hanno molti amici che lavorano nell'industria [*in industry*].
John: (**Their**) lavoro [*work*] è molto interessante?
Renzo: Sì, (**their**) affari [*business*] richiedono [*require*] molti viaggi

[*travels*].

John: Come viaggiano?

Renzo: In Italia usano (**their**) macchine, ma anche (**our**) treni sono molto comodi. Per i lunghi viaggi usano (**our**) linea aerea, l'Alitalia.

John: (**Your**) amici portano regali quando ritornano da un viaggio?

Renzo: Oh sì, (**our**) friend Graziella porta sempre regali. Io ho un cappello da cowboy del Texas che ha comprato [*she bought*] durante [*during*] (**her**) viaggio in America.

B. a. Complete the questions below with the appropriate form of:

il tuo, la tua, i tuoi, le tue

1. Come si chiama ... attrice [*actress*] preferita?
2. Chi è ... più grande amico?
3. Qual è ... macchina preferita?
4. Come si chiama ... ragazzo/a [*boy/girlfriend*]?
5. Chi è ... professore/professoressa d'italiano?
6. Quali sono ... "CD" più belli?
7. Come si chiamano ... sorelle?
8. Dove sono ... libri d'italiano?
9. Dov'è ... scuola?
10. Quando studi ... lezioni?

b. Ask the above questions to a partner: **ex.: Come si chiama la tua attrice preferita?**

c. Record your partner's answers on paper: **ex.: La mia attrice preferita è ....**

d. Share the answers with the rest of the class: **ex.: La sua attrice preferita è....**

CLAUDIO BAGLIONI: "DA ME A TE"

Musicale - 20,50 - Raidue

Claudio Baglioni (47 anni, nella foto), dopo lo stadio Olimpico di Roma, si esibisce anche in quello di San Siro, a Milano.

L'ORO DI NAPOLI

Film (1954) - 20,35 - Rete 4

Dai racconti di Giuseppe Marotta, un film a episodi con Sofia Loren (63 anni, nella foto), Totò, Vittorio De Sica.

DO WE REMEMBER?

A. Form sentences by choosing an item from each column. Remember to make necessary changes.

Ex.: Lui legge una lettera

noi	imparare	un libro
tu	parlare	otto ore
lui	andare	italiano
voi	avere	in Italia a luglio
loro	essere	una lettera
lei	scrivere	stanchi
io	leggere	dalle otto alle dieci
Renzo e Lucia	capire	undici anni
Io e Giuseppe	dormire	a nuotare in piscina
Enrico	studiare	bene il professore

B. Provide the correct form of **andare** for each sentence.

1. Ho bisogno di aspirine, ... in farmacia.
2. John ha fame, ... in cucina.
3. Noi siamo stanchi [*tired*], ... a dormire.
4. È venerdì sera, Renzo e John ... al cinema.
5. Fa molto caldo, io e Brian ... al mare.
6. Nevica e fa freddo, perché tu e Renzo non ... a sciare?
7. Il padre di John non sta bene, oggi non ... a lavorare.
8. La zia Lucia ha bisogno di soldi, ... in banca.

C. Dillo in Italiano. [***Say it in Italian***]

1. I'm not going to school because I am sick.
2. Gino, today I am walking [*andare a piedi*] to school because I don't have my car.
3. Maria, where is my Italian book?
4. Kids, where are your books?
5. Here are our notebooks [*quaderni*].
6. Mom, do you know where the newspaper [*il giornale*] is?
7. Our friends have been waiting for forty minutes.
8. Their friends live in Rome.
9. I like meat but I don't like fish.
10. Their mother always works.

D. Dov'è? Dove sono? Complete the following dialogues with the appropriate possessives.

Sig. Romano:	Lucia, sai dov'è (**my**) giacca nera?
Sig.ra Romano:	(**Your**) giacca è lì.
Sig.ra Silvestri:	Renzo, dov'è (**your**) ombrello?
Renzo:	Ecco (**my**) ombrello.
Sig. Wright:	Janice, non trovo (**my**) scarpe [*shoes*]. Dove sono?
Sig.ra Wright:	Stephen, (**your**) scarpe sono nell'[*in the*] armadio.
Sig.ra Wright:	John, sono qui (**your**) amici?
John:	Sì, (**my**) amici sono in cucina.

E. Complete these parallel sentences.

1. Your car is fast.	... macchina è veloce.
2. My house is old.	... casa è vecchia.
3. Her school is big.	... scuola è grande.
4. Where is your pencil?	Dov'è ... matita?
5. His sisters are not here.	... sorelle non sono qui.
6. My watch is old.	... orologio è vecchio.
7. Her brothers live in Italy.	... fratelli abitano in Italia.
8. My friends are leaving for Rome by plane.	... amici partono per Roma in aereo.

F. Scrivilo in italiano! [*Write it in Italian!*]

1. Arianna has been reading for twenty minutes.
2. We are going to Venice with our friends.
3. They are going to get their guitar.
4. My father always sings in the shower.
5. Laura plays the piano very well.
6. "Mamma" is an old Italian song.
7. You also play the guitar.
8. This is Laura's piano.
9. She plays a song for her aunt.
10. Renzo, Laura, where are your jeans?
11. Our house is small.
12. This is their car.
13. Here is our newspaper.

PERFORMANCE ACTIVITIES

E ORA IN ITALIANO

Laura, Brian, Renzo and John are having fun during a practice session with their musical instruments.

Renzo:	John, tu suoni così bene la chitarra. Vai a lezione regolarmente?
John:	Sì, ogni lunedì a scuola. Anche tu suoni molto bene.
Renzo:	Nella tua scuola c'è una banda musicale?
John:	Certo! Io suono la chitarra e mio fratello suona la tromba.
Laura:	Da quanto tempo suona la tromba, Brian?
John:	Da molti anni. E tu studi il piano a scuola?
Laura:	No, vado a lezione di piano al conservatorio.
Renzo:	Eh! Voi parlate troppo. Dobbiamo[*we must*] preparare il concerto.
Laura:	Hai ragione. Andiamo! Da capo [*From the beginning*]!

ASCOLTIAMO

Listen as your teacher reads aloud a setting in English followed by a passage in Italian which will be read twice; then choose the most appropriate response to the question based on the passage you have just heard.

1. What does the teacher want you to do?
    1. Buy a CD of Vivaldi's "Four Seasons."
    2. Bring money to buy a ticket for a concert.
    3. Study the life of Antonio Vivaldi.
    4. Listen to Baroque music while studying.

2. What is Renzo asking John?
    1. his birthday
    2. his advice
    3. to borrow his CD
    4. to organize a party

3. What does Maria need?
    1. help preparing dinner
    2. help with school work
    3. money to make a phone call
    4. a ride to get to the music lesson

4. What kind of class does this student have at the end of the day?
    1. Social Studies
    2. Science
    3. Music
    4. Computer Science

LEGGIAMO

A. Read the ad below and then provide the requested information.

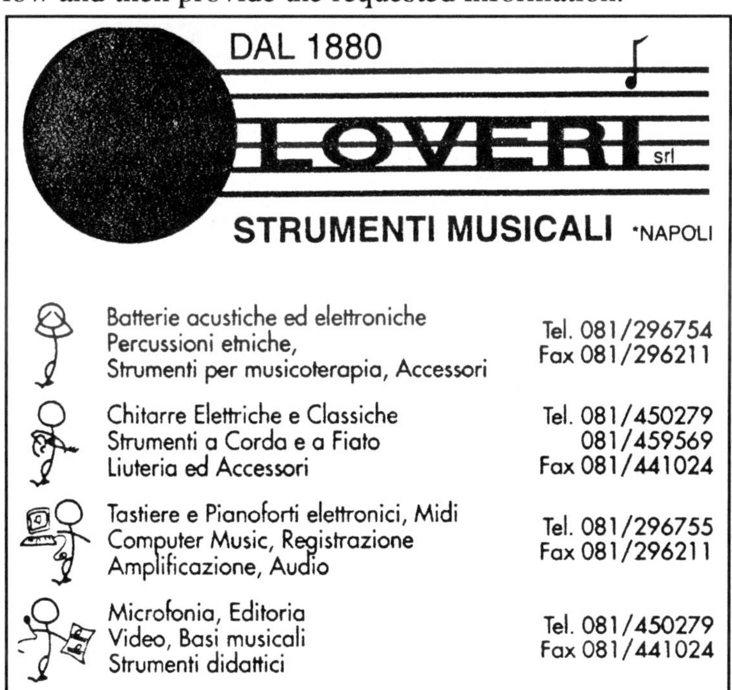

1. Find the following Italian musical terms.

a. percussion
b. string instrument
c. key boards
d. accessory
e. music therapy
f. wind instrument
g. amplification
h. drums

2. What number would you call to buy an electronic key-board?

B. According to the TV schedule below, at what time can you watch a musical?

1. at 2:00 PM
2. at 2:15 PM
3. at 7:30 PM
4. at 8:40 PM

TMC

14,15 Canzone pagana, film musicale (USA 1950) con Esther Williams, H. Keel
16,00 Tappeto Volante
17,35 Zap Zap estate, contenitore
19,30 Tmc News
20,40 Film
23,00 Film del ciclo "I magnifici di Telemontecarlo"
2,00 Felicita Colombo, film commedia (Italia 1937) con Dina Galli, Armando Falconi

C. After reading the article, choose the correct answer.

PER GLI AMANTI DELLA MUSICA

Desidero conoscere ragazzi/e che suonano piano, violino, clarinetto o flauto per organizzare un piccolo complesso. Scrivete a Giuseppe Del Monaco-Corso Verdi 26 - 33050 Fossanova (LT)

Che cosa desidera organizare questo ragazzo?

1. un piccolo club di musicisti
2. un circolo musicale scolastico
3. una piccola banda
4. un concerto

PARLIAMO

For each situation below, create a conversation with at least four exchanges.

1. You and your friend are in a music store trying to buy a CD for a friend's birthday. You discuss the kind of music that you like.

2. Your friend invites you to a concert but you have a previous commitment. Plan and discuss the possibility of going to another concert together.

3. This weekend your school is putting on a musical. Call up Giovanni, the Italian exchange student, and convince him to go with you, to either Friday night's or Saturday night's performance.

4. You parents don't want you to go to a rock concert by yourself. Call up your friend and ask her/him to go with you. Include the performers, date, time, place, possible transportation and so on.

SCRIVIAMO

1. Write a note to your friend and ask him/her if he/she is going to a rock concert with you. Include information about the event.

2. For your birthday you have received a CD of Andrea Bocelli, called *Romanza*. Write a thank-you note to your best friend, thanking her and expressing your appreciation for the gift.

3. Describe your favorite music group using at least five adjectives.

4. Write a letter to your friend about your plans for a vacation. Indicate the means of transportation that you will use for the trip and those available for activities at your chosen destination.

TEATRO PARIOLI

Domani ore 21,30
L'ALLEGRA BRIGATA in

Via col vento
un musical

Commedia musicale di
Gustavo Verde e Massimo Cinque
* * *
SPECIALE GIOVANI
L. 15.000
PRENOTAZIONI 80.35.23

ABOUT ITALY

MUSIC AND THE SILVESTRI FAMILY

All of Renzo's relatives love music. It is a family, as well an Italian, tradition.

Renzo and his friends have a passion for "rock". They all have collections of CD's and tapes. Sometimes, they go to one of the discos that open in the afternoon. They especially like those that project music videos on a large screen. They like to imitate the people performing and try to keep up with the "rappers". At home, rock music and videos are available to them through radio and TV.

Laura is not only fond of Beethoven and Chopin, she likes jazz, too. Like many of her friends, she is interested in folk and Afro-Latin music from South America and the Caribbean. Of course, they listen to the Italian "cantautori" [singer-songwriters] who are popular because their lyrics as well as of their music. Baglioni, Dalla, Venditti, Coccianti and Zucchero express the feelings, the desires and the fears of Italian young people, and even discuss problems related to sports, feminism and loneliness.

Unfortunately, Italian teenagers can not afford expensive concerts and entertainment very often. Since they can't find a regular part-time job (at most they baby sit or tutor younger children), they can only count on the allowance that their parents give them.

Mr. and Mrs. Silvestri are nice parents. Their children "educate " them about rock, folk and jazz. They only object when the noise is too loud. To tell the truth, they are more traditional and prefer opera and classical music. Mr. Silvestri also has an interest in old Italian songs, those from Naples and also those that express the unrest of the workers and the hardship of war in the mountains. He has his collection too, and every so often he can't resist the temptation to lecture his children about "his" kind od music. Parents are parents!

The world of music is full of Italian terms. Can the musicians in class tell you what these common musical terms mean?

a cappella	andante	crescendo	sostenuto
adagio	arpeggio	largo	staccato
allegro	coloratura	obbligato	vivace
forte	pianissimo	sonata	lento

MORE ABOUT MUSIC IN ITALY

Italian musical tradition is well known. It was a Benedectine monk, Guido d'Arezzo, around the year 1000 AD, who perfected the musical notation introducing the lines which are used to write music.

Italian is generally recognized as the international language of music and countless musical terms derive directly from it. The following expressions are common examples: *allegro, forte, opera, recitativo, aria, soprano, libretto, sonata, piano, pianissimo, adagio,* etc.

Opera,a dramatic musical representation, has its origin in the Italian renaissance and continues to thrill audiences all over the world. The "Teatro alla Scala", located in Milan, is one of the most important opera theaters, and it is the goal of singers and conductors to perform there.

Big orchestras, as well as small groups of musicians give innumerable performances of symphonic, chamber and Baroque music concerts in big cities and small towns, in famous concert halls, auditoriums and churches. In the warm summer months concerts are often given under the stars in the squares and even in ancient Roman and Greek theaters.

Jazz and pop music, like rock and rap, are very popular, especially with young people. This kind of music is available through CDs, cassettes, radio, TV and live concerts. Well-known *cantautori,* or singer-songwriters, such as Vasco Rossi, Zucchero, Claudio Baglioni, Lucio Dalla, Jovanotti and Andrea Bocelli, frequently entertain large crowds of Italian young and not so young people with their lyrics and music.

San Remo, a beautiful city on the Italian riviera, not far from Genoa, is the site of the annual *Festival di San Remo.* There, during the month of February, a song competition takes place, and the best participating Italian song is chosen by a jury. It is the biggest event for Italians who like popular music. A similar event takes place annually in the city of Naples, the *Festival della Canzone Napoletana,* and its objective is to choose the most beautiful Neapolitan song for that year.

CLASS DISCUSSION

1. For young musicians
   - A. What Italian musical terms do you read on your scores? What do they mean for your performance?
   - B. Do you know some kind of Italian music? What can you say about it?

2. If Renzo and Laura were your guests, what musical entertainment would you plan for them? Why?

3. Suppose that you plan to buy American CD's for your Italian friends. What would you buy and why?

Italians love music whether it is in the concert hall, in the theater, in a sidewalk café, at the disco, on the radio or on TV. Where have you heard Italian music? Do you know the name of the tune? Where, and when, do you hear music where you live?

CAPITOLO UNDICI: AL SUPERMERCATO
CHAPTER ELEVEN: AT THE SUPERMARKET

FUNCTIONS

Inviting someone to go somewhere
Accepting an invitation to go somewhere
Locating things and people
Inquiring about things
Indicating locations

LANGUAGE

The verb *venire*
Prepositions *di*, *a* and *da* + articles
Vocabulary for places in town
Jobs and occupations
Vicino a, *davanti a*
The verb *volere*

ABOUT ITALY

Grocery shopping

SITUATION

When John arrives home after practicing guitar with Renzo, he finds Laura there, and his mom, who is speaking on the phone with Mrs. Romano.

MRS. W.: Sì, Lucia, grazie! Sei molto gentile! **Veniamo** con piacere!
JOHN: Ciao, Laura. Come mai [*how come*] sei qui?
LAURA: **Vado** al supermercato con la tua mamma. **Vieni** anche tu?
JOHN: Al supermercato?
MRS. W.: Voglio fare la macedonia di frutta, la portiamo ai Romano domani sera. Andiamo a casa loro a cena.
JOHN: Va bene, **vengo** anch'io, **così** parlo italiano con Laura. Ma che cos'è la macedonia di frutta?
MRS. W.: It is a fruit salad. Gli Italiani prendono sempre la frutta per dessert. Andiamo al mercato **dei** Giannetti, hanno sempre **della** [*some*] bella frutta fresca.

At the supermarket Laura helps John practice his Italian.

JOHN: Dov'è la frutta?
LAURA: La frutta è sempre **davanti alla** verdura.
JOHN: Dove sono le mele?
LAURA: Sono **vicino alle** pere.
JOHN: Dove sono le fragole?
LAURA: Sono **davanti alle** ciliege.
JOHN: E le pesche?

LAURA:	Ci sono delle [*some*] pesche **vicino alle** banane.
MRS. W.:	Abbiamo bisogno di uva? Non la vedo.
LAURA:	È lì, **viene dal** Cile.

Back home they prepare the macedonia that must sit in the fridge overnight.

PAROLE DA RICORDARE

VERBS

vengo	I come
viene	s/he comes
vieni	you come
veniamo	we come
voglio	I want

OTHERS

così	so
dal	from the
dei	of the
della	some
fresco	fresh
sempre	always

NOUNS

il Cile	Chile
la ciliegia	cherry
la frutta	fruit
la macedonia di frutta	fruit salad
il mercato	market
la verdura	vegetables

USEFUL EXPRESSIONS

come mai?	how come?
davanti a	in front of
vicino a	near
Sei molto gentile!	You are very kind!
Veniamo con piacere!	We are pleased to come!
Vengo anch'io.	I'll come too.

PROVIAMOCI

A. Complete each sentence with the appropriate words from the dialog.

1. La signora Wright fa la ... con pere, mele, fragole, pesche, ciliegie e uva.
2. Laura dice: " ...al mercato con la tua mamma.... anche tu?"
3. John dice: "Va bene, ... anch'io, così parlo italiano con Laura."
4. Al supermercato la frutta è sempre ... verdura.
5. Le mele sono ... pere.
6. L'uva ... dal Cile.

B. Now read aloud the completed sentences above.

C. What would you say? Choose the appropriate utterance from the dialogue according to each situation below.

1. Your friend offers you a ride home in his father's car.
2. You are surprised to find your friend's sister at your house.
3. Your Italian neighbor invites you and your family to an Italian dinner party.
4. Somebody at the supermarket is asking you where the fruit is located.
5. Your relatives inform you that they are going to the circus.

The verb **VENIRE** *[to come]*

The verb **venire** is conjugated as follows:

io	**vengo**	I come, I am coming
tu	**vieni**	You come, you are coming
lui/lei	**viene**	he/she comes, he/she is coming
Lei	**viene**	you come, you are coming (polite)
noi	**veniamo**	we come, we are coming
voi	**venite**	you come, you are coming (pl.)
loro	**vengono**	they come, they are coming
Loro	**vengono**	you come, you are coming (polite, pl.)

When you talk about travels and mention cities, **venire** requires **da** and **andare** requires **a**.

Venire is also used when you join the person(s) you are talking to or that person joins you and/or other people.

1) Are you going to Boston tomorrow? I am going too (with you).
   Vai a Boston domani? **Vengo** anch'io.

2) I am going to class. Are you going (with me) too?
   Vado a lezione. **Vieni** anche tu?

PROVIAMOCI

A. Say where these people are coming from and where they are going.

Ex.: Mel Gibson viene da Sydney e va a Los Angeles.

1. Giulietta ... da Verona e ... a Venezia.
2. Io e Franco ... da Torino e ... a Genova.
3. Salvatore ... da Palermo e ... a Catania.
4. I Silvestri ... da Roma e ... a Boston.
5. Voi venite ... Filadelfia e ... a New York.
6. È vero che tu ... da Milano e ... a Bologna?
7. Tu e Gina ... da Reggio Emilia e ... a Firenze.
8. Io ... da Trieste e ... a Pisa.
9. Loro ... da Londra e ... a Parigi.

B. Say who is going where and who will join up. Follow the example.

Exs.: Paul: Vado a scuola. You and Mary: Veniamo anche noi.

1. You and Laura: .. al supermercato.	John: ...(io)
2. Mrs. Romano: ... a casa.	I ragazzi: ... (noi)
3. Mr. Wright: ... al concerto.	Mrs. Wright: ... (io)
4. Papà: ... a San Francisco.	Papà: ... (voi)?
5. John: ... in ristorante.	Renzo: ... (Jeff e Roger)?
6. Papà e Mamma: ... in vacanza.	I figli: ... (noi)

The preposition "DI" + *article*

In the dialogue Mrs. Wright says: "Andiamo al mercato **dei** Giannetti."

Dei is a contraction of two words: **di** + **i** which means *of the*.

Look at the following table to see how **di** combines with the other articles.

di +	il	lo	la	l’	i	gli	le
=	**del**	**dello**	**della**	**dell’**	**dei**	**degli**	**delle**

PROVIAMOCI

A. Select the appropriate contraction from the chart above.

1. La Ferrari è la macchina ... professore.
2. Il televisore non c’è nella [*in the*] camera ... ragazzi.
3. La casa ... zio di Renzo è molto bella.
4. I giorni ... settimana sono sette.
5. Questo è il motorino ... amico di Renzo.
6. Questi [*these*] non sono i libri ... studenti italiani.
7. È vero che c’è solamente [*only*] un letto nella camera ... bambine?
8. Le cene ... signora Romano sono molto buone.
9. Grazie ... libri e ... appunti [*notes*] d’italiano.

B. Di chi è? Di chi sono? Say what things belong to whom.

Ex.: piano / ragazza **Il piano è della ragazza.**

1. dischi / amici di Renzo
2. Lamborghini / Signor Martelli
3. orologio [*watch*] / cugino americano
4. stereo / amica della mamma
5. cane [*dog*] / vicini di casa [*neighbors*]
6. ombrello / signora Paolucci
7. giacca / studente di scambio [*exchange*]

Ricciolini d’oro mangia la pappa **del** bambino.

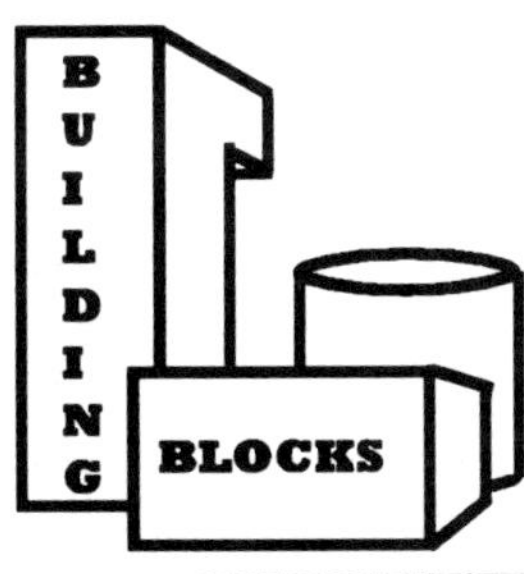

The prepositions "A" and "DA" + articles

Here is how **a** and **da** combine with all the articles.
They are very similar and with a little practice you will master them.

	il	lo	la	l'	i	gli	le
+ a =	**al**	**allo**	**alla**	**all'**	**ai**	**agli**	**alle**
+ da =	**dal**	**dallo**	**dalla**	**dall'**	**dai**	**dagli**	**dalle**

Exs.: Renzo telefona spesso **agli** amici.
Le fragole sono davanti **alle** ciliege.
Il treno parte **dalla** stazione centrale.
Il professore riceve una cartolina [*postcard*] **dagli** studenti.

PROVIAMOCI

A. Select the appropriate contraction. Choose from:

al, allo, alla, all', ai, agli, alle

1. Io preferisco non andare ... parco con Giulio.
2. Oggi lui non va ... università perché è chiusa [*closed*].
3. Giovanni scrive sempre ... zio americano a Natale.
4. Il professore d'italiano ripete la frase [*sentence*] ... studenti.
5. Gli amici telefonano ... ragazzi Wright.
6. Fra cinque minuti io vado ... stazione perché arriva la mia amica.
7. La banca apre ... nove e chiude ... quattordici.

B. Complete each sentence with an appropriate contraction. Choose from:

dal, dallo, dalla, dall', dai, dagli, dalle

1. Il nonno ritorna a casa ... ospedale oggi pomeriggio.
2. Io vengo a piedi ... concerto.
3. Lui viene ... studio del dottor Petri.
4. Noi torniamo ... vacanze fra due settimane.
5. Loro non vengono ... teatro, vengono ... stadio.
6. Vengono spesso ... Italia i cugini di Lucia?
7. L'autobus [*bus*] parte ... piazza [*square*] del mercato.
8. L'aereo arriva ... America alle 19:45.
9. Io ricevo molte telefonate ... amici inglesi.
10. Questo e-mail viene ... cugini italiani.

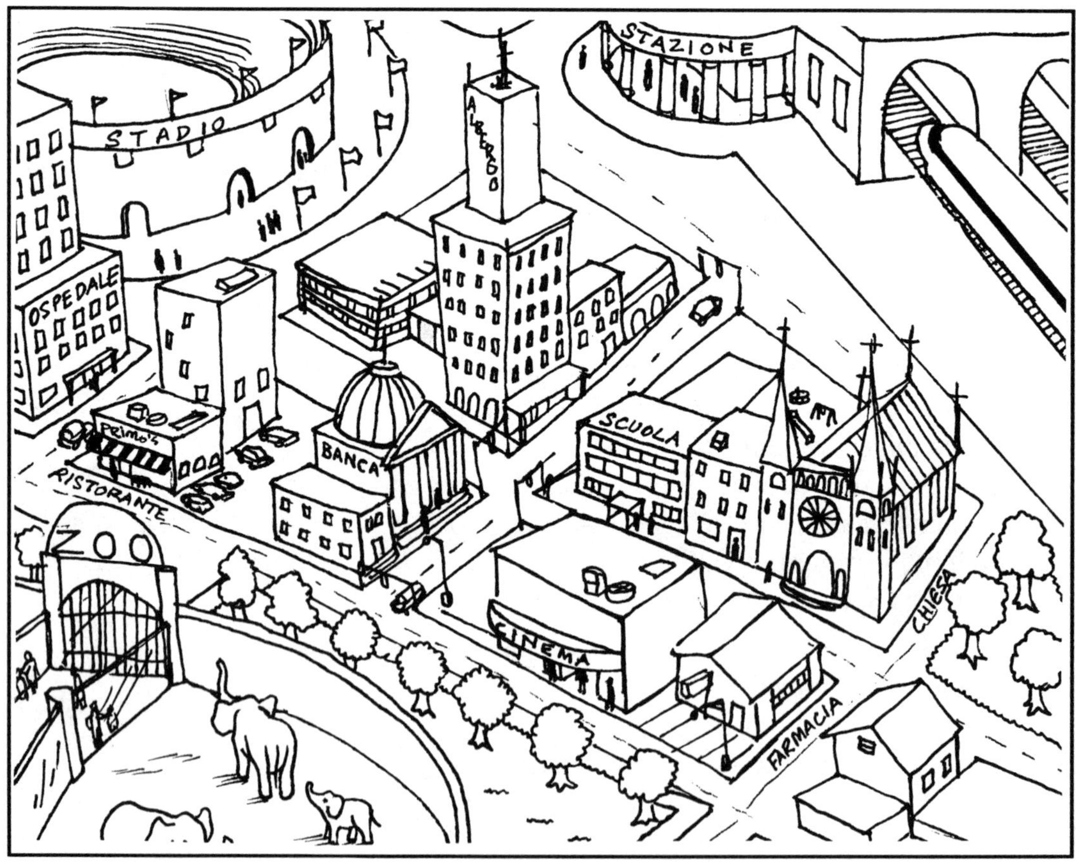

IN CITTÀ [*PLACES IN TOWN*]

ALIMENTARI [*GROCERIES*]

il negozio di frutta e verdura [*produce*]
la latteria [*dairy*]
la macelleria [*butcher shop*]
la salumeria [*deli*]
la panetteria [*bakery (bread)*]
la pasticceria [*pastry shop*]
il supermercato [*supermatket*]

ACQUISTI [*SHOPPING*]

la boutique [*ladies's fashion*]
la cartoleria [*stationery*]
il centro commerciale [*shopping mall*]
la libreria [*book store*]
il negozio [*store*]
la pelletteria [*leather shop*]
il negozio di abbigliamento[*clothing*]

LUOGHI PUBBLICI [*PUBLIC PLACES*]

la chiesa [*church*]
la fontana [*fountain*]
il marciapiede [*sidewalk*]
il municipio [*city hall*]
il museo [*museum*]
la piazza [*square*]
la scuola [*school*]
la stazione [*railroad station*]
la strada/ via [*street*]
la biblioteca [*library*]

SERVIZI [*SERVICES*]

l'albergo [*hotel*]
la banca [*bank*]
il bancomat [*automatic teller*]
il bar/caffè [*coffee shop*]
la farmacia [*pharmacy*]
la fermata dell'autobus [*bus stop*]
la gelateria [*ice cream shop*]
l'ospedale [*hospital*]
l'ufficio postale [*post office*]
il ristorante [*restaurant*]

DIVERTIMENTI [*ENTERTAINMENT*]

il cinema [*movie teather*]
la discoteca [*discothèque*]
il giardino pubblico [*park*]
lo stadio [*stadium*]
il teatro [theater]
lo zoo [*zoo*]

PROVIAMOCI

A. Look at the list of places around town and then tell where these people are going.

1. Mario va a vedere una partita di calcio allo ... Olimpico di Roma.
2. Noi questa sera andiamo a mangiare al ... "Da Alfredo".
3. È sabato sera. Ugo e Walter vanno al ... a vedere un film di Spielberg.
4. La mamma di Giuseppe sta molto male e il marito la porta all'... .

5. Gli amici di Renzo vanno alla ... a prendere il treno per Firenze.
6. Se [*if*] hai bisogno di aspirine perché non vai in ... ? È qui vicino.
7. I Silvestri alloggiano [*stay*] sempre all'... Danieli quando sono in vacanza a Venezia.
8. Renzo Silvestri ha quattordici anni e frequenta la ... media.
9. I signori Morelli vanno in ... perché hanno bisogno di soldi.
10. Mamma, ci sono delle giraffe bellissime allo ... . Ci andiamo domenica pomeriggio?
11. Quando siamo a Firenze visitiamo anche la ... di Santa Croce.
12. Ho bisogno di francobolli [*stamps*] e vado a piedi all'... . Non è molto lontano di qui.
13. Questa sera papà e mamma vanno al ... dell'opera

B. Dove abitano? Say where these people live using **vicino a +** the appropriate article.

Ex.: Roberto / la farmacia - **Roberto abita vicino alla farmacia.**

1. Fernando / il municipio
2. Annamaria / lo zoo
3. Alfredo / l'ospedale
4. Giovanni / la chiesa di San Giovanni
5. Luciana / i negozi di generi alimentari
6. Carlo / le scuole elementare e media
7. Arianna / l'ufficio postale
8. Filippo / la libreria

C. Dov'è? Dove sono? Say where these people are using **davanti a +** the appropriate article.

Ex.: Gli amici / il ristorante - **Gli amici sono davanti al ristorante.**

1. La zia Lucia / la farmacia, dove lavora suo cugino
2. Le amiche / la Banca Commerciale
3. Il papà di Brian / il municipio, dove ha un appuntamento con sua moglie
4. Il nonno / la chiesa e aspetta la nonna
5. La professoressa / l'ospedale, dove aspetta l'autobus
6. I bambini / i giardini pubblici, ma è ora di ritornare a casa
7. I ragazzi / il cinema, dove c'è un film interessante
8. Le signore / il centro commerciale e vanno al parcheggio a prendere la macchina

The verb VOLERE *[to want]*

"Volere" has its own conjugation.

io	**voglio**	I want
tu	**vuoi**	You want
lui / lei / Lei	**vuole**	he / she / you (pol.) want(s)
noi	**vogliamo**	we want
voi	**volete**	you (pl.) want
loro /Loro	**vogliono**	they / you (pol.pl.) want

PROVIAMOCI

A. Complete each sentence with the verb volere.

1. Io non ... mangiare adesso [*now*], grazie.
2. Robertino ... un aeroplanino.
3. Io e Laura ... un paio [*pair*] di jeans.
4. Tu e Renzo che tipo di musica ... ascoltare?
5. Lui ... andare a casa.
6. L'amico di John non ... studiare.
7. Che cosa (tu) ... vedere in TV?
8. Renzo e Laura ... vedere tante città italiane.
9. Jennifer ... dormire perché ha sonno.
10. Che cosa ... comprare Lei per sua moglie?
11. Io non ... parlare male di Jeff.
12. Tu che cosa ...?

B. Before leaving Italy, Renzo made a list of all the things his family and friends wanted from the States. Complete the list that follows by supplying the correct form of the verb **volere** in each sentence.

Io ... comprare un paio di scarpe Timberland. Lo zio ... un paio di occhiali da sole Ray Ban. Laura e la mamma ... i jeans Levi. Io e Robertino ... un cappello da baseball. Papà ... una macchina fotografica [*camera*]. La nonna ... un servizio di posate [*silverware*] Oneida.

C. Choices: Che cosa vogliono queste persone per il compleanno? Create sentences that tell what the people on the left want for their birthday. Use the choices from the second column.

People	Choices
1. I nonni ...	a. un telefono portatile [*cellular phone*]
2. La mamma ...	b. un videoregistratore [*V.C.R.*]
3. Il papà ...	c. un viaggio [*trip*] in Florida
4. Tu e Luisa ...	d. una cena in ristorante
5. Io ...	e. un biglietto [*ticket*] per la partita di baseball
6. Tu ...	f. un CD
7. Io e mia sorella ...	g. un videogioco [*video game*]
	h. una motocicletta
	i. un nuovo stereo
	j. una bicicletta

JOBS IN TOWN

il padrone di un negozio di alimentari	grocery store owner	**l'architetto**	architect
il padrone di un ristorante	restaurant owner	**il dottore/ medico**	physician
il cuoco	chef, cook	**il farmacista**	pharmacist
il cameriere	waiter		
il pasticciere	pastry maker	**il postino**	mail man
il barista	bartender	**il tassista**	taxi driver
		il commesso	salesclerk
il professore	teacher (secondary/college)	**l'impiegato**	employee
l'insegnante	teacher		
		l'attore	actor
il cartolaio	stationery vendor	**l'attrice**	actress
il librario	book-seller	**il/la cantante**	singer
il bibliotecario	librarian	**l'artista**	artist

USEFUL JOB TERMS

il colloquio	job interview	**la ditta**	company	**guadagnare**	to earn
il lavoro	work, job	**lo stipendio**	salary	**la carriera**	career

PROVIAMOCI

A. Who does what? The following sentences describe a trade or profession. Working with a partner tell what profession is being described. (You may consult your book.)

1. Gli Italiani vanno al suo negozio a comprare i dolci [*cakes*] in occasioni speciali.
2. Ha un negozio pieno di libri e riviste [*magazines*].
3. La persona che ti progetta [*designs*] la casa dei tuoi sogni [*your dream house*].
4. La persona che vedi sul palcoscenico [*stage*] a teatro.
5. Vai al suo studio [*office*] quando stai male.
6. Ti serve in ristorante e ti consiglia [*advises*] cosa mangiare.
7. Andiamo al suo negozio a comprare la carne.
8. Ascolti le sue lezioni a scuola e impari tante cose.
9. Quando hai fretta ti porta dove vuoi.
10. Papà dice che prepara un espresso molto buono.
11. Nel suo negozio compriamo tante medicine.
12. Lo aspettiamo sperando [*hoping*] di ricevere una lettera.
13. La persona che ti serve nei negozi.

C. Let's talk! Working with your partner and using the dialog below as a guide, create your own . Choose an occupation that you would like to pursue in life and talk about it with your friend. Include why a particular job appeals to you.

Luciana: Cosa vuoi fare da grande?
Angelo: Mi piace lavorare in una scuola. E tu?
Luciana: Io voglio diventare [*become*] musicista e suonare in un'orchestra famosa.
Angelo: Sì, tu suoni molto bene il violino. Io, invece, voglio lavorare con i bambini.
Luciana: Tu hai molta pazienza con i tuoi fratelli.
Angelo: È vero. Per questo [*That's why*] voglio fare l'insegnante di scuola elementare.

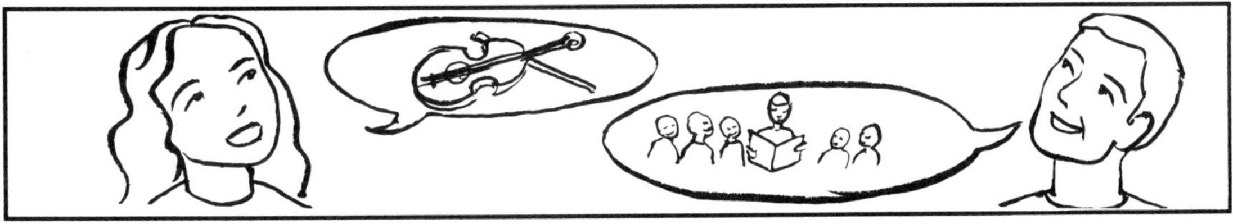

DO WE REMEMBER?

A. Read the sentences with the correct contraction in each blank.

1. Il concerto incomincia (a / le) ... nove.
2. La casa (di / lo) ... zio è grande.
3. Io vengo (da / la) ... cucina e vado in camera da letto.
4. A Natale scriviamo (a / gli) ... zii in Italia.
5. La famiglia Silvestri mangia sempre (a / l') ...una.
6. I ragazzi tornano (da / l') ... aeroporto.
7. Questa è la macchina (di / gli) ... amici di papà.
8. La casa (di / le) ... cugine di Tommaso è qui vicino.
9. Qual è la macchina (di / il) ... professore d'italiano?

B. Di chi è? Dove sono? Complete the following sentences according to the pictures.

1. La penna ... professore è (near) ... libro.
2. Il cane ... signori Jones è (in front of) ... casa.
3. Lui aspetta la sua ragazza (in front of) ... fermata dell'autobus.
4. La chitarra è (near) ... pianoforte.
5. Maria è (in front of) ... specchio.

C. Da dove vengono? [*Where do they come from?*]

Ex. Il panda del nostro zoo ... Cina. **Il Panda del nostro zoo viene dalla Cina.**

1. Il "goulash" ... Ungheria.
2. I pomodori ... nuovo mondo [*New World*].
3. Tu ... Stati Uniti.
4. Gli spaghetti ... Cina.
5. Noi ... centro commerciale.
6. Io ... studio del dottor Campanile.
7. Voi due ... lezione di piano.
8. Gli studenti di scambio ... Spagna.

D. Dove va? [*Where is he going?*] Tell where John's father is going.

Ex.: La Banca d'America: **Va alla banca d'America.**

1. il supermercato a fare la spesa
2. la cartoleria a comprare della carta da lettere [*stationery*]
3. le riunioni [*meetings*] con i suoi colleghi
4. l'università a fare lezione
5. l'ufficio postale a comprare i francobolli [*stamps*]
6. l'aeroporto a prendere sua sorella
7. l'appuntamento con il suo amico Luca
8. lo studio dell'avvocato Bruni
9. gli uffici del comune [*town hall*]
10. i giardini pubblici con Robertino

F. Nosy, nosy! You have a nosy friend. Answer his/her questions using **lo, la, li, le.**

Ex.: Aiuti **la mamma?** Sì, **la aiuto.**

1. Compri la frutta? Sì, ...
2. Mangi gli spinaci? No,...
3. Studi le lezioni? Sì, ...
4. Paghi il gelato? No, ...
5. Ascolti i genitori? Sì, ...

G. How do they travel? Provide a means of transportation.

1. Lo zio Giorgio va in Germania ...
2. Tua sorella parte dalla stazione centrale ...
3. I tuoi genitori vanno in ufficio ...
4. Tu vai a scuola ...
5. La nonna va in centro [*downtown*]...

H. In Italian, please! Say that...

1. you like meat.
2. you do not like fish.
3. you like broccoli.
4. you have class from 3:30 to 4:20.
5. your friend Jeannette is tall and beautiful, she is French and you like her a lot.

PERFORMANCE ACTIVITIES

E ORA, IN ITALIANO

On their way back home Mrs. Wright, Laura and John are having a conversation in the car.

Laura:	È molto interessante andare al supermercato americano. Mi piace.
John:	Perché?
Laura:	Ci sono molti servizi: la farmacia, il bancomat, la lavanderia... C'è tutto!
Mrs. W.:	C'è anche la possibilità di prendere a nolo [*rent*] una videocassetta.
Laura:	È vero. Il supermercato americano è molto comodo!
Mrs.W.:	Laura, a Roma dove andate a fare la spesa?
Laura:	Di solito facciamo la spesa vicino a casa perché il supermercato è lontano.
John:	E che negozi ci sono?
Laura:	Abbiamo di tutto: la salumeria, la panetteria, la latteria, la macelleria e anche un negozio di frutta e verdura.
Mrs. W.:	Ah! Allora non avete mai bisogno della macchina per fare la spesa.

ASCOLTIAMO

Listen as your teacher reads aloud a setting in English followed by a passage in Italian which will be read twice; then choose the most appropriate response to the question based on the passage you have just heard.

1. Where are Maria and Giovanna going tomorrow morning?
   a. to the supermarket
   b. to the airport
   c. to school
   d. to the restaurant

2. What is this person's profession?
   a. lawyer
   b. teacher
   c. nurse
   d. doctor

3. What does your friend do for her aunt?
   a. housework
   b. cooking
   c. drive
   d. keep her company

4. Che cosa vuole preparare la signora Romano?
   a. un piatto speciale
   b. una verdura
   c. un dolce
   d. una macedonia di frutta

5. Which picture shows Mario Antonelli's occupation?

LEGGIAMO

A. After reading the ad, answer the questions below.

> **INCOMINCIA LA TUA GIORNATA**
> **CON UN SUCCO DI FRUTTA.**
>
> Pesca, pera, albicocca, mela con tutto il sapore tipico della nostra terra. Una squisita bevanda il succo di frutta, ma anche un ottimo [*excellent*] alimento, ricco di vitamine, sali minerali, zuccheri semplici naturali: un gusto gradevole e tanta energia.
>
> Un succo di frutta è facile da bere, da solo o per accompagnare uno spuntino, è adatto ad ogni età e si può inserire in qualsiasi tipo di dieta. Un succo di frutta è sapore, energia, salute.

1. What does the ad tell you to do?

   a. To buy more fruit.
   b. To have fruit with your meals.
   c. To eat fruit in the morning.
   d. To drink more fruit juice.

2. Can you identify the Italian words in the ad that mean:

   a. day ...
   b. juice ...
   c. apricot ...
   d. taste ...
   e. earth ...
   f. beverage ...
   g. sugars ...
   h. snack ...
   i. age ...
   j. health ...

B. As you are leaving the city of Rome on your way to Florence, you notice a very large sign along the road which reads:

> SCARPE * PELLETTERIE * GIOIELLERIE * DOLCIUMI
> ABBIGLIAMENTO * ARTICOLI SPORTIVI * OTTICA
> AGENZIA ANNUNCI * IL MONDO DELLA CARTA
> AGENZIA VIAGGI * ENOTECA * PROFUMERIA
> SALUMERIA * PASTICCERIA * LIBRERIA * TELEFONIA

The sign indicates ....

1. a children's park
2. a museum
3. a mall
4. a zoo

C. The following information is a want ad from an Italian newspaper about a 16-year-old girl who is available to baby-sit. .

When does this girl prefer babysitting?

1. in the morning
2. in the afternoon
3. in the evening
4. at night

Una 16enne si offre come baby-sitter a Lucera (FG), preferibilmente solo al mattino. Se interessati telefonate al numero 0881/946388

PARLIAMO

For each situation below, create a conversation with at least four exchanges.

1. A guest speaks to the clerk at the reception desk of a hotel in your town. He/She wants to know what kind of entertainment there is in, or near, your community.

2. Two friends are shopping at the grocery store. One is unfamiliar with where things are but has a special meal in mind that he/she wants to prepare.

3. You are visiting your friend in Italy and are discussing where to go and buy the following items for Saturday's picnic: rolls, prosciutto, fresh fruit, beverages and dessert.

4. You and your friend are talking about what kind of work you would like to do when you finish college. Explain your choice of career.

5. You and your friend are in a deli in Italy. Discuss what to buy for tonight's party.

6. Your school will be having a career day. Explain to the new Italian exchange student who comes and what is done at an affair such as this.

SCRIVIAMO

1. Write a list of five occupations or professions you would consider learning about at an upcoming job fair.

2. You have just come back from grocery shopping during your stay in Catania. You realized that you left your umbrella in one of the stores in which you shopped. Make a list of the five food stores that you visited.

3. Write a note to the Italian exchange student describing the places of interest in the city or town where you live and that you would like him/her to see.

4. You have just arrived in Italy for an exchange program. Write a note to a newly-acquired friend asking him/her where and how you can shop in order to buy a birthday present for your mom.

5. You had made plans to go to the movies with your friend Friday night. Write an e-mail message to her saying that you prefer going to the mall. Mention that you need to look for a particular item.

ABOUT ITALY

GROCERY SHOPPING

When school is not in session, Laura and Renzo must help with some family chores. Since the fridge is not that big, they are frequently requested to buy groceries.

The supermarket is very large and has everything, but is rather far away. The open market, very colorful and full of produce and all kinds of other goods is far too. Fortunately, the neighborhood stores are well-supplied and, although more expensive, they provide personalized and reliable service.

Mrs. Silvestri shops at the supermarket for dry goods and some dairy products, but she prefers the local stores for fresh baked bread, milk, fruits and vegetables, and meat. She insists on buying *fresh* food. She also tends to forget things. Renzo or Laura may be called upon at the last minute to buy "four large, ripe, tomatoes to stuff with rice" or a big bunch of basil to make *pesto alla genovese*. Sometimes the list is longer and whoever is in charge has to stop at several places: at the greengrocer's for fruits and vegetables, at the baker's for some fresh bread, at the little bar where they also sell milk and eggs and, sometimes, at the butcher's.

Mrs Silvestri has a funny looking shopping bag that rests on a metal frame with wheels (*il carrello*, she calls it). It is very convenient, but Laura and Renzo hate it. They absolutely refuse to carry "that thing" and prefer to use *lo zainetto*, a sort of shoulder bag that students use to carry their books. If they meet a friend on the way back, they can always pretend they are going to the library.

Neighborhood vendors get an early start each morning.

Fresh vegetables are a favorite at the open markets.

In markets all over Italy one can purchase fine leather goods.

Special occasions call for a stop at the *pasticceria* for something sweet.

CAPITOLO DODICI: I WRIGHT VANNO IN ITALIA
CHAPTER TWELVE: THE WRIGHTS GO TO ITALY

FUNCTIONS

Formal introductions
Exchanging pleasantries
Showing appreciation

LANGUAGE

The verb *fare* plus idioms
The verb *potere*
Vocabulary for travel

ABOUT ITALY

Dealing with friends, peers, and adults

SITUATION

It is the evening of the dinner and "il gran concerto". It is also the occasion for Mrs. Romano to introduce the Wrights to her sister-in-law and family, the Silvestris.

MRS. R.: Roberto e Claudia, **vi** [*to you*] **presento i miei vicini di casa** e **cari** amici, i Wright: Steve, Janice, Brian, John e la piccola Jennifer.

MRS. S.: Piacere. Che bella famiglia!

MRS. W.: Il piacere è **tutto nostro**. Anche lei ha una bella famiglia.

MRS. S.: Ma lei parla bene l'italiano.

MRS. W.: Molto gentile! Con **l'arrivo** dei suoi figli, quest'estate facciamo **esercizio ogni** giorno.

MRS. R.: È vero. Ed è molto **utile** per loro perché **fra poco** vanno in Italia!

JOHN: Andiamo in Italia? **Fantastico**!

Mr. Wright explains to John that he has been invited to do some research at the University of Rome and expects the entire family to live in Italy for a year, starting in September. Brian is not very happy about it and Mrs. Romano explains.

MRS. R.: (*speaking to Mrs. Silvestri*) Brian non vuole venire perché ha un **lavoro** e fra poco **può** comprare una macchina **usata** e **far colpo sulle** ragazze.

At that moment, Laura comes down the stairs. She smiles at Brian and he blushes.

MRS. R.: Laura, ti presento Brian, il fratello di John.

LAURA:	Piacere. Sei simpatico come [*as*] tuo fratello?
BRIAN:	Huh? ...Well ...Ah ...
JOHN:	Just say, "Il piacere è tutto mio."
BRIAN:	Eel pea ya chair ray ay too toe me oh! (*rousing laughter from everyone*)

PAROLE DA RICORDARE

NOUNS

l'arrivo	arrival
l'esercizio	practice
il lavoro	work, job
il piacere	pleasure
il vicino	neighbor

ADJECTIVES

caro	dear,expensive
fantastico	great
ogni (inv.)	every
poco	little, few
tutto	all
usato	used
utile	useful

USEFUL EXPRESSIONS

Che bella famiglia!	What a nice family!
far colpo su	To impress
fra poco	shortly
molto gentile!	(you are/how) kind!
ogni giorno	every day

VERBS

presentare	to present, to introduce
può	s/he can

PROVIAMOCI

A. Tutto sui Wright [*All about the Wrights*]. **Vero o falso:** If it is false, correct it.

1. La bambina Wright si chiama Janice.
2. Ci sono cinque persone nella famiglia Wright.
3. Il signor Wright parla bene l'italiano.
4. I Wright vanno in Italia in dicembre.
5. Brian Wright vuole comprare una macchina nuova.

B. Complete each sentence with a word from the list below.

fratello in famiglia come vuole italiano vicini

1. La signora Romano presenta i ... di casa ai Silvestri.
2. I Wright hanno una bella ... .
3. La signora Wright parla bene l' ... .
4. Il signor Wright, la moglie e i figli vanno ... Italia.
5. Brian non ... andare in Italia.
6. Laura, ti presento Brian, il ... di John.
7. Brian è simpatico ... suo fratello.

C. Say the following in Italian.

1. (May) I introduce to you my neighbors.
2. What a nice family.
3. How kind!
4. We practice every day.
5. Shortly, the Wrights are going to Italy.
6. Brian works and he can buy a car.

The verb FARE *[to do,to make]*

We have already used the verb "**fare**".

Quanto **fa** tre più undici?
Tre più undici **fa** quattordici.

Che tempo **fa**?
Oggi **fa** cattivo tempo.

The verb "**fare**" translates the English *to do, to make*. It is used quite frequently and is important to know.

Here are all forms of the present tense of "**fare**".

io	**faccio**	I make/do	noi	**facciamo**	we make/do
tu	**fai**	you make/do	voi	**fate**	you (pl.) make/do
lui	**fa**	he makes/does	loro	**fanno**	they make/do
lei	**fa**	she makes/does			
Lei	**fa**	you (pol.) make/do	Loro	**fanno**	you (pol. pl.) make/do

Che cosa **fai** domani?
[*What are you doing tomorrow?*]

Gioco a baseball.
[*I am playing baseball.*]

Ragazzi, **fate** i compiti?
[*Kids, are you doing your homework?*]

No, guardiamo la TV.
[*No, we are watching TV.*]

Che cosa **fanno** gli amici di Renzo?
[*What are Renzo's friends doing?*]

Studiano l'inglese.
[*They are studying English.*]

When asked a question that contains "**fare**", the answer may or may not repeat that verb (just like in English).

Che cosa **fa** Ugo?
[*What is Ugo doing?*]

Fa una telefonata.
[*He is making a telephone call.*]

Che cosa **fai** domani?
[*What are you doing tomorrow?*]

Studio con Lucia.
[*I am studying with Lucy.*]

PROVIAMOCI

A. Complete with the correct form of **fare.**

1. Io ... gli spaghetti per cena; tu che cosa ...?
2. La mamma ... la pizza il sabato sera.

3. Voi ... le lasagne o gli gnocchi [*dumplings*]?
4. I Romano ... sempre una bella macedonia.
5. Zia, perché non ... gli spinaci? Mi piacciono molto.
6. Che cosa fa Lei per le vacanze?
7. Noi ... il vitello arrosto.
8. Chi ... la torta per il compleanno di Mauro?
9. Tu cosa ... stasera?

B. Answer the following questions according to the clues provided.

1. Che cosa fa la mamma quando il frigo è vuoto [*empty*]? (goes to the supermarket)
2. Che cosa fate tu e Gianni sabato? (play the guitar)
3. Che cosa fai quando hai fame? (eat)
4. Che cosa fanno gli studenti? (study)
5. Che cosa faccio io quando ho sonno? (go to sleep)
6. Che cosa fai per il compleanno di tuo padre? (buy a CD)
7. Che cosa fa Franco quando ha mal di testa? (takes an aspirin)

Special use of the verb "FARE".

The verb **"fare"** is very important. Not only does it mean **to make** or **to do**, it also combines with severel different expressions to take on entirely different meaning!

fare la doccia	to take a shower	**fare una domanda**	to ask a question
fare il bagno	to take a bath	**fare un favore**	to do a favor
fare colazione	to have breakfast		
		fare + (professione)	to be + a (profession)
fare una telefonata	to make a call		
fare una visita	to pay a visit	**fare una passeggiata**	to take a stroll
fare una festa	to have a party	**fare un giro**	to take a tour, to go for a ride
fare la conoscenza	to meet someone		
		fare una gita	to take a short trip
fare la spesa	to go grocery shopping	**fare le valige**	to pack suitcases
fare le spese	to go shopping (general)	**fare il biglietto**	to buy a ticket
fare un regalo	to give a gift	**fare un viaggio**	to take a trip
		fare una foto	to take a picture

PROVIAMOCI

A. Complete each sentence with an appropriate "**fare**" expression. Use the sketch as your cue.

1. La famiglia Costantini ...
2. Io e Grazia ...
2. Gina e Rosalba ...
4. Papà ...
5. Noi ...
6. Loro ...
7. Mario ...
8. Tu e Rosanna

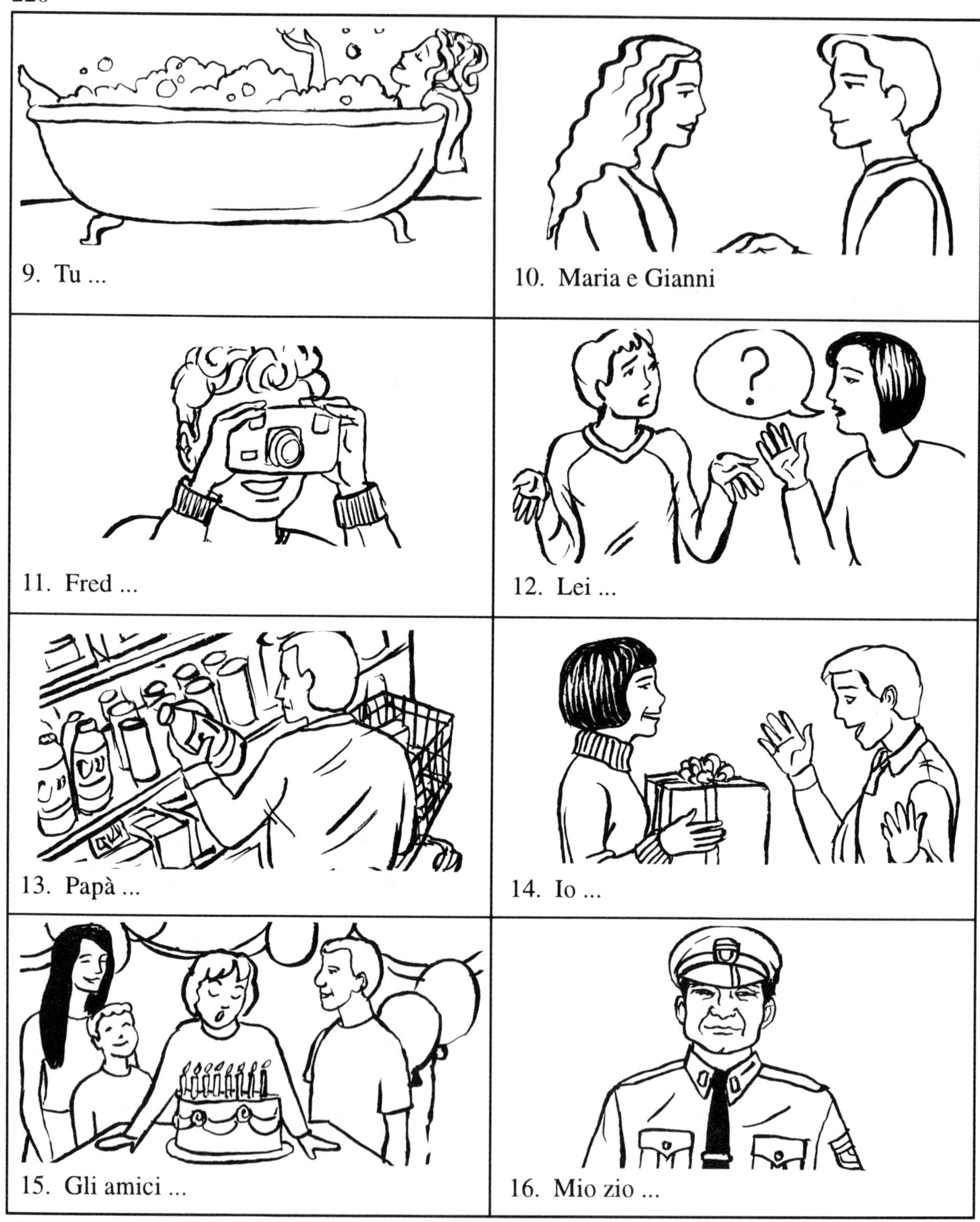

9. Tu ...

10. Maria e Gianni

11. Fred ...

12. Lei ...

13. Papà ...

14. Io ...

15. Gli amici ...

16. Mio zio ...

B. Now let's do things! Complete each sentence with an appropriate form of fare.

1. Tu che cosa ... la mattina, la doccia o il bagno?
2. Federico non ... mai [*never*] domande in classe.
3. Io e Ugo ... sempre molte foto quando siamo in viaggio.
4. I genitori di Renzo ... spesso una passeggiata la sera.
5. Dove ... la spesa la mamma di Renzo?
6. A che ora (tu) ... la festa per gli studenti di scambio?
7. Io ... sempre un regalo alla nomma per il suo compleanno.
8. La signora Tucci ... una festa per il marito che ritorna da un lungo viaggio [*trip*].
9. Maria, perché non ... l'architetto se [*if*] non ti piace fare la farmacista?
10. Io questa sera ... la conoscenza delle cugine di Vittorio.

C. Something about you! Answer the following personal questions.

1. A che ora fai colazione la mattina?
2. Chi fa le foto il giorno del tuo compleanno?
3. Perché fai domande al professore?
4. Quando fai un viaggio in Italia?
5. Dove fa la spesa la tua famiglia?
6. Quando fai il bagno, la sera o la mattina?
7. Fai il bagno o la doccia?
8. Cosa fai il quattro luglio?
9. Ti piace fare un giro in bicicletta o una passeggiata?
10. Preferisci fare un gita in macchina o in motocicletta?

D. Cosa fai? Give an appropriate response to the situations below.

Ex.: Sono le sette di mattina e vai in cucina. > **Faccio colazione.**

1. Il tuo migliore [*best*] amico non sta bene. >
2. Non capisci il professore. >
3. È il compleanno della tua amica. >
4. Non ti piace fare il bagno. >
5. Non hai tempo [*time*] di scrivere la lettera. >
6. È una bellissima giornata di giugno. >
7. Compri un biglietto aereo. >
8. Domani parti per l'Italia. >
9. Hai bisogno di latte, pane, formaggio, uova, pasta, etc. >
10. Insegni in un liceo. >

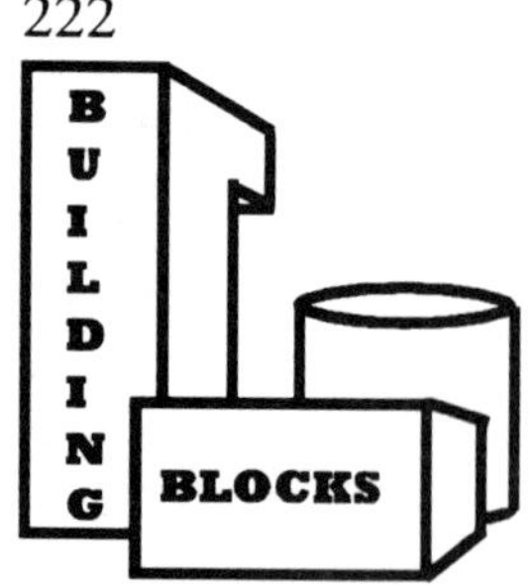

The verb POTERE *[to be able, can]*

In the dialog, Mrs. Wright says: "Brian non vuole venire perché ha un lavoro e fra poco **può** comprare una macchina usata e far colpo sulle ragazze."

The forms of "**potere**" in the present tense are as follow:

io	**posso**	I can	noi	**possiamo**	we can
tu	**puoi**	you can	voi	**potete**	you(pl.) can
lui	**può**	he can	loro	**possono**	they can
lei	**può**	she can			
Lei	**può**	you (pol.) can	Loro	**possono**	you (pol.,pl.) can

PROVIAMOCI

A. Complete the sentences below with the appropriate form of "**potere**".

1. Laura non ... andare in biblioteca perché ha mal di testa.
2. Noi ... venire oggi ma non domani.
3. Tu che cosa ... fare?
4. ... giocare anche voi a Hackey Sac.
5. Quando ... andare allo zoo i bambini?
6. Io non ... uscire [*to go out*] stasera.
7. Che cosa ... fare io se Gino non vuole studiare?
8. (Voi) Non ... andare a fare la spesa. Nevica troppo [*too much*].
9. I ragazzi non ... fare una festa, domani hanno un esame [*test*].
10. John e Renzo non ... comprare questo stereo, è troppo caro.
11. Perché non ... andare in Italia anche noi?
12. Perchè voi non ... pagare il viaggio?

B. Complete the following conversation with the correct forms of the verb "**potere**".

Renzo and John are planning a musical program.

Renzo: Mia sorella ... suonare il pianoforte mentre tu canti.

John: Ma io non ... cantare perché sono stonato [*tone-deaf*]. Se volete io ... suonare la chitarra.

Renzo: Ah!, anch'io suono la chitarra! Noi tre ... fare un trio. Tuo fratello ... far (*fare*) parte del complesso?

John: Lui ... suonare la tromba.

Sig.ra R.: (*Who has been eavesdropping*) Benissimo ragazzi, (voi) ... suonare e io e Claudia ... fare un dolce.

C. What can one do? Find solutions to the following questions in the list below and produce a complete Italian sentence.

1. What can you do if you win the lottery?
2. What can you do if your grades are bad?
3. What can people do on a rainy day?
4. What can I do if I have a headache?
5. What can Renzo buy as a souvenir of the U.S.A.?
6. What can you and I do when we are depressed?

a. andare in pizzeria
b. comprare una Ferrari
c. studiare di più [*more*]
d. andare a giocare a bowling
e. prendere un'aspirina
f. comprare un cappello da cow boy
g. guardare un film comico
h. fare il giro del mondo [*world*]
i. mangiare un grosso [*huge*] gelato
j. fare lo yoga

Vuoi fare merenda con un gelato?

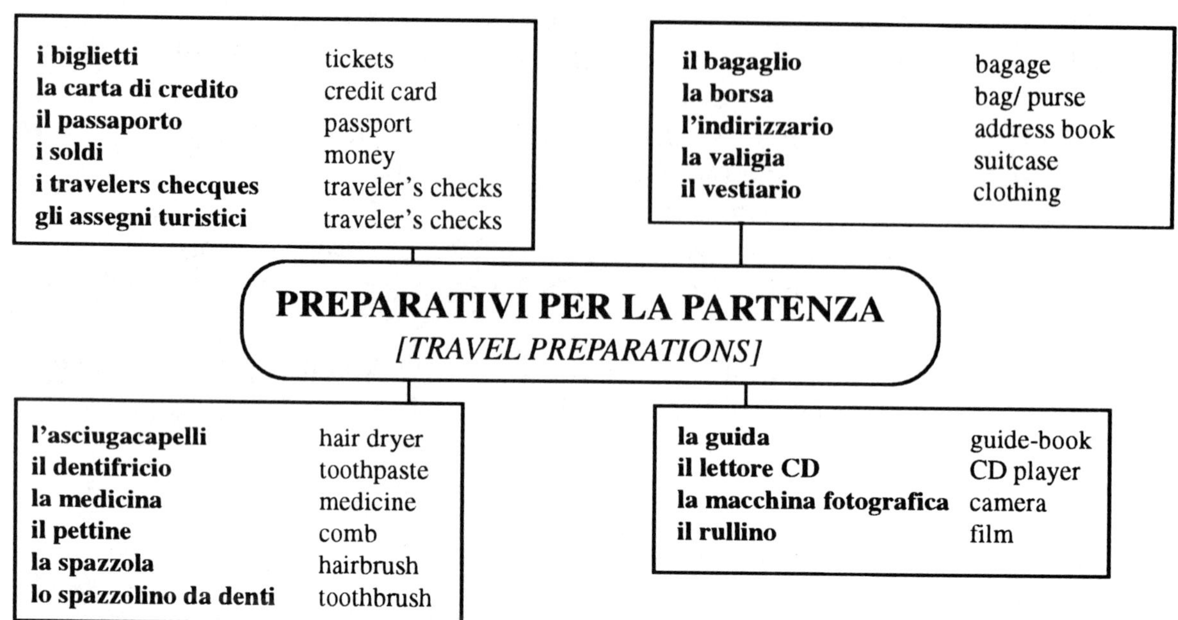

A. Complete each of the following with an appropriate word from the lists above.

1. Per entrare in Italia è necessario il ...
2. Per andare in aereo abbiamo bisogno del ...
3. Per fare foto usiamo la ...
4. Per comprare i souvenir, paghiamo con ...
5. Per portare le cose necessarie abbiamo le ...
6. Per asciugare [*to dry*] i capelli adoperiamo [*we use*] l' ...
7. Per pettinarsi [*to comb one's hair*] c'è ...
8. Per preparare l'itinerario usiamo la ...

B. Below is a list of things that have to be done before a big trip. The items are not in order. Put them in order and create a sentence for each with yourself as the subject [io]. (Later, your teacher and classmates can discuss in Italian the way you prepare for a trip.)

andare in banca	fare le valigie
comprare i biglietti	andare all'agenzia di viaggi
fare le spese	fare il passaporto
comprare i rullini	comprare gli assegni turistici
telefonare ai parenti	portare il cane al canile [*kennel*]
informare gli amici	prendere il tassì per l'aeroporto

C. The day after the big announcement, Mr. Romano talks to John. "Che cosa fate per il gran viaggio?" he asks. Help John answer the question by choosing the correct expression from the possible choices given for each statement.

Prima della mia partenza per l'Italia, faccio una __1__ alla nonna che abita lontano da qui.

Voglio parlare con mio cugino e gli [*to him*] faccio una __2__ perché non ho tempo di fargli una visita.

I colleghi di mio padre fanno una __3__ in ufficio per il suo viaggio. Loro gli fanno il __4__ di una bella valigia.

Mia madre è molto contenta e pensa alle cose necessarie per il viaggio. Domani noi facciamo il __5__ dei negozi della città. Oggi la mamma prende tutti i vestiti necessari per un anno in Italia e incomincia a fare le __6__.

Ora anche Brian vuole fare il __7__ in Italia. Prima [*before*] no. Quando Brian fa la __8__ di una bella ragazza non pensa a niente altro.

1.
a. valigia
b. visita
c. spesa
d. festa

2.
a. telefonata
b. doccia
c. domanda
d. conoscenza

3.
a. doccia
b. spesa
c. festa
d. domanda

4.
a. giro
b. regalo
c. bagno
d. biglietto

5.
a. viaggio
b. biglietto
c. favore
d. giro

6.
a. valigie
b. spese
c. foto
d. feste

7.
a. giro
b. favore
c. viaggio
d. regalo

8.
a. vista
b. conoscenza
c. domanda
d. festa

Now check your answers with those of another student.

DO WE REMEMBER?

A. Complete the following dialog between John and Renzo. Use appropriate verb forms. Choose from the list below.

va **piace** **c'è** **faccio** **vengo** **andiamo** **vuoi** **fai**

Renzo:	John, che cosa ... questa sera?
John:	Io non ... niente [*nothing*] di speciale. Perché?
Renzo:	... venire al cinema con me?
John:	Che film ...?
Renzo:	Un nuovo film di Disney.
John:	Mi ... l'idea. A che ora ...?
Renzo:	... bene alle sette?
John:	Benissimo. Allora ... io a casa tua alle sette meno dieci. Grazie. Ciao!
Renzo:	Ciao!

B. Working in pairs, create sentences by selecting an item from each column. You may create questions or statements. Remember to make necessary changes.

A	B	C
Io		gli spaghetti
Tu	**volere**	andare a dormire
Noi		venire con me
Loro		lavorare ogno giorno
Lucia	**venire**	la spesa al mercato
Laura		parlare con Renzo
Il signor Romano		in discoteca con Laura
I Wright	**andare**	comprare una macchina
Lui		un giro in bicicletta
Lei		In Italia per un anno
Chi	**fare**	con Brian in libreria
Jennifer		venire se vogliono
La sig.ra W.		già [*already*] a scuola
John ed io	**potere**	a scuola oggi.

C. In Italian please!

1. Say that you want to go out [*uscire*] but that you can't because it's late.
2. Say that John and Brian are not coming tonight.
3. Say that Mrs. Romano is making pasta for Sunday's dinner.
4. Ask Laura e Renzo if they are going to the movies with John and Brian.
5. Ask Brian what he is doing this afternoon.
6. Ask your friend Jonathan when he is leaving for Italy.

D. Respond in Italian to the following, using the verb **fare**.

Ex.: What do you do after working on a hot day? **Faccio la doccia.**

1. What does John do to get into the movie theater?
2. What do we do when we go on a trip?
3. What do people do when the fridge is empty [*vuoto*]?
4. What do I do when I want to remember a visit to a special place?
5. What do you and your family do in the kitchen in the morning?
6. What do you do for your birthday?
7. What do the students do when they don't understand?
8. What do you do for your friend when it is her birthday?
9. What do you do when your friend is in the hospital?

E. What can they do? Renzo is planning for the Wrights' visit to Rome. Using the verb **potere** and the information provided, create a sentence that shows what Renzo is planning for each person.

Ex.: io/presentare John ai miei amici.
Io **posso** presentare John ai miei amici.

1. I miei genitori/aiutare i signori Wright.
2. Laura/portare Brian in discoteca.
3. Robertino, tu/mostrare alla signora Wright dov'è il supermercato.
4. Noi/invitare i Wright a casa nostra.
5. Mamma, tu e papà/ portare John e me allo stadio.
6. La signora Wright/lasciare [*to leave*] la bambina con mia nonna quando esce [*goes out*].
7. Io/fare gli spaghetti all'amatriciana.
8. John, tu ed io/andare a sciare a casa di mio zio in montagna.

F. Scrivilo in italiano! How would you write in Italian that ...

1. you are going to the train station with your sister and your brother.
2. your grandmother is arriving this afternoon from Philadelphia.
3. your parents cannot come to the station. They are working.
4. here is grandmother! She is near the train. Hi, grandma!
5. she is not an old lady, she is rather [*piuttosto*] young and strong [*forte*].
6. she wants to walk home, but she can't. It is far and the suitcases are heavy [*pesanti*].

Rome's *Stazione Termini* is one of the busiest railroad stations in the world.

PERFORMANCE ACTIVITIES

E ORA IN ITALIANO

Renzo and Laura are very excited about their friends Brian and John spending a year in Rome. As they talk about the upcoming trip, they also make plans for the future.

Renzo:	La capitale italiana è stupenda. C'è la Roma antica...
Laura:	e poi c'è il centro con tutti i suoi negozi eleganti.
John:	Possiamo visitare il Colosseo, la Fontana di Trevi, il Vaticano?
Renzo:	Sì, e poi ci sono delle piazze fantastiche come Piazza Navona, Piazza di Spagna e Piazza San Pietro.
John:	Molti turisti visitano Roma, non è vero?

Renzo:	Sì, certo, vengono da tutte le parti del mondo; sono turisti europei, cinesi, giapponesi ...
Laura:	A Roma abbiamo musei interessanti, monumenti, palazzi...
John:	Possiamo andare al cinema qualche volta? Piace molto a Brian.
Laura:	Certo, e anche a concerti di musica classica e (*smiling*) di musica rock. (*to Brian*) Ti piace ballare?
John:	Ma certo! Brian vince sempre le gare di ballo [*dance contests*] a scuola!
Laura:	Fantastico! C'è una discoteca a cinque minuti da casa. Ci andiamo con gli amici.

ASCOLTIAMO

Listen as your teacher reads aloud a setting in English followed by a passage in Italian which will be read twice; then choose the most appropriate response to the question based on the passage you have just heard.

1. Why did your friend call?
   a. to invite you to her birthday party
   b. to say that she is not feeling well
   c. to tell you that she is not coming to your party
   d. to organize a birthday party for her mother

2. What is the travel agent telling you?

   a. Alitalia is offering a special discount ticket.
   b. Alitalia is offering a special menu in tourist class.
   c. You can pay upon departure.
   d. It is not possibile to fly this week.

3. What does the mother advise the son to do?
   a. to take a lot of pictures.
   b. to pack his suitcase tonight.
   c. to buy film in America.
   d. to limit the number of things to bring.

4. Che cosa suggerisce di fare l'agente di viaggio?
    a. cambiare la data della partenza
    b. cambiare la linea aerea
    c. partire d'estate
    d. comprare un biglietto turistico

5. Quale mezzo di trasporto suggerisce il signor Silvestri?

LEGGIAMO

1. You are in Italy visiting your relatives. You and your American friend would like to spend some vacation time on the Italian Alps. What number would you call to request some information?

    a. 1678-53039
    b. 1678-56072
    c. 1678-53040
    d. 1678-56071

TURISMO
NEL VENETO

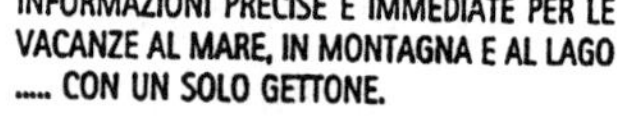

INFORMAZIONI LAGO
NUMEROVERDE
1678-56071

2. You would need to check this schedule if you are traveling by...

    a. bus
    b. streetcar
    c. train
    d. airplane

ORARI FERROVIARI

da CIVITAVECCHIA per GOLFO ARANCI:
partenza ore 9.30 arrivo ore 17.30
partenza ore 11.30 arrivo ore 19.30
partenza ore 21.30 arrivo ore 6.00
partenza ore 23.30 arrivo ore 8.00

da GOLFO ARANCI per CIVITAVECCHIA:
partenza ore 9.30 arrivo ore 17.30
partenza ore 11.30 arrivo ore 19.00
partenza ore 21.30 arrivo ore 6.30
partenza ore 23.30 arrivo ore 8.30

3. Which of the following hotels is right on the beach?

a.

RICCIONE
Hotel EXCELSIOR

Tel. 0541/644189-643800 - sulla spiaggia senza strade da attraversare - zona centrale - ascensore - parcheggio privato - colazione buffet - menù a scelta - camere servizi, balcone vista mare - Pensione completa bassa 43.000/48.000, media 55.000, alta 80.000 sconti bambini.

b.

RIMINI Hotel EDY

La tua casa al mare. Tel. 0541/380741, per una vacanza rilassante a soli 100 m. dal mare, ambiente rinnovato gestito dai proprietari. Colazione e contorni buffet, ricca cucina romagnola. Maggio, giugno, settembre 33.000 luglio e 22-28 agosto 40.000. Agosto interpellateci.

c.

CATTOLICA
Hotel GRAND PARADAIS

3 stelle. 50 mt. mare modernamente arredato, piscina idromassaggio, sala climatizzata, parcheggio custodito, 3 menù a scelta, specialità marinare, colazione buffet. Pensione completa Giugno 45.000 Luglio 45.000/55.000 Agosto 70.000 complessive Tel. 0541/963410 Fax 0541/830052.

d.

ABRUZZO MARE PULITO
MONTESILVANO SPIAGGIA - PESCARA
Hotel EXCELSIOR

Nella verde pineta - 30 metri mare - Compreso nel prezzo: spiaggia privata, ombrellone, sdraio, parcheggio recintato - Camere con servizi, balcone, telefono - scelta menù - Offerte promozionali famiglie - Bimbi fino 4 anni gratis - Informazioni 085-835510/4452658 - Fax 835087.

PARLIAMO

For each situation below, create a conversation with at least four exchanges.

1. Your partner takes the role of an exchange student from Rome. You will be visiting him this coming summer. You talk about things to do in Rome during your stay.

2. Working with your partner, discuss the details of a trip during spring break.

3. You and your Italian friend exchange information about plans for a vacation in Italy. Include specific suggestions for interesting activities while there.

4. You are leaving for Italy next week. You telephone your Italian neighbor and talk about your travel preparations: any last minute activities such as things to buy, things to pack, phone calls to make, things he/she can do for you during your absence, etc.

5. You have your ticket for Italy. Call up your friend and share with him/her this news and talk about the details of your trip.

SCRIVIAMO

1. Write a note to yur Italian friend to tell him/her about five things that you plan to bring on your trip to Italy.

2. Write a note to your Italian friend about five activities you would like to do while in Italy.

3. You will be flying to Italy next month. Write a short letter to your cousin detailing your arrival at Fiumicino in order to advise her about picking you up at the airport.

4. Write a note to your friend asking him if he can take care of your dog while you are away on vacation.

5. Write a letter to your Italian pen pal from Torino telling her about your plans to visit her. Describe your feelings about this.

ABOUT ITALY

DEALING WITH FRIENDS, PEERS AND ADULTS

Good manners take different forms in different places. English-speaking people are, in general, less formal than Italians. Let's consider a few situations.

It is 2:00 in the afternoon and in the elevator you meet Dr. Petri, who lives in the apartment next to yours in Rome. Since you are the younger one, you greet him first.

> You say: **Buon giorno** or **Buon giorno, dottore**.
> He says: **Buon giorno**, (your name).

Buon giorno means "good day". It is day until sunset. After dark you would say: **buona sera**, which means "good evenings". It is evening until you go to sleep. When you are about to go to bed you say: **buona notte.**

Notice that on the elevator you don't have to mention the name of the doctor; you do it only if you are in a crowded place and you want to get his attention. When the elevator has reached its destination floor, you take leave and...

You say: **Arrivederla** or **Arrivederla, dottore.**
He says: **Ciao**, (your name).

"Hi" and "hello" are used extensively in North America among people of all ages, but remember that those expressions are not translated in Italian with "**ciao**". **Ciao** is only to be used for family members, children, friends and some - but not all - peers. Never say "**ciao**" in Italy to an adult who is not a relative or a close family friend. It would sound ill-mannered.

The same rule applies to the use of **tu**, the informal second person. **Tu** is also reserved for family, children, friends and peers. Among your peers are your schoolmates [compagni di scuola], your friends' friends and, when you are older, fellow university students and work colleagues [colleghi d'università e di lavoro]. Again, don't use **tu** in Italy with an adult who is not a close family friend. Just wait until s/he asks you to do so.

In the future, you will see how people apply these rules and also notice how the American "you" is rendered in different situations in Italy.

The Italian caffè, or bar, is a good place to meet friends and aquaintances. How do you suppose the following people would say hello and good bye to each other?

1. Two old school chums
2. A lawyer and a client
3. A lady and a former dance instructor
4. A gentleman and a cute three-year-old
5. A teenager and his parish priest
6. The mayor and his constituents
7. A girl and someone from her gym
8. An industrialist and a union president
9. The pharmacist and a regular client
10. A woman and her sister-in-law

Capitolo dodici: I Wright vanno in Italia

CAPITOLO TREDICI: NUOVI AMICI
CHAPTER THIRTEEN: NEW FRIENDS

FUNCTIONS

Changing language register
Describing a home
Exchanging information and advice

LANGUAGE

Preposition *in* + articles
Vocabulary for the house
The verb *dovere*
Preposition *su* + articles
Sopra, sotto, and *dietro*
Vocabulary for public transportation

ABOUT ITALY

Where do people live?
How do Italians go to places?

SITUATION

Everyone is seated around the dining room table. Mr. Romano pours wine for the adults. Mrs. Romano makes sure that everyone has enough to eat. Mrs. Wright and Mrs. Silvestri get acquainted. John and Renzo make plans for the future. Brian stares across the table at Laura, who is playing with the baby.

MRS. S.: La prima cosa che **dobbiamo** fare è **darci del tu**.
MRS. W.: Grazie, è molto più facile per **me**.
MRS. S.: Avete una casa a Roma? Affittate un appartamento?
MRS. W.: Una **collega** di mio marito è **romana** e ha una casa in via Baglivi. Lei viene qui **da noi** e noi andiamo **da lei**. Facciamo uno ... **scambio**, vero?
MRS. S.: Sì. **Sai**, via Baglivi non è molto lontana da casa nostra. È una **zona centrale**.
MRS. W.: Sì? Mio marito dice che la casa è molto bella. Ha tre **camere da letto**, una **cucina** moderna, una **sala da pranzo**, un grande **soggiorno** e due **bagni**. C'è anche un **posto** per la macchina.
MR. R.: **Avete intenzione di** comprare una macchina?
MRS. W.: Sì, una macchina usata.
MRS. S.: **Però** la macchina non è **proprio necessaria**, ci sono **i mezzi di trasporto pubblici**.
MR. R.: Ma è comoda per fare gite. Ci sono **tante cose** da vedere in Italia.
MRS. W.: E anche per andare al supermercato.

PAROLE DA RICORDARE

NOUNS

l'appartamento	apartment
il bagno	bathroom
la camera da letto	bedroom
la casa	house
la cucina	kitchen
l'ingresso	entrance hall
la sala (stanza) da pranzo	dining room
il soggiorno	living room
il/la collega	colleague
la cosa	thing
il posto	place
lo scambio	exchange
la zona	section, area

ADJECTIVES

comodo	comfortable
lontano	far
moderno	modern
necessario	necessary
pubblico	public
romano	Roman (from Rome)

VERBS

affittare	to rent
dobbiamo	we have to/must
parcheggiare	to park
sai (sapere)	you know

USEFUL EXPRESSIONS

avere intenzione di...	to intend, to plan
da lei	at/to her place
da noi	at/to our place
fare gite	to take trips
dare del tu	to address someone with "tu"
dare del Lei	to address someone with "Lei"
mezzi di trasporto	means of transportation

OTHERS

me	me
però	but
proprio	really, exactly

PROVIAMOCI

A. Complete each sentence with a word from the list below.

gite camere Roma tu necessaria lontana appartamento

1. Ora la Signora Silvestri e la signora Wright si danno del ...
2. La famiglia Silvestri vive in un ... a Roma.

3. La casa dei Wright a ... è molto bella.
4. Via Baglivi non è molto ... dai Silvestri.
5. In casa Wright a Roma ci sono tre ... da letto.
6. La macchina è comoda per fare ...
7. A Roma la macchina non è proprio ...

B. Answer each question in complete sentence.

1. Dov'è la casa dei Wright a Roma?
2. Che zona è?
3. Com'è la casa? (describe it)
4. È lontana da casa Silvestri o è vicina?

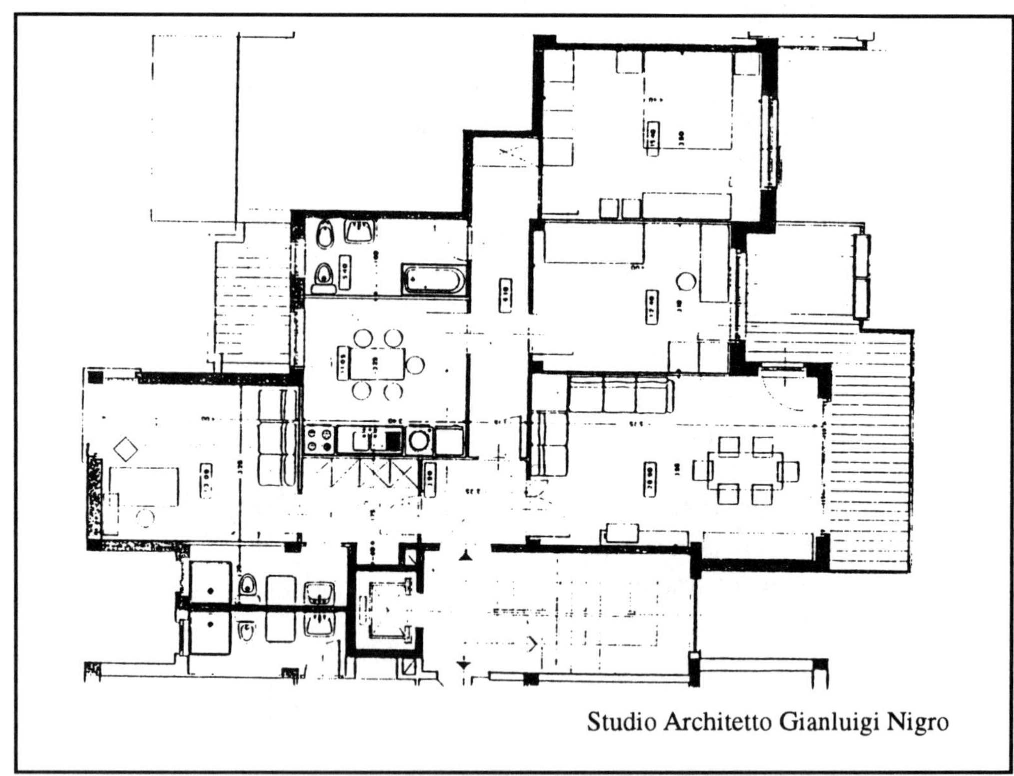

La casa dei Wright a Roma in via Baglivi.

C. In casa Wright ...

1. ci sono tre camere da ...
2. c'è una ... moderna.

3. c'è una sala da ...
4. c'è un grande ...
5. ci sono due ...
6. c'è anche un ... per la macchina.

D. Now describe your house. Begin by stating...

1. the location,
2. the age
3. the make-up of your house,
4. your favorite room,
5. size.

D. Answer the questions based on the ad.

Affito la mia casa (ora vivo a Roma) a Milano, in una bella piazza semicentrale (piazzale Libia). È un appartamento di 120 mq. arredato. Mi potete telefonare al mattino prima delle 9 al numero 06/6874231

1. Dove abita questa persona?
2. Che cosa affitta?
3. Dov'è la casa che affitta?
4. Quando puoi telefonare per chiedere informazioni?
5. Quanto è grande l'appartamento?

The preposition "in" + article

John's Dad likes to sing "in the shower". Remember, "Mio padre canta **nella** doccia."? "**Nella**" is a contraction of two words: "**in**" + "**la**", (in +the). The table below explains what to do when you want to say, "in the", for any kind of noun.

in +	il	lo	la	l'	i	gli	le
=	**nel**	**nello**	**nella**	**nell'**	**nei**	**negli**	**nelle**

If you apply the above table to the situations you are familiar with, you will come up with the following results:

... in John's room	... **nella** camera di John
... in the book	... **nel** libro
... in the closet	... **nell'**armadio

PROVIAMOCI

A. The influence of Italy and the Italians can be found in many facets of our lives. Produce complete sentences following the model.

Ex.: Troviamo l'influenza italiana **nell'**arte.

1. l'industria
2. la tecnologia
3. la scienza
4. lo sport
5. la moda
6. la cucina
7. le automobili
8. il cinema
9. l'architettura
10. i giocattoli

* Can you give examples for each of the areas mentioned?

B. Complete each sentence with the correct contractions. Choose from:

nel, nello, nella, nell', nei, negli, nelle

1. La signora Romano non mette lo zucchero ... caffé.
2. Il padre di John è ... ascensore [*elevator*] di casa.
3. Lo zio di Jeff lavora ... ufficio del signor Petrini.
4. D'estate ci sono sempre molte persone ... piscine pubbliche.
5. La domenica le partite di calcio hanno luogo [*take place*] ... stadi.
6. Ogni giorno i turisti entrano ... basilica di San Pietro.
7. Il libro di matematica è ... studio di papà.
8. ... scuole italiane ci sono lezioni sei giorni alla settimana.
9. La mamma mette la pasta ... piatto [*dish*] di John.
10. ... Albergo Miramonti non c'è una piscina.
11. I bambini giocano ... parchi e ... giardini.
12. Molti studenti stranieri vanno a dormire ... ostelli della gioventù [*youth hostels*].
13. Il lupo [*wolf*] mangia Cappuccetto Rosso ... cucina della nonna.
14. Il cane dorme ... automobile di papà.
15. Il papà di Renzo è ... studio del dottor Foschi.

Most people in Italy live in modern appartment buildings but unusual dwellings can be found in many parts of the country. Cone-shaped roofs are typical of the *Trulli* of the town of Alberobello in Puglia (l.). The Ca' D'Oro (r.) is one of the beautiful palaces found along the Grand Canal of Venice.

In casa [In the house]

In sala da pranzo	in the dining room
il tavolo	table
le sedie	chairs
il buffet	sideboard

In soggiorno	in the living room
il divano	couch
la poltrona	stuffed chair
la lampada	lamp
il televisore	television

In camera da letto	in the bedroom
il letto	bed
il comò	dresser
il comodino	night table
l'armadio	wardrobe

In bagno	in the bathroom
il lavandino	sink
lo specchio	mirror
la tazza (del gabinetto)	toilet
la vasca (da bagno)	bathtub
il bidè	bidet

In cucina	in the kitchen
il lavandino	sink
il frigorifero	refrigerator
la cucina a gas	gas range
la cucina elettrica	electric range
la lavastoviglie	dishwasher

Verbs of "going" (or "being") + places in the house require **in**.

Ex.: Dove andiamo a fare un panino? **Andiamo in cucina.**

PROVIAMOCI

A. Dove andiamo? Where are we going?

1. dormire? ...
2. mangiare? ...
3. guardare la TV? ...
4. fare la doccia? ...
5. cucinare? ...
6. studiare? ...
7. leggere? ...
8. fare il bagno? ...

B. Dove si trova...? [*Where does one find...*] Pieces of furniture do not necessarily belong in just one room. Ask your partner where the items listed below are in his/her house.

Ex.: un letto **Dove si trova un letto a casa tua?**
C'è un letto in camera.

1. un tavolo
2. un televisore
3. un armadio
4. una lampada
5. una poltrona
6. un lavandino
7. un divano
8. una sedia

The verb DOVERE *[to have to, must]*

Dovere is a verb similar to **volere** [*to want*] and **potere**[*to be able to*]. It is irregular and it is generally followed by an infinitive form.

Remember Mrs. Silvestri? - "La prima cosa che **dobbiamo** fare è darci del tu."

Dobbiamo means "we have to / must".

The forms of **dovere** are:

io	**devo** studiare	I have to study
tu	**devi** studiare	you have to study
lui/ lei	**deve** studiare	he/she has to study
Lei	**deve** studiare	you have to study (pol.)
noi	**dobbiamo** studiare	we have to study
voi	**dovete** studiare	you have to study (pl.)
loro	**devono** studiare	they have to study
Loro	**devono** studiare	you have to study (pol., pl.)

PROVIAMOCI

A. Complete each sentence with a form of **dovere**.

1. Noi ... studiare se vogliamo essere promossi [*to pass the course*].
2. Tu ... ascoltare bene in classe.
3. I Wright ... fare il passaporto per andare in Italia.
4. Voi ... fare bene l'esame d'italiano.
5. Signorina, Lei ... fare una telefonata al direttore.
6. Io ... parlare con lo zio Tom perché ho bisogno di soldi.
7. Laura e Brian ... andare a comprare la verdura.
8. Io e Renzo ... aiutare la zia.
9. Lui ... pulire la camera ogni [*every*] sabato.
10. Chi ... andare a fare la spesa oggi?

B. Working with a partner, supply the correct form of the verb **dovere**, then complete each sentence.

Ex.: prendere l'aspirina perché ha mal di testa (il signor Silvestri)
Il signor Silvestri **deve** prendere l'aspirina perché ha mal di testa.

1. fare la spesa al supermercato (Laura e Renzo)
2. fare più sport per la tua salute (tu)
3. andare in banca a prendere i soldi (papà)
4. telefonare ai nonni ogni weekend (io e Maria)
5. studiare la lezione d'italiano (i ragazzi)

6. mettere le biciclette in garage (noi)
7. andare a dormire (tu e tuo fratello)
8. preparare l'arrosto per la cena di questa sera (la mamma)

I mezzi di trasporto pubblici
[*Public means of transportation*]

A tavola, durante la cena dai Romano, la signora Silvestri dice: "A Roma la macchina non è proprio necessaria perché ci sono i mezzi di trasporto pubblici."

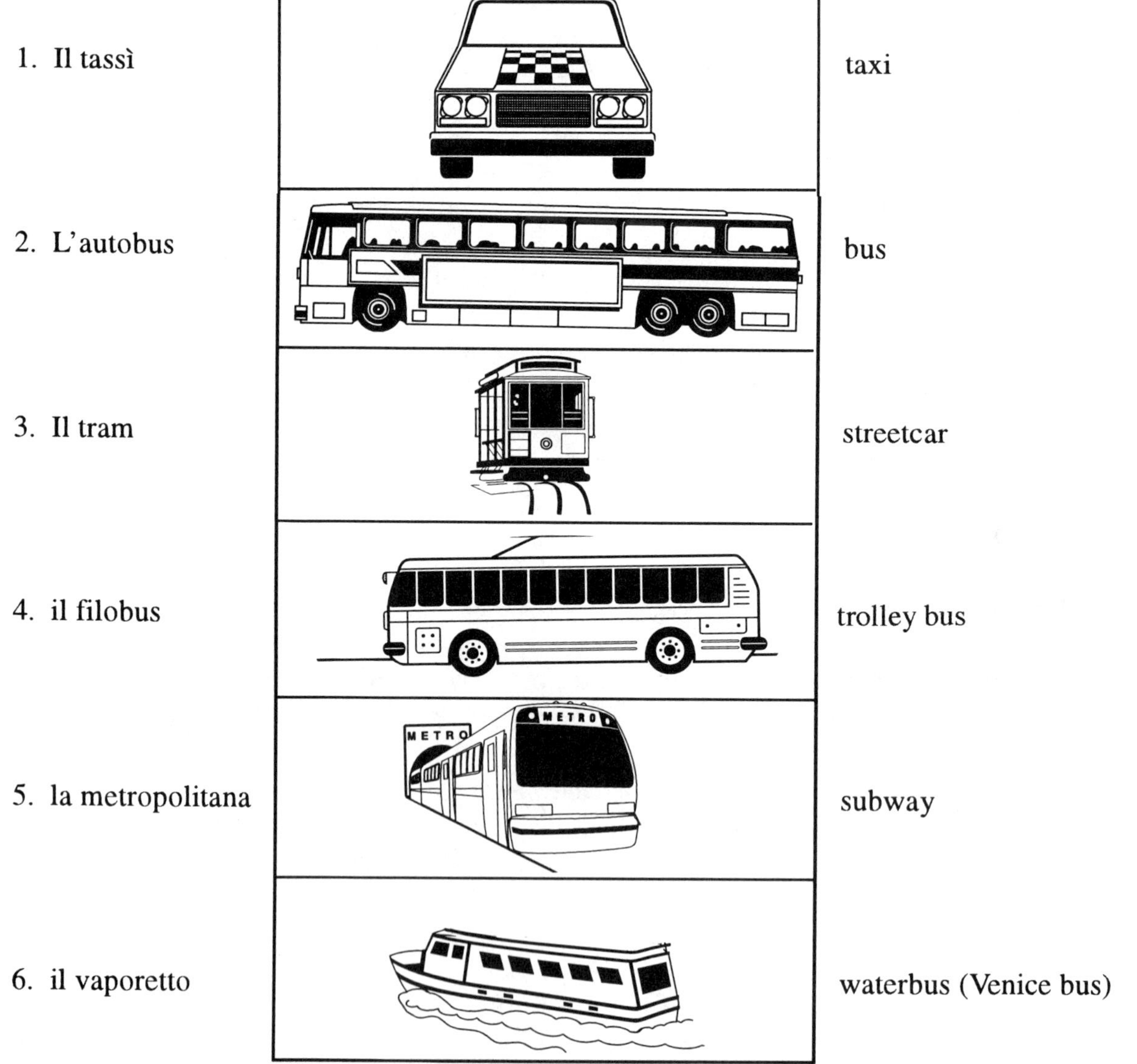

1. Il tassì	taxi
2. L'autobus	bus
3. Il tram	streetcar
4. il filobus	trolley bus
5. la metropolitana	subway
6. il vaporetto	waterbus (Venice bus)

LETTURA
[*READING*]

In città la gente [*people*] usa molto i mezzi di trasporto pubblici. Il **centro** [*downtown*] è servito essenzialmente da autobus e filobus. A Roma il tram si chiama **circolare** perché descrive un cerchio intorno al centro della città. Gli autobus, i filobus e i tram non sono cari, ma sono **lenti** [*slow*]. Chi ha fretta può prendere il tassì, però deve essere preparato a spendere molti soldi. Un mezzo di trasporto rapido ed economico è la **metropolitana** [*subway*], ma non c'è in **tutte** [*all*] le città. L'autobus di Venezia si chiama **vaporetto**, è una **barca a vapore** [*steamboat*] e trasporta molti [*many*] passeggeri.

PROVIAMOCI

A. Answer the following questions.

1. Quali sono i mezzi di trasporto pubblici del centro?
2. Come si chiama il tram a Roma?
3. Che svantaggio [*disadvantage*] hanno gli autobus, i filobus e i tram?
4. Cosa può fare chi ha fretta?
5. È economico il tassì?
6. Qual è il mezzo di trasporto rapido e non caro?
7. Come si chiama l'autobus di Venezia?

B. Complete with appropriate means of transportation.

1. A Venezia prendo il ... per andare dalla stazione a Piazza San Marco.
2. Il ... è un mezzo caratteristico della città di San Francisco.
3. Per andare da un posto [*place*] all'altro [*to the other*] a Roma è molto economico prendere la ....
4. Quando non vogliamo prendere l'autobus e non abbiamo la macchina possiamo andare in ...
5. Qual è il mezzo di trasporto pubblico più comune [*common*] della tua città? È ...
6. Il tuo mezzo di trasporto preferito è ...

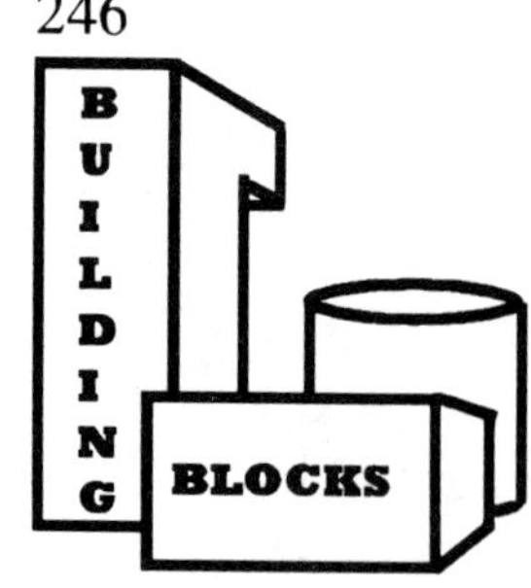

The preposition "su" + article [on the] and other means of locating things

1. The preposition su is used with definite articles when it comes before nouns. The table below will show you how it combines with articles.

su +	il	lo	la	l'	i	gli	le
=	**sul**	**sullo**	**sulla**	**sull'**	**sui**	**sugli**	**sulle**

Il libro è **sul** tavolo — The book is **on the** table

2. You may say exactly where something or somebody is by using:

sopra [*over, or on top*] **sotto** [*under, below*] **dietro** [*behind*]
davanti a [*in front of*] **vicino a** [*near*]

Il gatto [*cat*] spesso dorme **sul** tavolo, **sotto** la sedia o **dietro** il divano.
*Often the cat sleeps **on the** table, **under** the chair or **behind** the couch.*

PROVIAMOCI

A. Complete each sentence with the appropriate contraction with **su.**

1. ... casa dei Silvestri a Roma c'è l'antenna della televisione.
2. Il libro di musica di John non è ... scaffale [*bookshelf*].
3. Ci sono molti libri ... banchi [*desks*] degli studenti.
4. A dicembre non ci sono molte foglie [*leaves*] ... alberi [*trees*].
5. È vero che il giornale è ... comodino della mamma?
6. Le valige sono ... letti.
7. C'è tanto sale [*salt*] ... bistecca.
8. Ci sono tante macchie [*stains*] ... jeans di Robertino.
9. I Silvestri viaggiano ... aerei dell'Alitalia.

10. I gatti dormono ... sedie di cucina.
11. La foto di Laura è ... pianoforte.
12. I giovani turisti camminano spesso con lo zaino ... schiena.

B. Dov'è? Dove sono? Complete the sentences with the appropriate expression of location.

sotto **sopra** **dietro** **vicino a** **davanti a**

1. Gli uccelli volano [*fly*] ... la casa.
2. La bicicletta è ... l'albero.
3. Renzo è ... l'albero.
4. John è ... alla casa.
5. La zia di John è ... alla finestra.
6. L'albero è ...alla casa

C. Mrs. Romano has a small canary [*canarino*] . She loves to hear it sing in the morning. This morning while she was cleaning its cage, it escaped! Renzo, Laura e Robertino help catch it . Using the picture as a guide, tell where the bird lands before they capture it.

Ex.:  **Il canarino è sul televisore!**

Do We Remember?

A. Complete each blank with the correct preposition or contraction.

1. (Nel/In) ... Guinness Book of World Records ci sono informazioni interessanti.
2. Brian dorme (sul/su) ... divano del soggiorno.
3. La mamma prepara la cena (sulla/in) ... cucina.
4. Brian mette il vocabolario italiano (nello/in) ... zaino.
5. L'automobile (del/di) ... Signor Silvestri è usata.
6. Questa sera Claudia arriva (da/di) ... Boston.
7. Renzo legge (su/in) ... camera sua.
8. Robertino gioca (dietro/sopra) ... la casa della zia.
9. (In/Nei) ... musei italiani ci sono sempre tanti stranieri [*foreigners*].
10. Molti stranieri entrano ogni [*every*] giorno (nella/in) ... Basilica di San Pietro.

B. In the city. Where do you go when... (be sure to use an appropriate preposition)

1. you need to fill the doctor's prescription.
2. you have been injured.
3. you want to see many animals in one place.
4. you have to catch a train.
5. you have to make a deposit in your bank account.
6. you want to inquire about higher education.
7. you feel like taking a romantic stroll with your sweetheart.

8. you have to catch the local bus.
9. you need to buy fresh bread.

C. Make a list of things that you must do every weekend. Include the verb **dovere** with every activity.

D. Home sweet home! Provide the information requested below.

1. Name the rooms in your house.
2. Describe what you do in each room.
3. Make a list of items found in each room.

E. Matching: Can you recall common public means of transportation?

a.	b.
Il tram	waterbus
la metropolitana	streetcar
l'autobus	subway
il vaporetto	bus
il filobus	trolley bus

PERFORMANCE ACTIVITIES

E ORA IN ITALIANO

John and Renzo are talking about and comparing the houses in which they live.

Renzo:	John, mi piacciono tanto le case americane. Sono molto comode.
John:	E tu dove abiti a Roma?
Renzo:	Abito in un appartamento in via dei Villini, vicino al centro di Roma.
John:	Com'è? È grande? Ci sono molte stanze?
Renzo:	Sì, abbiamo tre camere da letto, un soggiorno, una sala da

	pranzo, una cucina, due bagni e una grande terrazza.
John:	Ma non sentite il rumore [*noise*] del traffico?
Renzo:	No, perché è una zona residenziale.
John:	C'è un giardino?
Renzo:	No, abbiamo una bella terrazza con tanti fiori.
John:	Ma dove vai a giocare?
Renzo:	Io e i miei amici andiamo a giocare a Villa Torlonia, non lontano da casa mia.

ASCOLTIAMO

Listen as your teacher reads aloud a setting in English followed by a passage in Italian which will be read twice; then choose the most appropriate response to the question based on the passage you have just heard.

1. What comment does the exchange student make about your house?

   a. The garden is rather small.
   b. Your bedroom is beautiful.
   c. The view from the house is impressive.
   d. The kitchen is very practical.

2. What does your friend like about her new vacation home?

   a. It is very large with a beautiful garden..
   b. She can swim and go out on the boat whenever she likes.
   c. There is enough room for many guests.
   d. It is close to town.

3. Che cosa piace molto al tuo amico?

   a. abitare lontano dal centro
   b. fare il bagno in piscina
   c. avere una camera bella e grande
   d. visitare i vecchi palazzi di Milano

4. Dov'è la banca?

   a. davanti alla stazione della metropolitana
   b. a Piazza del Risorgimento
   c. a destra dell'ufficio postale
   d. È molto vicina.

PARLIAMO

Working with your partner, create a conversation using the suggestions below.

1. You are vacationing in Venice with you best friend. Convince him/her to walk to the train station from Piazza San Marco instead of taking the "vaporetto."

2. You are talking to your friend who has just moved into a new apartment. Find out where it is, how big it is, the number and types of rooms, and his reaction to this new experience.

3. Now you have your own bedroom because your older sister moved out. Express your personal feelings to your friend about this new situation.

4. You and your cousin from Italy are exchanging and comparing information about housing in Italy and in the United States.

LEGGIAMO

1. While in Rome, you read this announcement in the newspaper.

What is the announcement about?

> Avvertiamo tutti i cittadini che oggi pomeriggio incomincia lo sciopero [*strike*] del personale dei mezzi di trasporto pubblico. Autobus, tram, filobus, tassì, e metropolitana non sono in servizio dalle 13,00 alle 18,00.

a. Various means of transportation available to the public.
b. Trains will be delayed starting at 1 PM.
c. Public transportation will come to a stop at 1 PM.
d. The public is requested to use mass transit.

2. The information provided below would be of interest to people looking ...

   a. for a new place to live.
   b. for a job in construction.
   c. for a house in downtown Torino.
   d. to rent a small house.

È una vera gioia vivere in questa residenza
di nuova costruzione
a venti minuti da Torino.
Di questo complesso residenziale fanno parte
ville con giardino e appartamenti di lusso.

SOGGIORNO
CUCINA E SALA DA PRANZO
QUATTRO CAMERE
TRE BAGNI
ATTICO
TAVERNA
GIARDINO
DOPPIO BOX

TEL: 03/15654982
FAX: 03/15642004

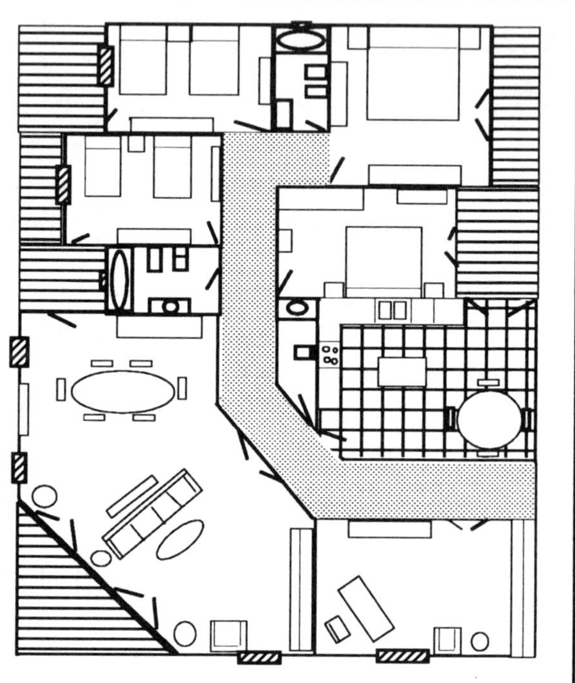

3. What is this ad about?

   a. renting an apartment.
   b. selling an apartment
   c. buying an apartment
   d. looking for an apartment

Vendo a Gaeta un appartamento composto da soggiorno con angolo cottura, camera e cameretta, bagno e terrazzo e posto auto. Il prezzo è di 110 milioni. Telefonatemi nelle ore di ufficio ai numeri 06/8335238-8392358

SCRIVIAMO

1. Describe your newly decorated room to your pen pal using at least five sentences.

2. Write a note to your Italian friend explaining five things you must do regularly.

3. You will have an exchange student living with you next September. Write a note to her describing your house. Give information as to the number of rooms, types of rooms, and the bedroom that she will occupy.

4. Write a note to your best friend describing your dream house.

ABOUT ITALY

WHERE DO PEOPLE LIVE

As we mentioned in Chapter 4, for the majority of Italians, "casa" means the apartment where they live. A large private home is called a **villa.** Smaller private homes are called **villino** or **villetta**.

Great Italian villas set the standard for beauty and elegance in private homes.

The Silvestri family owns a fairly large apartment in an apartment building. Their **palazzina** has six floors and they live at the very top; a desirable location because they are far up from the street traffic and have the luxury of a big terrace and lots of light.

This type of housing is also found in the country. Italy has emerged from World War II as an industrial nation, which means that most people work in factories or offices, and farming is not as extensive as it was sixty years ago. Old farmhouses are often turned into vacation places, and a great many people, farmers included, live in a town setting, in **palazzine** with all the modern conforts.

A typical neighborhood of villette

HOW DO ITALIANS GO TO PLACES

All young people would like a car, but there are a few problems. The minimum age for the driver's license is eighteen, the majority of young people have no money of their own, and gasoline is very expensive.

Renzo, Laura and their friends can use public transportation: **autobus,** [*busses*], **filobus** [*trolley busses*], **tram** [*street cars*], and **metropolitana** [*subway*]. The fare is reasonable, and there are very convenient monthly passes for frequent users. Single tickets must be bought ahead of time (at bars or newsstands) and punched by a machine (*l'obliteratore*) that stamps them with the date and the time of the ride. Those who live in Rome, Milan, Turin, or Naples have the additional convenience of the subway.

Laura has a moped. Renzo, according to his father, is too young for that; for the time being, he can only use his bicycle. Adults have cars. Everybody agrees that there are too many cars around, but nobody is willing to give up his own. During rush hours there are traffic jams in the big cities, just as in every other big city in the world like New York or Tokyo.

The exam that one has to pass to obtain a driver's license is a very tough one, and requires a good knowledge of the engine and how it works. Given the speed limit (65 to 80 miles per hour on highways), and the number of cars on the roads, the frequency of accidents in Italy is surprisingly low.

It goes without saying that Laura, Renzo and their friends can't wait to have a car of their own. Well, you can understand that, don't you?

This street-car makes a circle around the city of Rome.

The public busses in Rome are dependable but crowded.

Scooters are a popular way of getting around congested Italian streets.

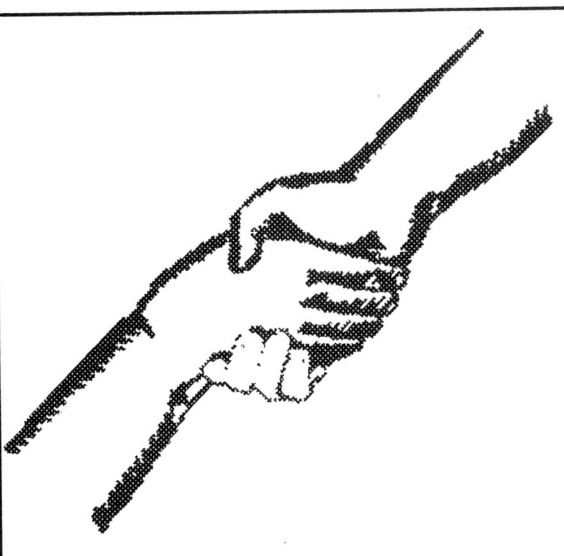

CAPITOLO QUATTORDICI: AL CENTRO COMMERCIALE

CHAPTER FOURTEEN: AT THE SHOPPING CENTER

FUNCTIONS

Planning to buy clothes
Commenting on prices and other things
Asking and giving street directions

LANGUAGE

Vocabulary for clothing
Expressing "some" with *di* + article
More on *di* + article
Vocabulary for street directions

ABOUT ITALY

Shopping in Rome

SITUATION

Laura would like to take advantage of the reasonable prices in the American clothing stores before returning to Rome. Brian would like to pick up a few things that will help him blend in with Italians his age. Laura is willing to give him advice and Brian wants to get to know her better. Neither can communicate with the other, so they reluctantly agree to let their younger brothers accompany them to the local mall to act as interpreters.

LAURA: Voglio comprare dei bei jeans.

JOHN: She wants to buy...

BRIAN: Jeans, that much I understood. There is a store down there on the left that has nice jeans that are pretty reasonable.

RENZO: Lui dice che c'è un negozio lì **a sinistra** che vende dei bei jeans a **buon mercato**.

LAURA: Fantastico! **Non vedo l'ora di vederli**. (to John) Che cosa vuole comprare Brian?

JOHN: She wants to know what you want to buy.

BRIAN: Shoes. Something confortable.

JOHN: Mio fratello vuole comprare delle **scarpe comode**.

LAURA: Allora deve comprare un **bel paio di** scarpe da barca americane. I miei amici vanno **matti per** le Timberland.

RENZO: Sì, è vero! Anch'io voglio un paio di Timberland.

In the jeans store, Laura comes out of the dressing room with a pair of new jeans on.

LAURA: Come sono belli! A Roma costano **il doppio**.
RENZO: Quanto costano?
LAURA: Trenta dollari.
BRIAN: Yeah, they are nice, but too long. (to John) "Lungo," right?
JOHN: "Lunghi". Not bad, Bri.
LAURA: No, **vanno bene**. Faccio un **risvolto** (*she makes a cuff*) ed **ecco fatto!**
RENZO: Sì, sì, hai ragione, anch'io faccio così.

PAROLE DA RICORDARE

NOUNS

il doppio double
il paio pair
il risvolto cuff
la scarpa shoe

VERBS

mi metto I put on
portare to wear

OTHERS

dei of the, some (masc. pl.)
delle of the, some (fem. pl.)

ADJECTIVES

bei beautiful (m. pl.)
bel beautiful (m. sing.)
comodo comfortable
matto crazy

USEFUL EXPRESSIONS

a buon mercato inexpensive
a destra to the right
andar bene to be O.K., to fit
a sinistra to the left
dritto straight ahead
ecco fatto there, it's done
non vedo l'ora (di) I can't wait (to)

PROVIAMOCI

A. Complete each sentence with a word from the list below.

matti **comode** **paio** **risvolto** **costano** **lì**

1. Laura va al negozio per comprare un ... di jeans.
2. Il negozio è ... a sinistra, davanti al cinema.
3. Brian vuole comprare un bel paio di scarpe ...
4. Gli amici di Laura vanno ... per le Timberland.
5. In Italia i jeans ... molto.

6. Laura fa un ... ai jeans perché sono lunghi.

B. Use the list of "Useful Expressions" in "Parole da ricordare" and tell how you would respond to the following situations in Italian.

1. You have just completed your big project for your Italian teacher.
2. You have just learned that your Italian teacher is going to treat the whole class to a party with Italian pastries.
3. Your Italian friends invites you to the movies and you can go.
4. A friend wants to know how much your jeans are. (They are inexpensive.)
5. A new student asks where the restrooms are. (They are to the right.)

L'ABBIGLIAMENTO

[ARTICLES OF CLOTHING]

Mrs. Silvestri realizes during her stay that clothing in the United States is much more reasonable in price than in Rome. What follows is a list of items Mrs. Silvestri purchased for her family in "**un negozio di abbigliamento**" [*a clothing store*].

√ *delle calze per Laura*	[stockings]
√ *dei calzini per Renzo e Robertino*	[socks]
√ *una camicetta per Lucia*	[blouse]
√ *delle camicie per mio marito*	[shirts]
√ *un cappotto per mio padre*	[winter coat]
√ *una giacca per mio cognato*	
√ *una gonna per me*	[skirt]
√ *un paio di guanti per mia madre*	
√ *un impermeabile per mio suocero*	[raincoat]
√ *un paio di pantaloni per mio fratello*	[slacks]
√ *un paio di scarpe Timberland per Renzo*	
√ *un vestito per Laura*	[dress or suit]*
√ *un paio di sandali per mia sorella*	
√ *una cintura per il mio vestito*	[belt]
√ *le scarpe da ginnastica per Renzo*	[sneakers]
√ *un paio di stivali per me*	[boots]
√ *una cravatta per Alberto*	[tie]
√ *un cappello per mio padre*	
√ *una borsa per la mia amica*	[purse]
√ *un costume da bagno per me*	[bathing suit]
√ *un paio di pantaloncini per mio nipote*	[short pants]

*vestito (da uomo) = man's suit *vestito (da donna) = dress or outfit

Che cosa compra?:

1. Che cosa compra la signora per suo marito? , per Laura?, per Renzo?, per Robertino?
2. Per chi compra una cravatta? , una borsa? , un cappotto? , una camicetta?
3. Quanti vestiti compra per Laura?

PROVIAMOCI

A. Working with a partner, identify each of the articles of clothing sketched below.
   a. Put your answers on a separate sheet of paper, including definite articles.
   b. Compare your list with that of another team. Do your lists match?

1.

4.

2.

5.

3.

6.

7.
12.
8.
13.
9.
14.
10.
15.
11.
16.

17. 

19. 

18. 

20. 

B. Che cosa ti metti quando ... Answer each question beginning with: "Mi metto ..."

Ex.: vai al mare? **Mi metto il costume da bagno.**

1. vai a una festa?
2. vai a scuola?
3. vai in discoteca?
4. fa freddo?
5. fa caldo?
6. piove?
7. nevica?
8. vai a un matrimonio [*wedding*]?

C. Complete with appropriate articles of clothing.

1. Le ragazze portano le calze, i ragazzi portano i ...
2. Quando deve essere elegante Brian si mette [*put on*] la ... e la ...
3. Quando piove portiamo [*we wear*] l'...e l'ombrello.
4. La camicetta è per la signora, mentre la ... è per il signore.
5. Laura va al mare con i ..., non con le scarpe.
6. Per giocare a tennis mettiamo le scarpe ...
7. In America i ... da baseball non sono a buon mercato.
8. Laura desidera comprare un paio di ... americani.

D. Tell what you would wear in the following situations. Mention several items of clothing. Begin each statement with, "Mi metto ..."

1. You are going to the beach and it is very hot.
2. You are getting ready for you sister's wedding reception.
3. It is Friday and you are getting ready to go out with friends.
4. You are getting dressed for a rainy day.
5. It is a very cold morning and you are getting ready to go out.
6. You are getting dressed for your very first job interview.

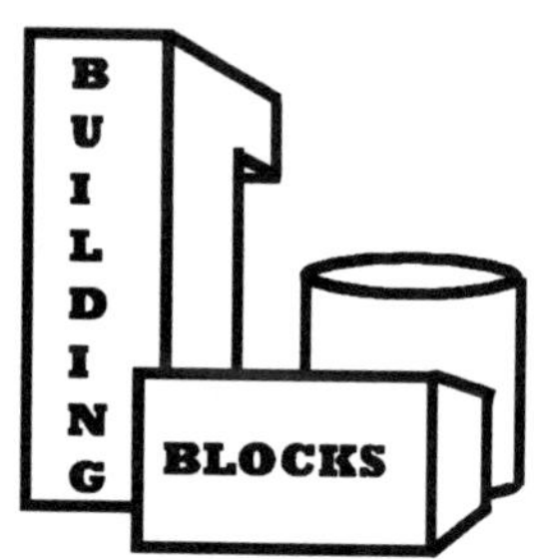

Expressing "some" with di + *articles*

Laura says: "Voglio comprare **dei** bei jeans."
John says: "Mio fratello vuole **delle** scarpe comode."
Mrs. Romano says: "I Giannetti hanno sempre **della** bella frutta fresca."

The contraction of **di + article** that you studied in Chapter 11 is also used to indicate "some".

Ex.: Ho ancora **dei** biglietti dell'autobus di Roma
*I still have **some** bus tickets from Rome.*

Voglio comprare **delle** belle sedie nuove per il soggiorno.
*I want to buy **some** nice new chairs for the living room.*

PROVIAMOCI

A. Express "some" in each sentence below.

1. Nelle boutique di via Frattina ci sono ... vestiti molto eleganti.
2. La signora Wright compra anche ... pesche.
3. C'è ... gelato al limone molto buono in frigo.
4. Domani sera a cena vengono ... studentesse, amiche di Brian.
5. Brian compra ... cioccolatini per Laura.
6. Ci sono sempre ... studenti che non studiano.
7. Ragazzi, volete ... fiori per la mamma o ... dolci [*sweets*]?

8. C'è ... zucchero in cucina? La zuccheriera [*sugar bowl*] è vuota [*empty*].
9. Renzo ha ... amici simpatici.
10. Laura compra ... bei jeans a buon mercato

Expressing possession with "di" or "di" + article

Several times we have used expressions like:

Sono la mamma **di** John.	I am John's mother.
La casa **dei** Romano è grande	The Romano's house is big.
È la Ferrari **del** professore	It is the professor's Ferrari.

Now we must remember that to express possession in this way in Italian we use the equivalent of "**of**" or "**of the**" and **NEVER** "**'s**".

PROVIAMOCI

A. Complete the sentences below in good Italian.

1. (The uncle's car) ... è davanti alla casa.
2. (The family's suitcases) ... sono in macchina.
3. (Brian's shoes) ... sono nuove e belle.
4. (The friends' party) ... è alle otto a casa loro.
5. (The boy's books) ... sono su una sedia in cucina.
6. (Mother's purse) ... è molto bella.
7. (My sister's car) ... è nera e non mi piace.
8. (Professor Bianch's lessons) ... non sono sempre facili.

B. Di chi è? [*Whose is it?*] Answer the following questions using the clues given.

Ex.: Di chi è questa camicia? (Robertino) **È la camicia di Robertino.**

1. Di chi è questa borsa? (Laura)
2. Di chi sono queste scarpe? (Renzo)
3. Di chi è questo biglietto? (la signorina)
4. Di chi sono queste valigie? (i Silvestri)

5. Di chi sono questi ombrelli? (le signore)
6. Di chi è questa casa? (l'avvocato Morelli)
7. Di chi sono questi libri? (lo zio Giovanni)
8. Di chi sono queste medicine? (il nonno)

PER TROVARE LA STRADA

[STREET DIRECTIONS]

You are in Piazza della Croce Rossa looking for the university (see the map on the next page). You ask for help from a passerby.

You: Scusi , per favore, che strada devo fare per andare all'università?

S/He: Devi **prendere** viale Castro Pretorio quasi [*almost*] **fino in fondo**, poi devi **girare a sinistra** su via Monzambano, **attraversare** Piazza Confienza e girare ancora [*again*] a sinistra su viale dell'università.

USEFUL EXPRESSIONS FOR GETTING AROUND TOWN

1.

Andare dritto
To go straight

Girare a sinistra
To turn left

Girare a destra
To turn right

Attraversare la piazza	*To cross the square*
Girare alla prima traversa	*To turn at the first block*
Girare alla seconda traversa	*To turn at the second block*
Girare all'incrocio	*To turn at the intersection*
Andare fino in fondo alla strada	*To go all the way down the street*

Girare all'angolo
To turn at the corner

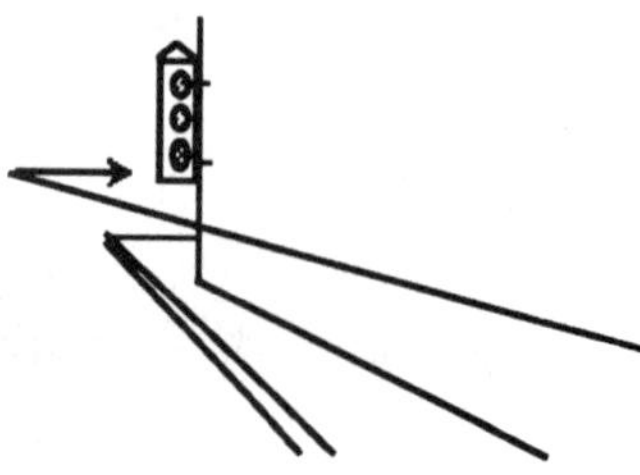

Girare al semaforo
To turn at the traffic light

2.

Dopo il ponte	*After the bridge*
Dietro la chiesa	*Behind the church*
Davanti alla fermata dell'autobus	*In front of the bus stop*
Vicino alla banca	*Near the bank*

3. "Street" or "avenue" in Italian are: **via, viale or corso**.

Exs.: **Via** Nazionale **Corso** Galileo Ferraris **Viale** Giulio Cesare.

4. Abbreviations: **V.** = Via **V.le** = Viale **C.so** = Corso
P.za = Piazza **L.go.** = Largo (similar to a square)

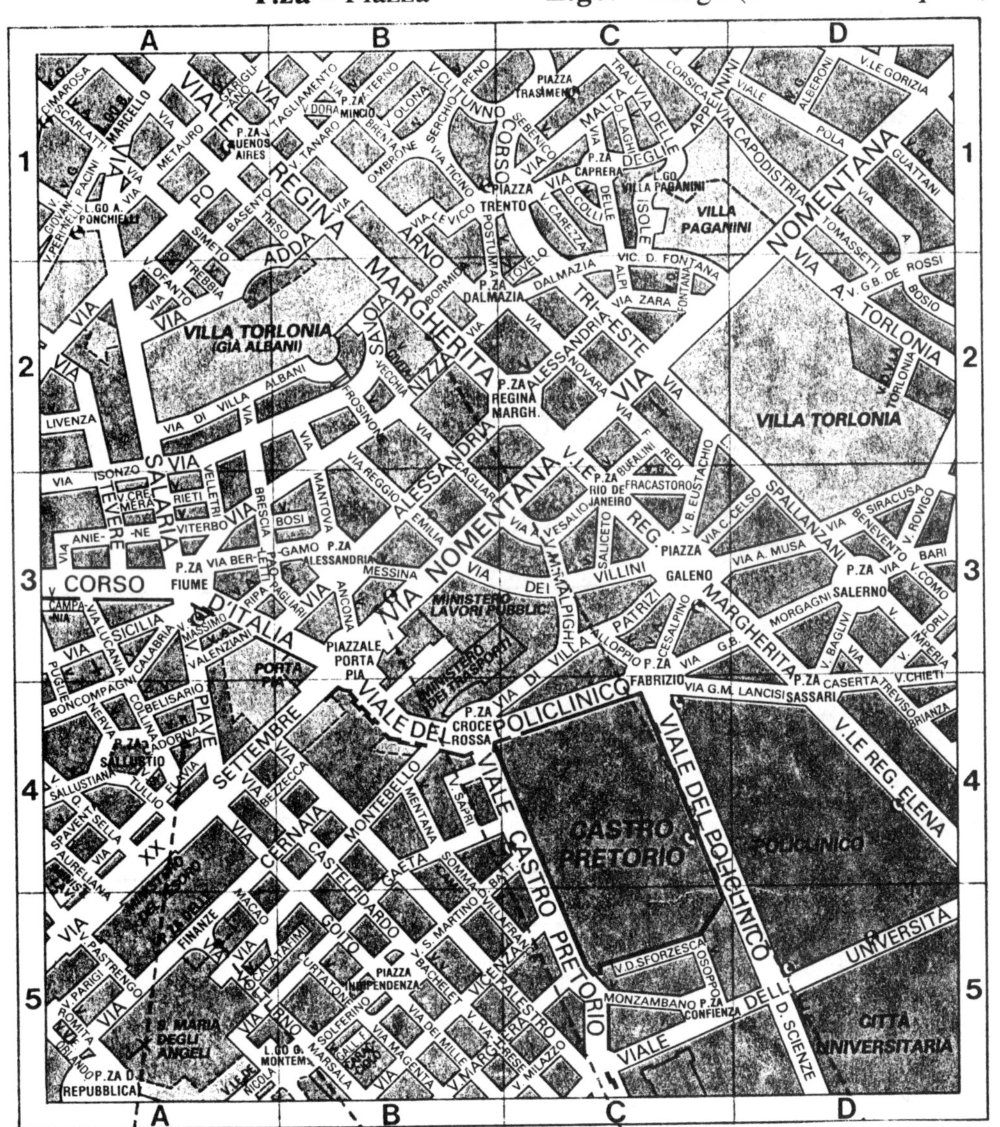

PROVIAMOCI

A. Getting there. Your family is hosting an exchange student and you are explaining to him/her how to get to places. Start with "Devi [*You must*]..."

1. You must go all the way down the street, then turn right.
2. You must go straight, then turn to the left at the traffic light.
3. You must turn right at the corner and go straight to the square.
4. You must cross the street [*strada*] and then go left.
5. You must go straight , and then turn right at the second light.
6. You must cross the square, continue on [*continuare su*] Kennedy Avenue and turn left at the second intersection.

B. Come si va allo zoo? [*How do you get to the zoo?*]

Mrs. Romano explains to Laura, who is grocery shopping with her:

> Dal supermercato, devi andare a sinistra e seguire via Washington fino al secondo incrocio. Poi devi girare ancora a sinistra e continuare su via Jefferson. Lo zoo è dopo l'ufficio postale a destra.
>
> [*From the supermarket you must go to the left and follow Washington Street to the second intersection. Then you must turn left again and continue up Jefferson Street, The zoo is after the post office on the right.*]

Here is a map of the downtown area. Trace the route.

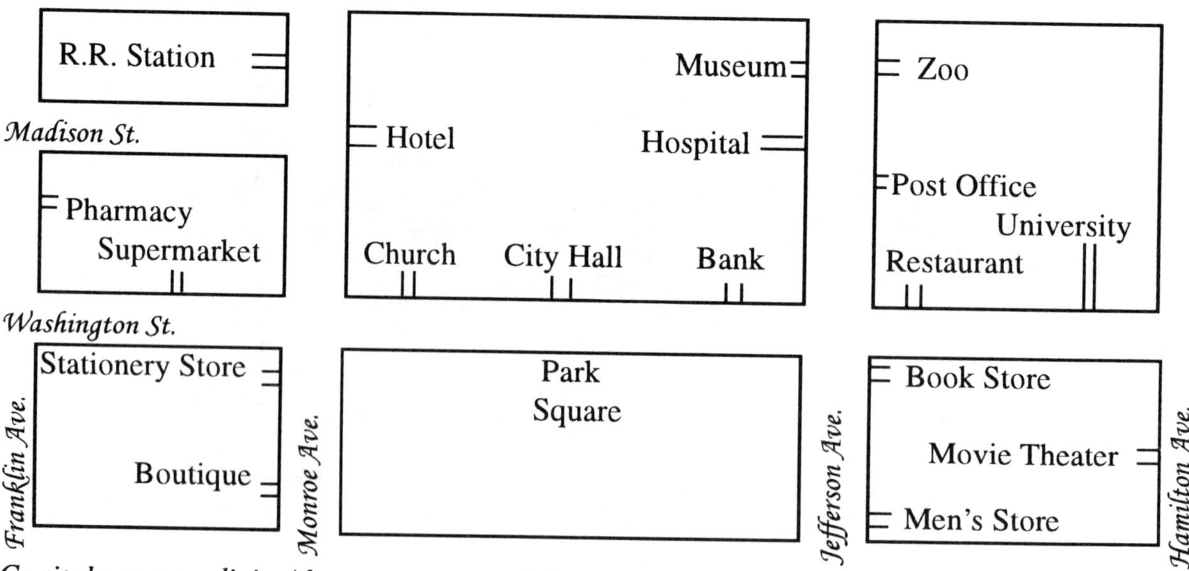

C. Using the simple map of the downtown area on the prevoius page, practice getting from one place to another in town.

D. Working with a classmate, ask/answer each other how to go to certain places on the map. Change roles several times.

E. Make your own map that shows how to go from your house to school, and explain it in Italian to a classmate.

F. Renzo plans to go from via dei Villini (next to piazza Galeno [3C] on the map of Rome) where he lives, to via Baglivi (next to Piazza Salerno[3D] to visit the Wrights. Write a short paragraph describing his route. Begin with: "Da casa sua, Renzo va a destra / sinistra in via ..."

G. Class activity: Each student will write the name of a store or building in big letters on a sheet of paper as directed by the teacher. The aisles between the rows of desks, as well as the spaces in front of the room and at the back are assigned street names. The teacher asks the students to give him/her instructions on how to get to a certain place. The student who holds the sought after place shows the class his/her sign. As class members give instructions in Italian, the teacher moves along the "streets". The teacher may participate several times and then turn his/her role over to a student.

This is a street address. In what ways are Italian addresses written differently than American ones?

DO WE REMEMBER?

A. Review descriptive adjectives and colors (Chapter 5), then...

a. Describe what you are wearing today. Use the verb "portare" [*to wear*].

b. Describe what your classmate to your right or left is wearing.

B. Explain to your classmate how to go to school from your house.

C. Complete the following exercise with an appropriate contraction of "di" + article" [*of the*].

1. Dov'è la macchina ... zio? È lì a sinistra, davanti alla farmacia.
2. Questa non è la casa ... Rossi, è la casa ... Morelli.
3. Mi piace andare nella barca ... professor Cesarotti.
4. I libri ... studenti sono sulla cattedra [*teacher's desk*] ... professoressa.
5. Le scarpe ... bambine sono care.

D. Brian ha bisogno di tante cose. Complete each line of the dialogue by supplying the appropriate contranctions of "di + article".

Brian:	Ho bisogno ... macchina.
Mamma:	Sì, ma hai bisogno ... permesso di papà.
Brian:	E poi ho bisogno ... chiavi [*keys*] ... macchina.
Mamma:	Se [*if*] vai al centro commerciale ho bisogno ... mia medicina.
Brian:	Sì, va bene, però [*however*] io ho bisogno ... soldi per comprarla.

E. John and Renzo agree to pick up a few things for their families at the market. Once there, they help each other remember what everyone wants. Help complete each sentence below from that conversation.

Ex.: la mamma / le belle mele. **La mamma vuole delle belle mele.**

1. La zia / le nuove ricette [*recipes*] per fare i dolci
2. Tua sorella Laura / le bibite per i suoi amici.
3. Papà / il prosciutto di Parma per l'antipasto
4. Brian / le patatine "chips"
5. Lo zio Alberto / la frutta fresca per la macedonia

6. La zia Lucia / il formaggio per i panini
7. La mamma/ la carne di vitello da fare arrosto

PERFORMANCE ACTIVITIES

E ORA IN ITALIANO

Laura, Brian, John and Renzo are at a local mall shopping for clothes to bring back to Italy.

Laura:	Quante belle cose ci sono in questo negozio. Voglio comprare tutto.
Renzo:	E anche i prezzi sono buoni. A Roma tutto è molto più caro.
John:	Ah sì?
Laura:	Io ho bisogno di una camicetta, un paio di jeans Levi e una gonna. Spero di avere abbastanza soldi.
John:	Non ti preoccupare, noi abbiamo soldi anche per te.
Renzo:	(*to John*) John, dove sono le scarpe? Io cerco un paio di Timberland.
John:	Sono in quell'angolo lì, a sinistra.
Laura:	Sì, le vedo, sono lì in fondo.
Renzo:	Va bene. Perché non andiamo prima [*first*] a vedere le scarpe?
Laura:	D'accordo. Su, andiamo!

ASCOLTIAMO

Listen as your teacher reads aloud a setting in English followed by a passage in Italian which will be read twice; then choose the most appropriate response to the question based on the passage you have just heard.

1. What is the customer looking for?

   a. a bigger size blouse
   b. a different color blouse
   c. a better quality blouse
   d. a less expensive blouse

2. What does your cousin need?

   a. a bathing suit
   b. a long skirt
   c. an elegant outfit
   d. a jacket

3. What is the passerby telling you to do?

   a. to go all the way down, then turn right.
   b. to go all the way down, then turn left.
   c. to go all the way down the street.
   d. to go straight, then turn left at the first light.

4. Perché la tua amica non compra la borsa?

   a. Il colore è brutto.
   b. Costa troppo.
   c. Non è il suo stile.
   d. È piccola.

5. Di che cosa ha bisogno la tua amica?

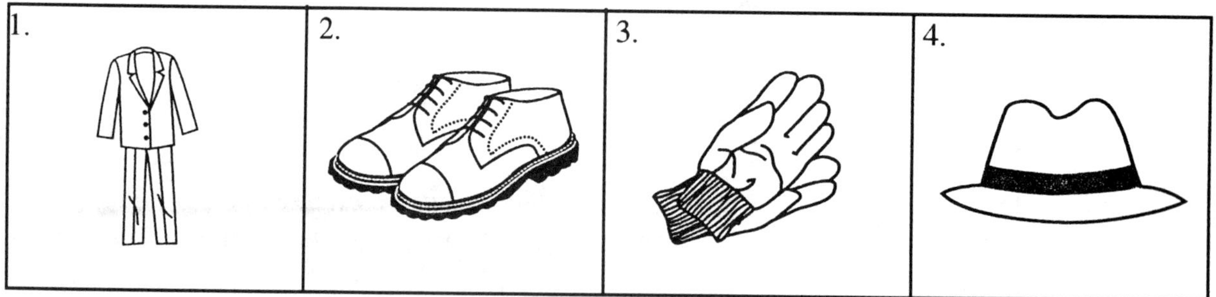

LEGGIAMO

1. Your cousin is having a baby shower. Where would you go to buy a baby gift?

a. ABITI DA SPOSA E CERIMONIA VIA FABIO MASSIMO 46	b. *CENTRO MODA* **MARINI** UOMO DONNA BAMBINO NEONATO
c. **MAMPIERI** IL POSTO GIUSTO DOVE SCEGLIERE LA MODA	d. *Piante e Fiori* *Addobbi per Cerimonie*

2. According to the information in this ad below, this store is...

   a. moving to a different location.
   b. having an end of season sale.
   c. liquidating all the merchandise.
   d. closing for store restoration.

3. Carissimo Giuseppe,

Sono contentissimo della tua venuta negli Stati Uniti il venticinque giugno. Io spero di venire all'aeroporto ma ho bisogno di sapere l'ora di arrivo dell'aereo. Non vedo l'ora di vederti. Salutami tutti. A presto.

John

Che cosa vuole sapere John?

a. A che ora parte l'aereo.
b. A che ora arriva l'aereo.
c. Il giorno dell' arrivo.
d. La linea aerea

PARLIAMO

1. You and your partner are going to the mall, and you are discussing how to get there. You start the conversation.

2. Call your partner on the phone to obtain directions how to get to his/her house for supper. You start the conversation.

3. Your partner is the salesclerk in a clothing store. You are shopping for a gift for your friend. Talk about something appropriate you might consider purchasing.

4. You are wearing something that your partner really likes and he/she wants to know where you bought it and how to get there. Your partner starts the conversation.

5. Your partner is wearing something which you don't like very much, and you try to convince him/her to wear something else. You start the conversation.

SCRIVIAMO

1. Make two lists of things you need for each of the following trips:

   a. You are going to spend a week at the beach.
   b. You are going to Italy with your family in July.

2. Write a thank you note for a shirt/blouse which you received as a graduation gift.

3. Write a note to the exchange student giving directions on how to get from his house to your house for Saturday night birthday party.

4. You will be leaving soon for Italy as an American exchange student. Your host parents asked you to write a short letter describing the clothing that you will be wearing upon your arrival at the airport.

ABOUT ITALY

SHOPPING IN ROME

Laura loves to shop and she plans to take her new friends shopping in Rome. She knows that Mrs. Wright would like to look at clothing. For that, Laura will first take her guest to LA RINASCENTE, a large department store where you are free to browse, find out what is in fashion and read price tags. In the majority of other stores you cannot wander around; as you enter, a salesperson meets you, ready to show you the items that interest you.

The most elegant and expensive stores are downtown. Via Condotti, via Frattina and piazza di Spagna are known for elegant designers' boutiques; in the area you can find: Armani, Biagiotti, Gucci, Valentino, Krizia, Versace and others. Neighborhood clothing stores are more affordable and quite nice. There are some chain stores like Benetton or Jeans West. Additionally UPIM and STANDA, are discount department stores.

Laura has plans for the rest of the family, too. One Sunday she will take everybody to Porta Portese. It is a square next to the Tiber river, whose name derives from the gate, or door [*porta*], in the nearby walls that were built to protect the old city of Rome. On Sunday morning a huge flea market is held at Porta Portese. There, one can find just about anything; furniture, clothing, electronics, jewelry, even art works. It is a crowded, colorful place full of interesting items and people.

Laura will have some advice for her friends: don't fall in love with everything you see! Remember, if you want to buy something here; bargain! In town, however, you may see signs that read PREZZI FISSI, which means, "prices are as marked".

Elaborate window displays entice shoppers to enter fashionable stores.

Capitolo quattordici: Al centro commerciale

CAPITOLO QUINDICI: LA PARTENZA
CHAPTER FIFTEEN: THE DEPARTURE

FUNCTIONS

Taking leave
Formal requests
Requesting services
Interpreting written information

LANGUAGE

The present perfect tense
Vocabulary for air travel
A general review and practice

ABOUT ITALY

Going abroad

SITUATION

The big day has finally arrived. The Wrights are leaving for Italy. Mr. and Mrs. Silvestri have already returned to Italy, but the Silvestri children convinced their parents to let them stay with zia Lucia until the Wrights leave. Now they are leaving on the same plane. Mrs. Romano has come to the airport.

MRS. R.:	Ecco **siamo arrivati**. (To Laura and Brian) Bravi **avete già trovato** un **carrello** per i **bagagli.**
LAURA:	Ora andiamo a **consegnare** le valigie **al banco d'accettazione** e prendiamo la **carta d'imbarco**. Renzo, dove hai il biglietto e il passaporto?
RENZO:	Li ho qui, nello zaino.
LAURA:	**Ho capito**, ma perché quando **siamo usciti** di casa non **hai aiutato** con le valigie?
MRS. W.:	Non ti preoccupare, Laura, va tutto bene.
MR. W.:	Su, dobbiamo andare, è ora!
MRS. W.:	Arrivederci , Lucia. Grazie di tutto!
MRS. R.:	**Ma figurati!** Ieri sera **ho parlato** con mio fratello; vi aspetta all'aeroporto. Arrivederci, e buon viaggio!
THE SILVESTRIS:	Ciao zia! Ti aspettiamo a Roma! A presto!

Dopo dieci minuti i nostri amici hanno trovato i loro posti. Papà e mamma Wright sono nella zona centrale con Robertino e Jennifer; i ragazzi sono dalla parte dei finestrini: John vicino a Renzo e Brian vicino a Laura. Tutti **hanno allacciato** la **cintura di sicurezza**.

È bello partire! Buon Viaggio! In questo momento, l'**assistente di volo**, annuncia la partenza dell'aereo.

PAROLE DA RICORDARE

NOUNS

il carrello	cart
il bagaglio	luggage
il finestrino	window
la parte	side
il posto	seat
la zona	section
il banco d'accettazione	check-in counter
la carta d'imbarco	boarding pass
l'assistente di volo	flight attendant

VERBS

hai aiutato	you (have) helped
ho capito	I (have) understood
hanno allacciato	they (have) fastened
siamo arrivati	we (have) arrived
siamo usciti	we (have) left
consegnare	to hand in
annuncia	announces

USEFUL EXPRESSIONS

Allacciare la cintura di sicurezza	To fasten the seat belt
È ora.	It is time.
Ma figurati!	Oh, don't mention it!
Uscire di casa	to leave home

PROVIAMOCI

A. Complete each sentence with the appropriate word or words from the dialogue above.

1. Laura e Brian hanno trovato un ... per i bagagli.
2. Renzo ha il biglietto e il passaporto nello ... .
3. Quando sono usciti di casa, Renzo non ha aiutato con le ... .
4. Appena arrivano all'aeroporto, i nostri amici vanno a ... le valigie al ... .
5. Per entrare nell'aereo è necessario avere la ... .
6. I signori Wright hanno i loro posti nella ... centrale con i bambini.
7. Brian è ... a Laura, John è vicino ... Renzo.
8. Tutti hanno allacciato la ... .

B. Answer each question in complete sentence according to the dialogue.

1. Che cosa usano i passeggeri per portare i bagagli al banco d'accettazione?
2. Quale documento è necessario per entrare in aereo?
3. Chi non ha aiutato con le valigie quando sono usciti di casa?
4. Dove ha il passaporto e il biglietto Renzo?
5. Che cosa dice la signora Romano quando i suoi parenti partono?
6. Dopo quanto tempo trovano i loro posti in aereo?
7. Cosa devono allacciare i passeggeri?
8. Chi annuncia la partenza?
9. Dove vanno i nostri amici?

Il passato prossimo con "Avere"
The present perfect tense with "To have"

The present perfect tense allows you to express and understand "what happened" in the past. You will master it in the second volume of ***AMICI***; here you will find a simple outline of its formation and use.

In the dialogue you have read:

hanno allacciato	they fastened
hanno trovato	they found
ho capito	I understood
non hai aiutato	you didn't help

1. Notice that where in English you would use a one-word verb (fastened, found, understood, helped), Italians say the equivalent of "they have fastened, they have found, I have understood, you have not helped". In other words: they use the auxiliary, or helping verb "to have" plus the past participle of the main verb. (That happens in English too: at the beginning of the dialogue we read: "The big day **has** finally **arrived**.")

2. To produce the present perfect tense you need the second part of the verb, that is the "past participle". This happens in English too! For instance, if Mrs. Romano were speaking in English, she would have said, "I **have spoken** to my brother." In Italian she said, "**Ho parlato** con mio fratello."

The Italian past participle of regular verbs is very easy. It is formed by replacing the endings of the infinitive with

-ato (for verbs ending in -are)	compr-**are**	compr-**ato**
-uto (for verbs ending in -ere)	ricev-**ere**	ricev-**uto**
-ito (for verbs ending in -ire)	fin-**ire**	fin-**ito**

Now, here is something you can say knowing what you are doing:

Il signor Wright **ha comprato** i biglietti aerei.
Noi **abbiamo ricevuto** una telefonata dall'Italia
Voi **avete finito** l'esame d'Italiano.

PROVIAMOCI

A. Write out the past participles of the following verbs.

parlare	ricevere	dormire	imparare	ascoltare	ripetere
capire	avere	telefonare	mantenere	seguire	preferire
insegnare	dovere	sentire	suggerire	servire	credere
abitare	studiare	giocare	cantare	usare	nuotare

B. Compare your work with that of a friend.

C. Read the following sentences aloud.

a.
1. Robertino, hai mangiato tutta la pizza?
2. Brian ha comprato un paio di scarpe Timberland.
3. Renzo ha trovato un amico in America.
4. I ragazzi hanno giocato a Hacky Sac.
5. Voi avete ricevuto l'invito alla festa della scuola?
6. Io ho ripetuto la domanda al professore.
7. Antonio ha avuto mal di testa tutto il giorno.
8. Noi abbiamo venduto l'appartamento al mare.
9. Voi non avete sentito suonare il telefono?
10. I Romano hanno servito un pranzo ai loro nuovi amici.
11. La tua amica ha dormito durante tutta la lezione.
12. Hai capito le regole [*rules*] del passato prossimo?

b. Working with a friend express in English the meaning of the sentences above.

D. Your turn. Now complete the following sentences by providing the appropriate past participle.

1. Sabato John ha (suonare) ... nella banda.
2. Per andare in centro Gabriella e Marta hanno (usare) ... la mia macchina.
3. Ragazzi, come avete (festeggiare) ... i 18 anni di Marina?
4. Io non ho (guardare) ... la televisione per una settimana.
5. Barbara, perché non hai (salutare) ... gentilmente il dottore?
6. Perché voi avete (vendere) ... la nuova Vespa?
7. Noi abbiamo (ricevere) ... tante cartoline dall'Italia.
8. Loro non hanno (credere) ... alle tue parole [*words*].
9. Non hai (capire) ... che devi studiare di più?
10. Avete (sentire) ... la bella notizia [*news*]? Andiamo in Italia.
11. Ora abbiamo (finire) ... di studiare per l'esame.
12. Carlo, tu hai (dormire) ... poco, hai (giocare) ... con il computer tutta la notte?
13. Oggi voi avete (pulire) ... bene la vostra camera.

E. Your turn again! In the following examples, the auxiliary (helping) verb has been taken out. You must supply the correct form of **avere** for each.

1. I miei studenti ... imparato tanto italiano.
2. Ragazzi, ... studiato per l'esame?
3. Il signor Wright ... ricevuto un'offerta di lavoro [*job offer*] in Italia.
4. Gianni, ... giocato a calcio domenica?
5. Io non ... sentito il tuo nuovo CD.
6. Io e Anna ... preferito restare a casa questa sera.
7. ... telefonato Mario?
8. Quali materie ... studiato voi?
9. Loro non ... parlato molto.
10. Che dolce (voi) ... servito ieri sera?
11. La piccola Jennifer ... dormito durante tutto il viaggio.
12. In aereo i ragazzi ... ascoltato la musica.
13. È vero che tu e Filippo ... avuto l'influenza?

F. The whole verb! Now you must supply both parts of the "Passato Prossimo" for the following examples.

1. Io (ricevere) ... un regalo per il mio compleanno.
2. I bambini (mangiare) ... tutto il gelato.
3. La signora non (capire) ... l'assistente di volo.
4. (Tu / aiutare) ... i tuoi amici a fare le valigie.
5. (Noi / trovare) ... subito un carrello all'aeroporto.
6. Tu e Luca (comprare) ... i biglietti per il concerto.
7. Io (finire) ... di studiare a mezzanotte.
8. Il professore (ripetere) ... la spiegazione [*explanation*].
9. Loro (ricevere) ... una telefonata dall'Italia.
10. Renzo, perché non (pulire) ... la tua camera prima di partire?

Il passato prossimo con "Essere"
The present perfect tense with "To be"

A few Italian verbs are conjugated with the auxiliary **essere**. The most common are:

andare	**venire**	**ritornare**	**restare**
arrivare	**partire**	**entrare**	**uscire**

Now you can say:

I nostri amici **sono arrivati** all'aeroporto.
Ragazze, a che ora **siete uscite**?

The past participle of verbs conjugated with "essere" agrees with the subject.

Ex. : Ragazz**e**, a che ora siete uscit**e**?

"Ragazze" is feminine plural, "uscite" has the feminine plural ending, like an adjective. If the subject of the verb were "ragazzi," the sentence would say:

Ragazz**i**, a che ora siete uscit**i**?

PROVIAMOCI

A. Read the following sentences aloud.

1. Io e la mamma siamo andate a fare la spesa al supermercato.
2. I giovani Silvestri sono tornati in Italia con i loro amici americani.
3. La zia Lucia è restata in America.
4. I signori Wright sono partiti con i ragazzi Silvestri.
5. A che ora sono arrivate all'aeroporto le tue amiche?
6. Appena [*as soon as*] la signora Wright è entrata in aereo ha avuto bisogno di un'aspirina.

B. Working with a friend, find the reasons for the endings of the above past participles.

C. Working with a friend express the meaning of the above sentences in English.

D. Your turn. Complete the following sentences by providing the appropriate forms of "**essere**".

1. Io ... partita da Catania alle sei di mattina.
2. Lui ... arrivato allo studio del dottor Foschi alle dieci.
3. Lorenzo, Franco, perché ... ritornati tanto tardi ieri sera?
4. Le ragazze ... andate a cena al ristorante cinese.
5. Anna ... entrata nel bar dell'università e ha incontrato Luigi.
6. A che ora (voi) ... arrivati all'aeroporto?
7. Tu ... arrivato in treno o in macchina?
8. Noi non ... usciti sabato sera, ... andati a dormire presto.

E. Your turn again. Complete the following sentences in writing by providing the appropriate past participles.

a.
1. Franca e Teresa sono (partire) ... per le vacanze.
2. Gli amici di Giovanna sono (venire) ... al mare con noi.
3. Zia Lucia, perché sei (restare) ... In America? Perché non sei (venire) ... con noi?
4. Questa mattina il professore è (arrivare) ... a scuola in ritardo [*late*].
5. Renzo, John, quando siete (andare) ... alle Cascate del Niagara?
6. Appena Carlo è (entrare) ... in casa ha incominciato a piovere.

7. Tutta la famiglia è (uscire) ... presto oggi per andare al mare.
8. Io e Davide siamo (andare) ... a vedere un film interessante.
9. Nonno, perché tu e Robertino siete (ritornare) ... così presto? Non siete (restare) ... al parco?
10. Abbiamo invitato Chiara e Cristina alla nostra festa, ma loro non sono (venire) ... .

b. Now check the endings of the past participles with a partner.

c. Now read aloud your completed sentences.

F. The whole verb! Form the "passato prossimo" of the following examples by supplying the appropriate forms of both parts of the verbs.

1. I Wright (uscire) ... da casa alle dieci di mattina.
2. La famiglia (arrivare) ... a New York di pomeriggio.
3. Il signor Romano (andare) ... all'aeroporto con sua moglie.
4. Renzo, noi (venire) ... da casa per salutarvi.
5. Perché (voi/entrare) ... nel bar dell'aeroporto? Avete sete?
6. Io (restare) ... con i bagagli mentre gli altri [*the others*] (andare) ... al bar.
7. Tu (ritornare) ... al bar a comprare una pizzetta.

IN AEREO
ON THE AIRPLANE

A. Requesting services. When flying, especially on long trips, travelers are confined in small areas and are often in need of certain services provided by the airline personnel. Take the part of the Wright family and the Silvestri children as they express their needs. Use the words provided in the list below.

aspirina	aspirin	**cuffia**	earphones
bicchiere d'acqua	glass of water	**cuscino**	pillow
coperta	blanket	**gabinetto**	rest room

Robertino: Io non sto molto comodo [*comfortable*] in questa poltrona, ho bisogno di un ...
John: Io desidero ascoltare la musica e ho bisogno della ...
Sig.ra W: Scusi, signorina, ho mal di testa; ha un'... per piacere?

Sig. W: C'e` una ... lì? Ho freddo.

Renzo: (*to the flight attendant*) No, grazie, non prendo un'altra Coca-Cola. (*to Brian*) Se bevo troppo, poi devo andare in ...

Laura: Io ho molta sete. Signorina, un ... per favore.

B. Renzo e John: As the Wright family begins the long transatlantic flight, Renzo and John keep each other occupied.

a. Using a page from the airline's magazine, Renzo asks John the time of day in various cities around the world. How do you think John responds?

Ex.: A Roma sono le nove di sera (or le ventuno)

1. A Mosca
2. A Manila
3. A Citta` del Messico
4. A Singapore
5. A Londra
6. A Rio De Janeiro
7. A Los Angeles
8. A Bombay
9. A Sydney

Honolulu (A.M.)

Halifax (P.M.)

Bombay (A.M)

Los Angeles (Noon)

New York (P.M.)

Rio De Janeiro (P.M)

Singapore (A.M.)

Denver (P.M.)

London (P.M.)

Moscow (P.M.)

Manila (A.M)

Mexico City (P.M)

Rome (P.M)

Tokyo (A.M.)

Sydney (A.M.)

b. Renzo quizzes John on his knowledge of the calendar.

1. In che giorno della settimana è Natale?
2. Che giorno è il primo dell'anno?
3. Che giorno è il primo giovedi di luglio?
4. Quali mesi hanno cinque domeniche?
5. In quali mesi il tredici viene di venerdì?
6. Che giorno della settimana è il dieci aprile?
7. Qual è la data e il giorno del tuo compleanno?

	Gen	Feb	Mar	Apr	Mag	Giu	Lug	Ago	Set	Ott	Nov	Dic	
1	Giov	Dom	Dom	Merc	Ven	Lun	Merc	Sab	Mart	Giov	Dom	Mart	1
2	Ven	Lun	Lun	Giov	Sab	Mart	Giov	Dom	Merc	Ven	Lun	Merc	2
3	Sab	Mart	Mart	Ven	Dom	Merc	Ven	Lun	Giov	Sab	Mart	Giov	3
4	Dom	Merc	Merc	Sab	Lun	Giov	Sab	Mart	Ven	Dom	Merc	Ven	4
5	Lun	Giov	Giov	Dom	Mart	Ven	Dom	Merc	Sab	Lun	Giov	Sab	5
6	Mart	Ven	Ven	Lun	Merc	Sab	Lun	Giov	Dom	Mart	Ven	Dom	6
7	Merc	Sab	Sab	Mart	Giov	Dom	Mart	Ven	Lun	Merc	Sab	Lun	7
8	Giov	Dom	Dom	Merc	Ven	Lun	Merc	Sab	Mart	Giov	Dom	Mart	8
9	Ven	Lun	Lun	Giov	Sab	Mart	Giov	Dom	Merc	Ven	Lun	Merc	9
10	Sab	Mart	Mart	Ven	Dom	Merc	Ven	Lun	Giov	Sab	Mart	Giov	10
11	Dom	Merc	Merc	Sab	Lun	Giov	Sab	Mart	Ven	Dom	Merc	Ven	11
12	Lun	Giov	Giov	Dom	Mart	Ven	Dom	Merc	Sab	Lun	Giov	Sab	12
13	Mart	Ven	Ven	Lun	Merc	Sab	Lun	Giov	Dom	Mart	Ven	Dom	13
14	Merc	Sab	Sab	Mart	Giov	Dom	Mart	Ven	Lun	Merc	Sab	Lun	14
15	Giov	Dom	Dom	Merc	Ven	Lun	Merc	Sab	Mart	Giov	Dom	Mart	15
16	Ven	Lun	Lun	Giov	Sab	Mart	Giov	Dom	Merc	Ven	Lun	Merc	16
17	Sab	Mart	Mart	Ven	Dom	Merc	Ven	Lun	Giov	Sab	Mart	Giov	17
18	Dom	Merc	Merc	Sab	Lun	Giov	Sab	Mart	Ven	Dom	Merc	Ven	18
19	Lun	Giov	Giov	Dom	Mart	Ven	Dom	Merc	Sab	Lun	Giov	Sab	19
20	Mart	Ven	Ven	Lun	Merc	Sab	Lun	Giov	Dom	Mart	Ven	Dom	20
21	Merc	Sab	Sab	Mart	Giov	Dom	Mart	Ven	Lun	Merc	Sab	Lun	21
22	Giov	Dom	Dom	Merc	Ven	Lun	Merc	Sab	Mart	Giov	Dom	Mart	22
23	Ven	Lun	Lun	Giov	Sab	Mart	Giov	Dom	Merc	Ven	Lun	Merc	23
24	Sab	Mart	Mart	Ven	Dom	Merc	Ven	Lun	Giov	Sab	Mart	Giov	24
25	Dom	Merc	Merc	Sab	Lun	Giov	Sab	Mart	Ven	Dom	Merc	Ven	25
26	Lun	Giov	Giov	Dom	Mart	Ven	Dom	Merc	Sab	Lun	Giov	Sab	26
27	Mart	Ven	Ven	Lun	Merc	Sab	Lun	Giov	Dom	Mart	Ven	Dom	27
28	Merc	Sab	Sab	Mart	Giov	Dom	Mart	Ven	Lun	Merc	Sab	Lun	28
29	Giov		Dom	Merc	Ven	Lun	Merc	Sab	Mart	Giov	Dom	Mart	29
30	Ven		Lun	Giov	Sab	Mart	Giov	Dom	Merc	Ven	Lun	Merc	30
31	Sab		Mart		Dom		Ven	Lun		Sab		Giov	31

c. Renzo and John enjoy listening to the different music channels offered on the in-flight music service through the headsets that plug into the arms of the seats. Looking around themselves, they try to imagine which program each fellow passenger is listening to by the expression or reaction each displays. Complete the following sentences with the correct form of the verb, **ascoltare**.

(Renzo is playing air guitar)
John: (*to his dad*) Renzo ... la musica rock.

(John is directing an orchestra from his seat)
Renzo: Tu ... la musica classica.

(The couple across the isle is holding hands)
John: Loro ... la musica romantica.

(John and Renzo are shaking their heads vigorously to a beat)
John: Noi ... la musica Rap

(Two boys behind Renzo and John seem to be having a sword fight)
Renzo: Voi due ... la musica di Hollywood.

(Mrs. Wright glares at the boys to stop them from disturbing others)
Sig.ra W.: Io ... la musica New Age.

C. Laura e Brian: Laura attempts to help Brian with his Italian. After a brief review of the indefinite articles, **un, uno, una** and **un',** she opens the on-board magazine to the pages that show the merchandise sold at the airplane's "boutique." She tells Brian what each item is called, and he is supposed to provide the indefinite article. You assume the role of Brian.

Ex.: Laura: cravatta Brian: **una cravatta**

1. profumo
2. accendino [*lighter*]
3. penna
4. orologio
5. spilla [*pin*]
6. foulard [*scarf*]
7. cintura
8. costume da bagno

D. Mezzi di trasporto: The boys notice several ads for Italian-made cars in the magazine that the flight attendant gave them. This initiates a conversation about the kinds of vehicles that are in Renzo's family. Complete Renzo's story by providing the necessary possessive expressions.

(My) ... padre ha un'Alfa Romeo e (my) ... madre ha una piccola Fiat. Quando lei deve viaggiare per (her) ... ditta [*company*] usa (their) ... Lancia. (My) ... genitori sono molto contenti di questo sistema perché la Lancia è più comoda per i viaggi lunghi. (My) ... sorella ha una motoretta, una Vespa. Tutti (her) ... compagni di scuola hanno la moto. Tu sei ancora troppo giovane per avere una motoretta, ma (your) ... fratello è grande abbastanza. Se (your) ... genitori ti comprano un motorino, possiamo fare delle gite con (our) ... amici.

E. L'arrivo [*The arrival*]: Upon arriving at Fiumicino airport, our friends hear the following announcement: "Attenzione, prego! Il signor Steven Wright è gentilmente pregato di rivolgersi al banco informazioni Alitalia. Grazie." [*Attention, please! Mr. Steven Wright is kindly requested to go to the Alitalia information desk. Thank you.*] Now you assume the role of Mr. Wright and provide the necessary responses.

Clerk:	Prego?
Mr. W.:	(Identify yourself)
Clerk:	Ah, sì! C'è un messaggio per Lei. I suoi amici l'aspettano al bar dell'aeroporto.
Mr. W.:	(Thank the clerk, tell him/her that s/he is very kind, then ask where the bar is)
Clerk:	Appena passata la dogana [*customs*], giri a destra. Il bar è lì vicino a sinistra.
Mr. W.:	(Say that you understand and ask if your friends have been waiting a long time [*molto*].
Clerk:	No, no. Il messaggio è qui da dieci minuti.
Mr. W.:	(Say very well, thank the clerk again and wish him/her a good day.)
Clerk:	Prego. Buon giorno e benvenuto in Italia!

F. An application: The boys find a page of their magazine with an application for a credit card. With Renzo's help, John tries to fill in all the information. Working with a partner, guess what is required in each section.

MODULO DI RICHIESTA PER DIVENTARE TITOLARE DI UNA CARTA DI CREDITO INTERNAZIONALE

INFORMAZIONI PERSONALI

Nome	Cognome	Nazionalità
Indirizzo abitazione		
Cap Località		Tel. casa ( )
Comune di nascita		Data di nascita

INFORMAZIONI FINANZIARIE

Nome della banca	Agenzia	Nº Conto
Indirizzo	Località	Addebito diretto _Sì _No

INFORMAZIONI DI IMPIEGO

Datore di lavoro	
Indirizzo	Tel. ufficio ( )
Cap Località	Allegato in busta chiusa __ Cedola stipendio __ Dichiarazione dei redditi
Qualifica	

RICHIESTA PER CARTA SUPPLEMENTARE PER UN COMPONENTE DEL NUCLEO FAMILIARE

Nome	Cognome
Grado di parentela	Data di nascita
Comune di nascita	Se già in possesso di una carta di credito indichi il Nº

HO LETTO ATTENTAMENTE IL REGOLAMENTO GENERALE DELLA CARTA DI CREDITO INTERNAZIONALE SUL RETRO E FIRMO ACCANTO ALL'X.

FIRMA (X)	DATA
FIRMA DEL FAMILIARE (X)	DATA

G. While waiting for the passaport control and the customs procedure, our friends look around and see various advertisements and instructions. Here are some for you.

a. Read the ad for the Hotel Ristorante San Paolo. Tell what services are offered by looking at the symbols and using "**c'è**" or "**ci sono**".

b. Read the following ad and answer the questions in complete Italian sentences.

1. Quanti negozi Fiordaliso ci sono?
2. In quale negozio puoi comprare le cose per i bambini?
3. In quali città sono questi negozi?
4. Come si dice in italiano "do it yourself?"
5. Try to find the Italian words for:
    a. hardware
    b. sea
    c. housewares
    d. toys
    e. gifts
    f. garden
    g. infantware

Dove si trova un negozio
Fiordaliso
si trova la garanzia di
qualità e prezzi ragionevoli

I negozi *Fiordaliso* sono:

La Torre
Genova
via XX Settembre 115
Tel.: 542•413

La Sirena
Napoli
p.zza Trento e Trieste 65
Tel.: 4181•22

Il Martello
Pisa
c.so Italia 72
Tel.: 23•017

Babylandia
Roma
via Cassia 1046
Tel.: 23•017

Casa Bella
Milano
via Fabio Filzi 25
Tel.: 669•700•19

I negozi *Fiordaliso* trattano

• ABBIGLIAMENTO • CASALINGHI • FAI DA TE • FERRAMENTA • GIARDINO/MARE • GIOCATTOLI • PRIMA INFANZIA • REGALI •

d. Simboli internazionali. Can you identify the following symbols? Make an educated guess, then compare your answers with those of a classmate.

1. Informazioni [*information*]
2. Donne [*ladies' room*]
3. Uomini [*men's room*]
4. Scale [*stairs*]
5. Parcheggio [*parking*]
6. Divieto di parcheggio [*no parking*]
7. Pronto soccorso [*first aid*]
8. Ascensore [*elevator*]
9. Gabinetti [*restrooms*]
10. Vietato fumare [*no smoking*]

A

B

C

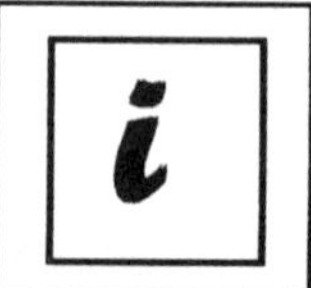

D

E

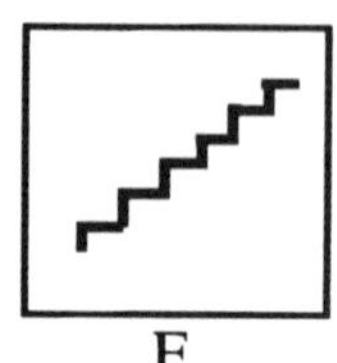

F

G

H

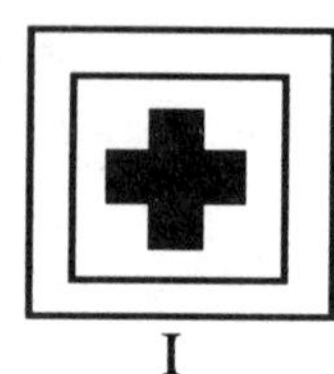

I

J

PERFORMANCE ACTIVITIES

E ORA IN ITALIANO

Now the plane is flying along the eastern coast of the United States and the captain informs the passengers about their location over the mainland. They will soon be approaching Nova Scotia and then continue for the long crossing of the Atlantic Ocean in order to reach Europe and finally Italy. The Wright and the Silvestri children are excited about their journey and talk about the experience.

Renzo:	(*to John and Brian*) Sono proprio contento di ritornare in Italia con voi. Ho passato delle vacanze veramente stupende in America.
John:	Ed io questa estate ho trovato un vero amico.
Laura:	(*to Brian and John*) I vostri genitori sono delle persone molto care e simpatiche. Siamo fortunati.
Brian:	Sei gentile Laura!
Renzo:	Non vedo l'ora di accompagnarvi in giro per Roma.
John:	(*to Renzo*) Abitiamo vicino al Colosseo? Ci sono le catacombe sotto la casa?
Renzo:	(*laughing*) Non ti preoccupare, le catacombe sono lontane.
Laura:	Sapete che per andare dall'aeroporto di Fiumicino a casa, dobbiamo attraversare la città? È un' occasione per vedere molti momumenti interessanti.
John:	Fantastico! Voi avete conosciuto un po' del mio paese e adesso noi possiamo conoscere l'Italia.

ASCOLTIAMO

Listen as your teacher reads aloud a setting in English followed by a passage in Italian which will be read twice; then choose the most appropriate response to the question based on the passage you have just heard.

1. What is this announcement about?

   a. to return to your seat
   b. to buckle your seat belt
   c. to remain seated
   d. to put your belongings under your seat

2. What is this person concerned about?

   a. not having enough time in Italy
   b. feeling sick on the airplane
   c. not being able to find her relatives
   d. not being able to speak Italian

3. Cosa può fare Pino?

   a. prendere l'aereo
   b. prendere la metropolitana
   c. andare ad aspettare al bar
   d. telefonare ai suoi genitori

4. Di che cosa ha bisogno Laura?

   a. di bere
   b. di un cuscino
   c. di una coperta
   d. di mangiare

LEGGIAMO

1. The ad below details information about vacationing ....

   a. at a campground
   b. in the mountains
   c. at the seashore
   d. at a luxury resort

Incanto di mare, di accoglienza e libertà!

Vacanze che ricorderai nel tempo. Distese di spiaggia mai affollate. L'invito dell'acqua chiara e pura. Rilassante serenità. Vita attiva di sport e scoperte. I tuoi ragazzi si divertono, protetti.

Mare Tunisia è ospitalità totale. Alberghi generosi. Spazi da star bene. Cucina tipica o italiana, a volontà. Un sogno vicino, a portata di mano.

Sì, inviatemi gratis più informazioni.

Nome________________________________
Città______________________ **CAP**________
Indirizzo______________________________

Spedire il coupon a: ENTE NAZIONALE TUNISINO PER IL TURISMO
• 20123 MILANO - VIA BARACCHINI, 10
TEL. 02/86453026 FAX 02/862752
• 00187 ROMA - VIA CALABRIA, 25
TEL. 06/42010149 FAX 06/42010151

2. When would the magazine need the information requested in this ad?

a. when subscribers move
b. when subscribers go on vacation
c. when subscribers want vacation information
d. when subscribers apply for a contest

COMUNICAZIONE AI NOSTRI ABBONATI

PER CHI QUESTA ESTATE CAMBIA INDIRIZZO

Tutti i nostri abbonati che questa estate trascorreranno le vacanze in un qualsiasi luogo di villeggiatura (solo in Italia) e desiderano ricevere le loro copie in abbonamento al nuovo indirizzo, possono farne richiesta compilando questo coupon e inviandolo in busta chiusa, con anticipo di almeno 20 giorni rispetto alla data di partenza, a Rusconi Editore - Servizio Abbonamenti - Viale Sarca 235 - 20126 - Milano.

ABBONAMENTO A

....

Cognome e Nome ....
Codice Abbonato ....
Indirizzo attuale ....
Cap ....Città..................................Prov..........
per il periodo da..................................a..........................
gg/mm/aa gg/mm/aa
desidero ricevere la mia copia all'indirizzo seguente:
c/o ....
Via /P.zza ....
Cap ....Città..............................Prov..........
Automaticamente allo scadere del periodo sopraindicato, l'abbonamento sarà inviato di nuovo all'indirizzo attuale.
Data ....Firma..
Se preferite potrete chiedere il cambio di indirizzo anche per telefono (02/6619.3195) o tramite fax (02/6619.2469).

3. Families staying at at these hotels, will receive...

a. a free breakfast
b. an extra day at no charge
c. complimentary accomodations for a young child
d. free baby sitting services

Dal 5 Settembre il primo bambino è gratis, sconto del 50% per fratellini e sorelline.*

E per tutta la stagione vantaggi speciali per tutta la famiglia! Prenotare presso Riccione Hotels, nel cuore della Riviera Adriatica, conviene ed assicura qualità, competenza e professionalità.

* offerta valida per bambini fino ai 6 anni d'età in stanza con due adulti.

4. What is the most economical airfare offered to get to this resort?

a. L. 90.000
b. L. 100.000
c. L. 150.000
d. L. 250.000

Hotel Club & Residence

SCIACCA (Agrigento)

Mezza pensione in Hotel
Luglio £. 90.000/100.000 al giorno
Agosto £. 100.000/140.000 al giorno
Sette giorni in Residence
Giugno da £. 110.000 a persona
Luglio da £. 170.000 a persona

In esclusiva per Torre Macauda il:
VOLA CON NOI! con la collaborazione
di **AIR SICILIA**
Sabato Volo A/R £. 250.000
Domenica Volo A/R £. 150.000

informazioni e prenotazioni
Tel. 0925 968500 • fax 0925 968905

SCRIVIAMO

1. Write a letter to your pen pal in Italy describing your vacation in Florida during your winter break.

2. You have just learned that your family is planning to go to Italy next summer. Write a note to your friend telling him/her your feelings about it.

3. You are planning to go to Italy in July. Write a note to a friend asking his/her advice about what you need to do or buy to get ready for your trip.

4. You have just arrived in Rome with your student group. Write a postcard to your parents describing your flight (for example: the film that you saw, the food that you ate, the people that you met, the view from the window...).

5. You stayed a week with your uncle and aunt in Palermo. You have just returned home. Write a note thanking them for their hospitality and kindness.

PARLIAMO

1. Your family has planned a vacation in Italy. Discuss your plans with a friend.

2. You are flying to Italy. You have just met the person next to you. You exchange information about your respective trips overseas.

3. Your partner is a travel agent in Rome. You come to the agency to plan a weekend trip to Florence. You talk about the details of the trip.

4. Your family is planning a trip to Italy. Your grandmother doesn't want to come. Let you, or your partner, take the role of the grandmother and convince her to join your family on the trip.

5. You go to the information desk at the airport in Fiumicino and ask how to get to your hotel in Rome. Discuss the different means of transportation available and what would be the most economical and convenient.

ABOUT ITALY

GOING ABROAD

Prior to their departure for Italy Mr. and Mrs. Wright have taken the time to explain to John and Brian a number of things that are important when traveling overseas. Electrical appliances in Italy work on 220 volts, not 110, as in the United States, and unless you use a voltage converter, you will burn out the motor of a hair dryer or curling iron. Plugs and sockets are also different, so you need an adapter plug.

There are many other aspects of everyday life that John and Brian need to understand when living in another country: they already know about telling time based on the 24 hour clock, and European sizes for clothing. Also, the metric system is used for measuring length, weight and volume: kilometers instead of miles, kilograms instead of pounds, and liters instead of quarts. Mrs. Wright remembers from her own experience in Italy that thermometers measure degrees in centigrade, not Fahrenheit.

John and Brian will undoubtedly be a little nervous about the new experiences that await them in Italy, but they feel reassured knowing that Renzo and Laura will be around to coach and help them during their time in Rome.

An American plug and socket.

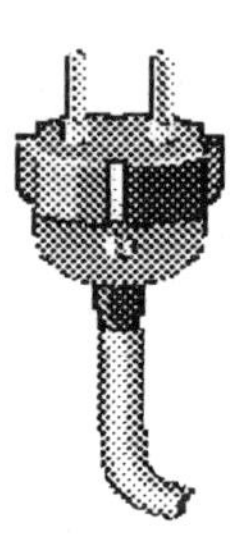

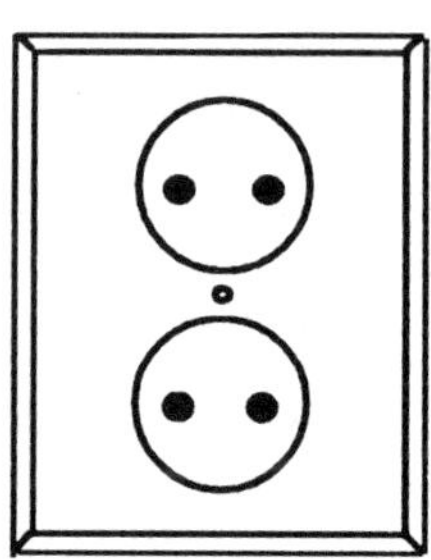

A European plug and socket.

Signs along the highway show distance in meters in Italy.

Raidue

12.05 Il nostro amico Charly
Telefilm "Il salvataggio"
13.00 Tg2 Giorno Notiziario
13.30 Tg2 Costume e Società
14.00 Un caso per due
15.10 Hunter Telefilm
16.05 Law & Order - I due volti della giustizia Telefilm
16.30 Tg2 Flash Notiziario

Italian television schedules use the 24 hour system.

The normal body temperature of a human being is between 35.6° C and 37.2° C, or 96° F and 99° F.

VOCABOLARIO ITALIANO-INGLESE

This vocabulary contains contextual meanings of words used in this book. Numbers in parentheses indicate the chapters in which each word appears for the first time.

A

a (10) at
abitare (60) to live, to dwell
l'abbigliamento (11) clothing
l'abito (14) dress/suit
l'accendino (14) lighter
l'acqua (9) water
gli acquisti (10) shopping
l'acquario (7) aquarium
adesso (4) now
l'aereo (10) airplane
l'aeroporto (10) airport
l'affare *m.* (10) business
affatto (9) at all
affittare (13) to rent
l'agenzia (6) agency
 _di viaggi (6) travel agency
l'agosto (7) August
aiutare (6)to help
l'aiuto (6) help
l'albergo (11) hotel
l'albero (13) tree
l'albicocca (9) apricot
gli alimentari (11) groceries
allacciare (14) to fasten
allegro (9) cheerful
l'allenamento (6) scrimmage
allora (7) then
alto (5) tall
amare (5) to love
americano (5) American
l'amica (5) friend
l'amico (5) friend
anche (9) also
ancora (10) still, yet
andare (10) to go
l'angelo (14) angel
l'angolo (14) corner
l'anniversario (6) anniversary
l'anno (3) year
annunciare (15) to announce
l'antichità (5) antiquity
antico (5) ancient
l'antipasto (9) "antipasto"
antipatico (5) unpleasant
anziano (5) elderly
aperto (6) open
l'apertura (6) opening
l'appartamento (6) apartment
appena (15) as soon as
l'appunto (11) note
l'aprile, *m.* (7) April
aprire (9) to open
l'arancia (9) orange
l'aranciata (2) orange soda
arancione (5) orange (color)
l'architetto (3) architect
l'architettura (13) architecture
l'armadio (2) closet
arrivare (6) to arrive
arrivederci (1) good bye
arrivederLa (1) good bye
l'arrivo (12) arrival
l'arrosto (6) roast-beef
arrosto (9) roasted
l'arte, *f.* (6) art
l'artista, *m.,f.* (5) artist
l'ascensore, *m.* (15) elevator
l'asciugacapelli, *m.* (12) hair dryer
ascoltare (6) to listen
aspettare (7) to wait for
l'assegno (12) check
 _turistico (12) travelers' cheque
l'aspirina (13) aspirin
l'assistente di volo (15) flight assistant
l'attico (13) penthouse
l'attore *m.* (10) actor
attraversare (14) to cross
attraverso (5) through
l'attrice *f.* actress
l'autobus, *m.* (8) bus

l'automobile, *f.* (2) automobile
l'autunno (7) fall
avaro (8) stingy
avere (3) to have
l'avvocato (3) lawyer
azzurro (5) sky blue

B

Babbo Natale (8) Santa Claus
il bagaglio (14) baggage
il bagno (12) bathroom
ballare (6) to dance
il bambino (8) child
la banana (9) banana
la banca (11) bank
il banco (13) desk
  d'accettazione (15) check-in counter
il bancomat (11) ATM machine
la banda (7) band
la bandiera (5) flag
la barca (10) boat
il barista (11) barman
basso (5) short (in height)
bello (5) beautiful, handsome
bene (3) well
benissimo! (2) very well!
benvenuto! (2) welcome!
la bevanda (9) drink
bianco (5) white
la bibita (9) soft drink
la biblioteca (6) library
il bibliotecario (11) librarian
il bicchiere (14) glass
la bicicletta (10) bicycle
il bidet (13) bidet
il biglietto (6) ticket
biondo (5) blond
la birra (9) beer
il biscotto (9) cookie
il bisogno (3) need
la bistecca (9) beef-steak
blu (5) navy blue
la bocca (8) mouth
bollito (9) boiled
la borsa (12) bag
la boutique (11) boutique
il braccio (8) arm
il Brasile (5) Brazil
bravo (3) good
i broccoli (9 broccoli
bruno (5) dark
brutto (5) ugly
il buffet (13) sideboard
buonanotte (1) good night
buonasera (1) good evening
buongiorno (1) good day
buono (1) good
il burro (9) butter

C

il caffè (9) coffee
il calcio (6) soccer
caldo (3) warm, hot
il calendario (2) calendar
calmo (8) tranquil
la calza (14) stocking
il calzino (5) sock
la camera (2) room
il cameriere (11) waiter
la camicetta (5) blouse
la camicia (5) shirt
la campagna (5) country
canadese (5) Canadian
il canarino (13) canary
il cancellino (2) eraser
il cane (8) dog
il canile (12) kennel
il cannolo (8) "cannolo"
cantare (6) to sing
il/la cantante (11) singer
la canzone (6) song
il capello (8) hair
capire (9) to understand
il cappello (14) hat
il cappotto (14) winter coat
carino (5) pretty
la carne (9) meat
caro (12) dear, expensive
il carrello (15) cart
la carriera (11) career
la carta (2) paper
  _geografica map
  _d'imbarco (15)

boarding pass
il cartolaio (11) stationery vendor
la cartoleria (11) stationery store
la cartolina (11) postcard
il cartoncino (7) card
la casa (6) house
la cassa (6) cash
la cassetta (7) cassette
il castello (6) castle
la cattedra (2) teacher's desk
cattivo (5) bad
il cavallo (10) horse
la cena (9) supper
cento (9) one hundred
centro (8) center, downtown
_**commerciale** (11) mall
cercare (7) to look for
il cerchio (13) circle
certamente (9) of course
il cestino (2) wastebasket
che cosa ? (2) what?
che (2) who, that
chi? (1) who?
la chiave (14) key
chiedere (8) to ask (for)
la chiesa (11) church
il chilometro (8) kilometer
la chitarra (7) guitar
chiudere (8) to close
chiuso (6) closed
ciao (1) hi, bye
il cibo (9) food
la ciliegia (11) cherry
il cinema (11) cinema
cinese (5) Chinese
cinquanta (4) fifty
cinque (1) five
la cintura (14) belt
il cioccolato (9) chocolate
cioè (4) that is
la città (7) city
la colazione (9) breakfast
il/la collega (13) colleague
il colloquio (11) conversation
_**di lavoro** job interview
come (12) as, like
come? (3) how?
comico (12) comic
il commesso (11) salesclerk
il comò (2) dresser
il comodino (13) night table
comodo (13) comfortable
il compagno (8) pal
il compito (12) homework
il compleanno (6) birthday
comprare (7) to buy
comune (13) common
con (10) with
il concerto (6) concert
il coniglio (8) rabbit
la conoscenza (12) acquaintance
conoscere (8) to know
consegnare(15) to hand in
consigliare (11) to advise
la coperta (14) blanket
coprire (9) to cover
il coro (6) chorus
correre (8) to run
il corsivo (8) cursive
il corso (14) main street
corto (5) short (lengthwise)
la cosa (13) thing
cosa? (2) what?
così (3) so
il costume costume
_**da bagno** (14) swimsuit
la cravatta (14) tie
la credenza (13) cupboard
credere (8) to believe
crescere (14) to grow
la crociera (10) cruise
la cucina (9) kitchen
_**a gas** (13) gas range
_**elettrica** (13) elec. range
la cuffia (14) earphones
la cugina (4) cousin
il cugino (4) cousin
il cuoco (11) cook, chef
il cuscino (14) pillow

D

da (10) from, by
dai, su! (9) come on!
la data (7) date
davanti a (11) in front of
decidere (8) to decide

il decollo (14) takeoff
il dente (3) tooth
desiderare (6) to desire
il dessert (9) dessert
destra (14) right-hand
di (2) of
il dicembre (7) December
diciannove (4) nineteen
diciassette (4) seventeen
diciotto (4) eighteen
dieci (1) ten
dietro (13) behind
difficile (5) difficult
il direttore (3) director
la direttrice (3) director
il disco (11) record
la discoteca (11) "disco"
discutere (8) to discuss
la ditta (11) company
il divano (13) sofa
diviso (:) (6) divided
la doccia (10) shower
docile (8) docile
dodici (4) twelve
la dogana (15) customs
dolce (9) sweet
il dolce (9) cake
il dollaro (7) dollar
la domanda (8) question
domandare (7) to ask
domani (7) tomorrow
la domenica (7) Sunday
la donna (15) woman
dopo (14) after
il doppio (14) double
dormire (9) to sleep
il dottore (1) doctor
la dottoressa (3) doctor
dove? (3) where?
dovere (13) to have to, must
il dramma (4) drama
dritto (8) straight
due (1) two
durante (10) during

E

e (1) and

economico (14) inexpensive
l'educazione *f.* (6) upbringing
  _fisica (6) physical ed.
  _tecnica (6) technology ed.
l'elefante, *m.* (5) elephant
elegante (8) elegant
energico (8) energetic
enorme (5) enormous
entrare (7) to enter
l'erba (7) grass
l'esame, *m.* (5) exam
esatto (6) exact
l'esercizio (12) practice
essenzialmente (13) mainly
essere (5) to be
l'estate, *f.* (7) summer
estero (14) foreign, (abroad)

F

facile (5) easy
la faccia (5) face
la Facoltà (3) university school
il fagiolino (9) string bean
il fagiolo (9) bean
la fame (3) hunger
la famiglia (4) family
fantastico (12) great, fantastic
fare (12) to do/make
la farfalla (9) butterfly
la farmacia (11) pharmacy
il/la farmacista (11) farmacist
il favore (12) favor
(il) febbraio (7) February
la fermata (11) stop
la festa (12) party
festeggiare (6) to celebrate
la figlia (4) daughter
il filobus (13) trolley bus
la filosofia (3) philosophy
la fine (8) end
la finestra (2) window
il finestrino (15) window
finire (9) to finish
i fiocchi flakes
  _di granoturco (9) corn flakes
il fiore (9) flower
la foglia (7) leaf

il fondo (14) bottom, end
la fontana (11) fountain
il formaggio (9) cheese
forte (8) strong
la fotografia (2) picture
il foulard (14) scarf
fra (9) between, among
la fragola (9) strawberry
francese (5) French
la Francia (5) France
il francobollo (11) stamp
la frase (11) sentence
il fratello (4) brother
il fratellastro (4) stepbrother
freddo (3) cold
frequentare (7) to attend
fresco (7) cool, fresh
la fretta (3) hurry
il frigo(rifero) (9) refrigerator
fritto (9) fried
la frutta (8) fruit
fumare (14) to smoke
fuori (9) out(side)

G

il gabinetto (6) rest room
la gamba (8) leg
la gara (12) contest
il gelato (7) ice cream
il genero (4) son-in-law
generoso (8) generous
(il) gennaio (7) January
la gente (10) people
gentile (8) kind
la geografia (6) geography
la Germania (5) Germany
il ghiaccio (7) ice
già (8) already
la giacca (14) jacket
giallo (5) yellow
giapponese (5) Japanese
il Giappone (5) Japan
il giardino (6) garden
giocare (6) to play
il giocattolo (13) toy
il gioco (6) game
il giornale (8) newspaper
la giornata (7) day
il giorno (1) day
giovane (5) young
il giovedì (7) Thursday
girare (14) to turn
giro (12) tour
gita (15) excursion, trip
giugno (7) June
gli (5) the
gli gnocchi (12) dumplings
la gola (3) throat
la gonna (5) skirt
grande (5) big, large
  _magazzino (10) dept. store
grasso (5) fat
grazie (3) thanks
grigio (5) gray
grosso (8) big
guadagnare (11) to earn
il guanto (2) glove
guardare (6) to look
la guida (12) guide

I

i (5) the
ieri (7) yesterday
imparare (7) to learn
l'impermeabile, *m.* raincoat
l'impiegato/a (11) employee
in (10) in, at
in umido (9) stewed
l'incrocio (14) intersection
indossare (14) to wear
l'industria (13) industry
l'informazione *f.* information
l'ingegnere *m. f.* engineer
l'Inghilterra (5) England
inglese (5) English
l'ingresso (13 entrance hall
l'insalata (9) salad
insegnare (7) to teach
insieme(6) together
insultare (8) to insult
intelligente (5) intelligent
interessante (5) interesting
l'intervista (7) interview
invece (6) instead

l'inverno (7) winter
io (3) I
irlandese (5) Irish
l'Italia (5) Italy
italiano (5) Italian

L

la (4) the
il lago (5) lake
la lampada (2) lamp
il largo (14) town square
le lasagne (12) lasagna
lasciare (12) to leave behind
il latte (9) milk
la latteria (11) dairy store
la lavagna (2) blackboard
  _luminosa overhead projector
il lavandino (13) sink
la lavastoviglie (13) dishwasher
lavorare (7) to work
il lavoro(13) work,job
le (5) the
leggere (8) to read
lei (3) she
lento (13) slow
la lettera (7) letter
le Lettere (3) humanities
il letto (2) bed
il lettore CD (11) CD player
la lezione (6) lesson, class
lì (1) there
libero (6) free
il libraio (11) book-seller
la libreria (11) book store
il libro (2) book
lieto (9) glad
liquido (9) liquid
lontano (7) far
il loro (10) theirs
loro (3) they
(il) luglio (7) July
lui (3) he
il lunedì (7) Monday
lungo (5) long
lupo (13) lupo

M

ma (3) but
la macchia (13) stain
la macchina (10) car
  _fotografica (11) camera
la macedonia (9) fruit salad
la macelleria (11) butcher shop
la madre (4) mother
il magazzino warehouse
  _grande dept. store
(il) maggio (7) May
la maglietta (5) T-shirt
magro (5) thin, skinny
mai (9) never
il maiale (9) pork
male (3) badly
la mamma (2) mother
mandare (7) to send
mangiare (7) to eat
la mano (8) hand
mantenere (15) to maintain
il manzo (9) beef
il marciapiede (11) sidewalk
il mare (7) sea
il marito (4) husband
la marmellata (9) jam
marrone (5) brown
il martedì (7) Tuesday
(il) marzo (7) March
la matematica (6) mathematics
la matita (2) pencil
la matrigna (4) stepmother
il matrimonio (14) marriage
la mattina (6) morning
matto (14) crazy
la medicina (11) medicine
il medico (11) physician
la mela (9) apple
meno (6) minus
mentre (9) while
il mercato (8) market
il mercoledì (7) Wednesday
la merenda (9) snack
il mese (7) month
il messaggio (14) message
messicano (5) Mexican
la metropolitana (13) subway
mettere (8) to put, place
la mezzanotte (6) midnight
mezzo (6) half

il mezzogiorno (6) noon
migliore (12) better
il migliore best
la minestra (9) soup
il minuto (8) minute
mio (4) my
la moda (13) fashion
il modellino (2) model toy
moderno (5) modern
la moglie (4) wife
molto (7) very, much
il mondo (10) world
la montagna (7) mountain
morbido (6) soft
la motocicletta (7) motorcycle
la motoretta (14) scooter
il motorino (7) moped
il municipio (11) city hall
il museo (7) museum
la musica (6) musica

N

napoletano (8) Neapolitan
il naso (8) nose
la nave (10) ship
la nebbia (7) fog
il negozio (8) store
il neonato (14) newborn
nero (5) black
nervoso (8) nervous
nevicare (7) to snow
il nipote (9) nephew/grandchild
noi (3) we
la nonna (4) grandmother
il nonno (4) grandfather
nostro (10) ours
la notizia (9) news
la notte (6) night
novanta (9) ninety
nove (1) nine
(il) novembre (7) November
la nuora (4) daughter-in-law
nuotare (6) to swim
nuovo (5) new
nuvoloso (7) cloudy

O

l'oceano (8) ocean
l'occhio (8) eye
l'offerta (15) offer
offrire (9) to offer
oggi (7) today
ogni (12) every
l'Olanda (5) Holland
olandese (5) Dutch
l'olio (9) oil
l'ombrello (7) umbrella
l'onorevole *m.,f.* honorable
l'ora (6) hour, time
l'orecchio (8) ear
l'orologio (14) watch
l'orto (7) vegetable garden
l'ospedale, *m.* (11) hospital
ottanta (9) eighty
otto (1) eight
l'ottobre, *m.* (7) October

P

il pacco (7) package
il padre (4) father
il padrone (11) owner
il paese (8) country
pagare (6) to pay
il paio (14) pair
il palcoscenico (11) stage
la pallacanestro (7) basketball
la pancia (9) belly
il pane (9) bread
la panetteria (11) bakery
il panino (9) sandwich
i pantaloncini (5) shorts
i pantaloni (5) pants, slacks
il Papa (6) Pope
il papà (4) daddy, father
parcheggiare (13) to park
parcheggio (15) parking lot/space
il parco (6) park
il/la parente (7) relative
parlare (6) to speak/talk
la parola (8) word
la parte (15) side
la partenza (12) departure

partire (9) to leave (for a trip)
partita (6) game, match
passare (10) to pass/to spend (time)
il passaporto (12) passport
il passeggero (14) passenger
la pasta (9) "pasta"
la pasticceria (11) pastry shop
il pasticciere (11) pastry maker
la patata (9) potato
la patatina (9) potato chip
il patrigno (4) stepfather
pattinare (7) to skate
la paura (3) fear
la pazienza (3) patience
pazzo 10) crazy
la pecora (8) sheep
la pelletteria (11) leather shop
pendente (1) leaning
la penna (6) pen
pensare (10) to think
il pepe (9) pepper
per (10) in order to, through
per (x) (6) times
la pera (9) pear
perché (6) why, because
perdere (8) to lose
perfetto (2) perfect
però (13) but
la persona (4) person
pesante (12) heavy
la pesca (9) peach
pescare (10) to fish
il pesce (9) fish
il pettine (12) comb
piacere (12) pleasure
piacere! (2) pleased to meet you!
il piano (10) piano
piantare (7) to plant
il piatto (9) dish
la piazza (11) town square
piccolo (5) small, young
il piede (3) foot
pigro (8) lazy
la pioggia (7) rain
piovere (7) to rain
la piscina (6) swimming pool
più (7) more
piuttosto (12) rather
la pizza (8) pizza
la pizzetta (9) small pizza
poco (12) little, few
poi (7) then, afterwards
polacco (5) Polish
la politica (8) politics
il poliziotto (12) policeman
il pollo (9) chicken
la Polonia (5) Poland
la poltrona (13) armchair
il pomeriggio (6) afternoon
il pomodoro (9) tomato
il ponte (14) bridge
la porta (2) door
portare (7) to carry/bring/wear
portoghese (5) Portuguese
le posate (9) silverware
la posizione (14) position
postale (11) postal
il poster (4) poster
il postino (11) mailman
il posto (13) place
potere (12) to be able, can
povero (5) poor
il pranzo (9) dinner
preferire (9) to prefer
pregare (14) to request, to pray
prendere (8) to take, get
preparare(9) to prepare
prepotente (8) bossy
presentare (9) to introduce
presto (6) soon
la primavera (7) spring
prima (12) before
primo (6) first
il problema (8) problem
il professore (1) professor
la professoressa (1) professor
il profumo (14) fragrance
il programma (4) program
promettere (8) to promise
il pronto soccorso (15) first aid
proprio (13) really
il prosciutto (9) ham
lo psichiatra (12) psychiatrist
pubblico (13) public
pulire (9) to clean
il pullover (5) sweater

Q

il quaderno (10) notebook
quale? (8) which (one)?
quando (6) when
quanto? (1) how much?
quaranta (4) forty
il quarto (6) quarter
quattordici (4) fourteen
quattro (1) four
quello (8) that
questo (2) this
qui(1) here
quindici (4) fifteen

R

la radio (10) radio
il ragazzo (10) young man
la ragione (3) reason
il ragioniere (3) accountant
rapidamente (6) fast
rapido (13) fast
rastrellare (7) to rake
il re (4) king
il regalo (10) gift
la regola (15) rule
la religione (6) religion
restare (7) to stay/remain
ricco (5) rich
ricevere (8) to receive
richiedere (10) to require
la ricreazione (6) mid-morning school break
ridere (9) to laugh
la riga (2) ruler
ripetere (8) to repeat
il riso (9) rice
rispondere (8) to respond
il ristorante (2) restaurant
il risvolto (14) cuff
ritornare (6) to come back/return
la riunione (11) gathering
la rivista (2) magazine
robusto (5) husky
romano (13) Roman
il romanzo (8) novel
rosa (5) pink
rosso (5) red
il rullino (12) film
russo (5) Russian

S

il sabato (7) Saturday
la sala (13) large room
  _videogiochi video arcade
il sale (13) salt
la salumeria (11) delicatessen
salutare (6) to greet
salve! (2) hello (fam.)
il sandalo (14) sandal
lo scaffale (13) bookshelf
la scala (15) stairway
lo scambio (13) exchange
la scarpa (5) shoe
scegliere (14) to choose
la schiena (3) back
lo schienale (14) back of chair
sciare (7) to ski
la scienza (6) science
la scrivania (2) desk
scrivere (8) to write
la scuola (6) school
scusa! (4) excuse me! (fam.)
se if
secondo (6) second
la sedia (2) chair
sedici (4) sixteen
seguire (9) to follow
sei (1) six
il semaforo (14) traffic light
sempre (8) always
sentire (9) to hear
la sera (6) evening
sereno (7) clear
serio (8) serious
servire (9) to serve
il servizio (14) service
sessanta (9) sixty
la sete (3) thirst
settanta (6) seventy
sette (1) seven
(il) settembre (7) September
la settimana (8) week
sfacciato (8) insolent
sgarbato (8) rude

sì (2) yes
la signora (1) lady, Mrs., ma'am
il signore (3) gentleman, Mr, Sir
la signorina (3) Miss, young lady
simpatico (5) likeable, nice
sinistra (14) left-hand
il soggiorno (13) living room
il sole (7) sun
i soldi (8) money
soltanto (9) only
il sonno (3) sleep
sopra (13) over, on top
la sorella (4) sister
la sorellastra (4) stepsister
sorpreso (10) surprised
sotto 13) under
la Spagna (5) Spain
spagnolo (5) Spanish
la spalla (8) shoulder
la spazzola (12) brush
lo specchio (2) mirror
spedire (9) to send
spendere (8) to spend
spensierato (8) carefree
sperare (11) to hope
la spesa (12) grocery shopping (food)
spesso (9) often
la spiaggia (7) beach
la spiegazione (15) explanation
la spilla (14) brooch/pin
gli spinaci (9) spinach
lo sportello (15) window
la sposa (14) bride
lo spuntino (6) snack
la squadra (6) team
lo stadio (8) stadium
stanco (10) tired
stasera (7) this evening
lo stato (8) state
la stazione (11) station
lo stipendio (11) salary
lo stivale (14) boot
lo stomaco (3) stomach
stonato (12) tone-deaf
la storia (6) history, story
la strada (14) road, street
straniero (5) foreign
strano (7) strange
lo studente (2) student
la studentessa (2) student
studiare (6) to study
studio (11) study
  _medico doctor's office
stupido (5) stupid
su (10) on
su! (8) come on!
suggerire (9) to suggest
suo (4) his, hers, its
la suocera (4) mother-in-law
il suocero (4) father-in-law
suonare (6) to play
superiore (8) superior
il supermercato (6) supermarket
la sveglia (2) alarm clock
la Svizzera (5) Switzerland
svizzero (5) Swiss

T

il tacchino (7) turkey
tagliare (7) to cut
il tappeto (2) rug
tardi (1) late
il tassì (10) taxi
il tassista (11) taxi driver
il tatuaggio (5) tattoo
la taverna (13) basement
il tavolo (8) table
la tazza (9) cup
il teatro (11) theater
la tecnologia (13) technology
tedesco (5) German
telefonare (6) to phone
la telefonata (12) phone call
il telefonino (2) cell phone
il telegramma (7) telegram
il televisore (5) TV set
il tempo (11) time
  _atmosferico weather
tenere (14) to keep
la testa (3) head
il tifoso (6) fan (sports)
timido (8) shy
il tipo (8) kind, guy
tirare (6) to pull
tornare (6) to come back/return
la torre (2) tower

la torta (9) cake
il torto (3) wrong
la tovaglia (9) tablecloth
tra (10) between, among
il tram (10) streetcar
il tramezzino (9) sandwich
il trasporto (13) transportation
la traversa (14) intersection
tre (1) three
tredici (4) thirteen
il treno (10) train
trenta (4) thirty
il trio (10) trio
troppo (5) too much
trovare (7) to find
tu (3) you
tuo (4) yours
tutto (12) all

U

l'ufficio (6) office
uguale (=) (6) equals
un (2) a
una (2) a
undici (4) eleven
l'università (4) university
uno (1) one
l'uomo (15) man
l'uovo (9) egg
  le uova (9) eggs
usare (6) to use
usato (12) used
uscire (12) to go out
utile (12) useful
l'uva (9) grapes

V

la vacanza (8) vacation
la valigia (12) suitcase
il vaporetto (13) steamboat
la vasca (13) tub
vecchio (5) old
vedere (8) to see
veloce (8) fast
vendere (8) to sell
il venerdì (7) Friday
venire (11) to come
venti (4) twenty
il vento (7) wind
verde (5) green
la verdura (9) vegetables
vero (5) true
verticale (14) vertical
il vestito (5) dress, suit
la via (14) street
viaggiare (7) to travel
il viaggio (6) travel, trip
il viale (14) avenue, boulevard
il vicino (12) neighbor
vicino (13) near
vicino a (7) near (something)
il videogioco (10) videogame
il videoregistratore (11) VCR
vietato fumare (15) no smoking
il vigile (8) policeman
vincere (8) to win
il vino (9) wine
viola (5) violet
il violino (6) violin
la visita (12) visit
visitare (7) to visit
il vitello (9) veal
la vittoria (6) victory
vivere (8) to live
la voglia (3) wish/desire
voi (3) you (pl.)
volare (3) to fly
volere (11) to want
vostro (10) yours (pl.)

Z

lo zaino (2) backpack
la zia (1) aunt
lo zio (4) uncle
la zona (13) section, area
lo zoo (7) zoo
lo zucchero (9) sugar

ENGLISH-ITALIAN VOCABULARY

A

a un, uno, una (2)
accountant ragioniere (3)
acquaintance conoscenza (12)
actor attore (10)
actress attrice (10)
address indirizzo (4)
to advise consigliare (11)
after dopo (14)
afternoon pomeriggio (6)
agency agenzia (6)
airplane aereo (10)
airport aeroporto (10)
alarm clock sveglia (2)
all tutto (12)
already già (8)
also anche (9)
always sempre (8)
American americano (5)
ancient antico (5)
and e (1)
angel angelo (14)
anniversary anniversario (6)
to announce annunciare (15)
"antipasto" antipasto (5)
antiquity antichità (5)
apartment appartamento (6)
apple mela (9)
apricot albicocca (9)
April aprile (7)
aquarium acquario (7)
arcade sala videogiochi (10)
architect architetto (3)
architecture architettura (13)
arm braccio (8)
armchair poltrona (13)
arrival arrivo (12)
to arrive arrivare (6)
art arte (6)
artist artista, *m.,f.*(5)
as, like come (12)
as soon as appena (15)
to ask (for) chiedere (8)
to ask domandare (7)
aspirin aspirina (13)
at a (10)
at all affatto (9)
ATM machine Bancomat (11)
to attend frequentare (7)
August agosto (7)
aunt zia (1)
automobile automobile (2)
avenue, boulevard viale (14)

B

back of chair schienale (14)
back schiena (3)
backpack zaino (2)
bad cattivo (5)
badly male (3)
bag borsa (12)
baggage bagaglio (14)
bakery panetteria (11)
banana banana (9)
band banda (7)
bank banca (11)
bartender barista (11)
basement taverna, cantina (13)
basketball pallacanestro (7)
bathroom bagno (12)
to be essere (5)
to be able, can potere (12)
beach spiaggia (7)
bean fagiolo (9)
beautiful, handsome bello (5)
bed letto (2)
beef manzo (9)
beefsteak bistecca (9)
beer birra (9)
before prima (12)
behind dietro (13)
to believe credere (8)
belly pancia (9)
belt cintura (14)
better migliore (12)
between, among fra, tra (10)
bidet bidet (13)
big grosso (8)
big, large grande (5)
birthday compleanno (6)
black nero (5)
blackboard lavagna (2)
blanket coperta (14)
blond biondo (5)
blouse camicetta (5)
boarding pass carta d'imbarco (15)
boat barca (10)
boiled bollito (9)
bold sfacciato (8)
book libro (2)
bookshelf scaffale (13)

bookstore libreria (11)
bookseller libraio (11)
boot stivale (14)
bossy prepotente (8)
bottom, end fondo (14)
boutique boutique (11)
boy ragazzo (1)
Brazil Brasile (5)
bread pane (9)
breakfast colazione(9)
bride sposa (15)
bridge ponte (14)
broccoli broccoli (9)
brooch spilla (14)
brother fratello (4)
brown marrone (5)
brush spazzola (12)
bus autobus (8)
business affare (10)
but ma (3), però (13)
butcher shop macelleria (11)
butter burro (9)
butterfly farfalla (9)
buy comprare (7)
bycicle bicicletta (10)

C

cake dolce (9)
cake torta (9)
calculator calcolatore (2)
calendar calendario (2)
camera macchina fotografica (15)
Canadian canadese (5)
canary canarino (13)
"cannolo" cannolo (8)
canzone song (8)
car macchina (10)
card cartoncino (7)
career carriera (11)
carefree spensierato (8)
to carry/bring portare (7)
cart carrello (15)
cash cassa (6)
cassette cassetta (7)
castle castello (6)
CD player lettore CD (11)
to celebrate festeggiare (6)
cellular phone telefonino (2)
center, downtown centro (8)
chair sedia (2)
check-in counter banco d'accettazione (15)
cheerful allegro (9)
cheese formaggio (9)
cherry ciliegia (11)
chest (of drawers) comò, cassettiera (4)
chicken pollo (9)
child bambino (8)
Chinese cinese (5)
chocolate cioccolato (9)
to choose scegliere (14)
chorus coro (6)
church chiesa (11)
cinema cinema (11)
circle cerchio (13)
city hall municipio (11)
city città (7)
to clean pulire (9)
clear sereno (7)
clever bravo (4)
to close chiudere (8)
closed chiuso (6)
closet armadio (2)
clothing abbigliamento (11)
cloudy nuvoloso (7)
coffee caffè (9)
cold freddo (3)
colleague collega (13)
comb pettine (12)
to come venire (11)
to come/go back tornare (6)
come on! dai, su! (9)
comfortable comodo (13)
comic comico (12)
common comune (13)
company ditta (11)
concert concerto (6)
cook cuoco (11)
cookie biscotto (9)
cool, fresh fresco (7)
contest gara (12)
corn granoturco (9)
corner angolo (14)
country paese (8)
cousin (m.) cugino (4)
cousin (f.) cugina (4)
to cover coprire (9)
CPA ragioniere (3)
crazy pazzo (10)
to cross attraversare (14)
cruise crociera (10)
cuff risvolto (14)
cup tazza (9)
cupboard credenza (13)
cursive corsivo (8)
customs dogana (15)
to cut tagliare (7)

D

daddy papà (4)
dairy store latteria (11)
to dance ballare (10)
dark blue blu (5)
dark bruno (5)
date data (7)
daughter figlia (4)
daughter-in-law nuora (4)
day giornata (7)
day giorno (1)
dear caro (12)
December dicembre (7)
to decide decidere (8)
delicatessen salumeria (11)
department store grande magazzino (10)
departure partenza (12)
to desire desiderare (6)
desk scrivania (2), banco (13)
desk (teacher's) cattedra (2)
dessert dessert (9)
difficult difficile (5)
dinner pranzo (9)
director (f.) direttrice (3)
director (m.) direttore (3)
"disco" discoteca (11)
to discuss discutere (8)
dish piatto (9)
dishwasher lavastoviglie (13)
divided diviso (:) (6)
to do/make fare (12)
docile docile (8)
doctor (f.) dottoressa (3)
doctor (m.) dottore (1)
dog cane (8)
dollar dollaro (7)
door porta (2)
drama dramma (4)
dress vestito/abito (8)
dress/suit vestito (5)
dresser comò (2)
drink bevanda (9)
dumplings gnocchi (12)
during durante (10)
Dutch olandese (5)

E

ear orecchio (8)
early presto (6)
to earn guadagnare (11)
earphones cuffia (14)
easy facile (5)
to eat mangiare (7)
egg uovo (9)
eight otto (1)
eighteen diciotto (4)
eighty ottanta (9)
elderly anziano (5)
electric range (13) cucina elettrica
elegant elegante (8)
elephant elefante (5)
elevator ascensore (15)
eleven undici (4)
employee impiegato (11)
end fine (8)
energetic energico (8)
engineer ingegnere (3)
England Inghilterra (5)
English inglese (5)
enormous enorme (5)
to enter entrare (7)
entrance hall ingresso (13)
equals uguale (=) (6)
eraser cancellino (2)
evening sera (6)
every ogni (12)
exactly esattamente (6)
exam(ination) esame (5)
exchange scambio (13)
expensive caro (12)
explanation (15) spiegazione
excursion gita, trip (15)
excuse me! (fam.) scusa! (4)

F

face faccia (5)
fall autunno (7)
family famiglia (4)
fan tifoso (6)
far lontano (7)
fashion moda (13)
fast, adv. rapidamente (6)
fast adj. rapido (8)
to fasten allacciare (14)
fat grasso (5)
father padre (4)
father-in-law suocero
favor favore (12)
fear paura (3)
February febbraio (7)
fifteen quindici (4)
fifty cinquanta (4)
film rullino (12)

filosophy filosofia (3)
to find trovare (7)
to finish finire (9)
first primo (6)
  _aid pronto soccorso (15)
fish pesce (9)
five cinque (1)
flight volo (15)
  _attendant assistente di volo
flower fiore (9)
to fly volare (2)
fog nebbia (7)
to follow seguire (9)
food cibo (9)
foodstuff alimentari (11)
foot piede (3)
foreign straniero (5)
forty quaranta (4)
fountain fontana (11)
four quattro (1)
fourteen quattordici (4)
fragrance profumo (14)
France Francia (5)
free libero (6)
French francese (5)
Friday venerdì (7)
fried fritto (9)
friend amico/a (5)
from, by da (10)
fruit frutta (8)
fruit salad macedonia (9)

G

game gioco (6)
garden giardino (6)
gas range cucina a gas (13)
generous generoso (8)
gentleman signore (3)
geography geografia (6)
German tedesco (5)
Germany Germania (5)
gift regalo (10)
girl ragazza (1)
glad lieto (9)
glass bicchiere (14)
glove guanto (2)
to go andare (10)
to go out uscire (12)
good bravo, buono (2)
good day buongiorno (1)
good evening buonasera (1)
good bye arrivederci (1)
good bye arrivederLa (1)
good night buonanotte (1)
grandchild nipote (9)
grandfather nonno (4)
grandmother nonna (4)
grapes uva (9)
grass erba (7)
gray grigio (5)
great fantastico (12)
green verde (5)
to greet salutare (6)
to grow crescere (14)
guide guida (5)
guitar chitarra (7)
gymnastic ginnastica (8)

H

hair capello (8)
  _dryer asciugacapelli (12)
half mezzo (6)
ham prosciutto (9)
hand mano (8)
to hand in consegnare (15)
hat cappello (14)
to have avere (3)
to have to, must dovere (13)
he lui (3)
head testa (3)
to hear sentire (9)
heavy pesante (12)
hello! (fam) salve! (2)
help aiuto (6)
to help aiutare (6)
here qui (1)
hi, bye ciao (1)
his, hers, its suo (4)
history storia (6)
Holland Olanda (5)
homework compito (12)
honorable onorevole (3)
to hope sperare (11)
horse cavallo (8)
hospital ospedale (11)
hotel albergo (11)
hour, time ora (6)
house casa (6)
how much? quanto? (1)
how? come? (3)
Humanities "Lettere"(3)
hunger fame (3)
hurry fretta (3)
husband marito (4)
husky robusto (5)

I

I io (3)
ice ghiaccio (7)
ice cream gelato (7)
if se (11)
in, at in (10)
in front of davanti a (11)
in order to per (10)
inexpensive economico (14)
information informazione (8)
insolent sfacciato (8)
to insult insultare (8)
intelligent intelligente (5)
interesting interessante (5)
intersection traversa/incrocio (14)
interview intervista (7)
_**job**- colloquio di lavoro
to introduce presentare (9)
Irish irlandese (5)
Italian italiano (5)
Italy Italia (5)

J

jacket giacca (14)
jam marmellata (9)
January gennaio (7)
Japan Giappone (5)
Japanese giapponese (5)
job lavoro (7)
July luglio (7)
June giugno (7)

K

kennel canile (12)
key chiave (14)
kilometer chilometro (8)
kind gentile (8)
kind of guy tipo (8)
king re (4)
kitchen cucina (9)
to know conoscere (8)

L

lady signora (1)
lake lago (5)
lamp lampada (2)
large room sala (13)
"lasagna" lasagne (12)
late tardi (6)
to laugh ridere (9)
lawyer avvocato (3)
lazy pigro (8)
leaf foglia (7)
leaning pendente
to learn imparare (7)
leather shop pelletteria (11)
to leave behind lasciare (12)
to leave (for a trip) partire (9)
left-hand sinistra (14)
leg gamba (8)
lesson, class lezione (6)
letter lettera (7)
librarian bibliotecario (11)
library biblioteca (6)
lighter accendino (14)
likeable simpatico (5)
liquid liquido (9)
to listen ascoltare (6)
little, few poco (12)
to live vivere (8)
to live, to dwell abitare (6)
living room soggiorno (13)
long lungo (5)
to look guardare (6)
to look for cercare (7)
to lose perdere (8)
to love amare (5)
love amore (5)
ma'am signora (1)
magazine rivista (2)
mailman postino (11)
mainly essenzialmente (13)
to maintain mantenere (15)
main street corso (14)
to make/do fare (12)
man uomo (15)
map carta geografica (2)
March marzo (7)
market mercato (8)
marriage matrimonio (14)
match partita (6)
mathematics matematica (6)
May maggio (7)
meat carne (9)
medicine medicina (11)
message messaggio (14)
Mexican messicano (5)
midnight mezzanotte (6)
milk latte (9)
minus meno (6)
minute minuto (8)
mirror specchio (2)
Miss signorina (3)
model modellino (2)
modern moderno (5)0

Monday lunedì (7)
money soldi (8)
month mese (7)
moped motorino (8)
more più (7)
morning mattina (6)
mother mamma (2)
mother-in-law suocera (4)
motorcycle motocicletta (7)
mountain montagna (7)
mouth bocca (8)
Mrs. signora (1)
museum museo (7)
musica musica (6)
my mio (4)

N

Neapolitan napoletano (8)
near vicino (a), (7)
need bisogno (3)
neighbor vicino (12)
nephew nipote (9)
nervous nervoso (8)
never mai (9)
new nuovo (5)
newborn neonato (14)
news notizia (9)
newspaper giornale (8)
night notte (6)
night table comodino (13)
nine nove (1)
nineteen diciannove (4)
ninety novanta (9)
noon mezzogiorno (6)
nose naso (8)
no smoking vietato fumare (15)
note appunto (11)
notebook quaderno (10)
novel romanzo (8)
November novembre (7)
now adesso (4)

O

ocean oceano (8)
October ottobre (7)
of course certamente (9)
of di (2)
offer offerta (15)
to offer offrire (9)
office ufficio, studio (11)
often spesso (9)
oil olio (9)
old vecchio (5)
on su (10)
one (1) uno
one hundred cento (9)
only soltanto (9)
open aperto (6)
to open aprire (9)
opening apertura (6)
orange arancia (fruit) (9)
orange arancione (color) (5)
orange soda aranciata (2)
ours nostro (10)
out(side) fuori (9)
over, on top sopra (13)
owner padrone (11)

P

package pacco (7)
pair paio (14)
pal compagno (8)
pants, slacks pantaloni (5)
park parco (6)
to park parcheggiare (13)
parking lot/space parcheggio (11)
party festa (12)
passenger passeggero (14)
passport passaporto (12)
pasticceria pastry shop (11)
pasticciere pastry maker (11)
patience pazienza (3)
to pay pagare (6)
peach pesca (9)
pear pera (9)
pen penna (14)
pencil matita (2)
penthouse attico (13)
people gente (10)
pepper pepe (9)
perfect perfetto (2)
person persona (4)
pharmacist farmacista (11)
pharmacy farmacia (11)
phone call telefonata (12)
phone telefonare (6)
phys. ed. educazione fisica (6)
physician medico/dottore (11)
piano piano (10)
picture fotografia (2)
pillow cuscino (14)
pin spilla (15)
pink rosa (5)
pizza pizza (8)
place posto (13)

to plant piantare (7)
to play giocare, suonare (6)
pleasure piacere (12)
Poland Polonia (5)
policeman vigile (11)
Polish polacco (5)
politics politica (8)
poor povero (5)
pork maiale (9)
Portuguese portoghese (5)
position posizione (14)
postal postale (11)
poster poster (4)
potato patata (9)
  _chip patatina
practice esercizio (12)
to prefer preferire (9)
to prepare preparare (9)
pretty carino (5)
problem problema (8)
professor (f) professoressa (1)
professor (m) professore (1)
program programma (4)
to promise promettere (8)
psychiatrist psichiatra (12)
public pubblico (13)
to pull tirare (6)
to put, place mettere (8)

Q

quarter quarto (6)
question domanda (8)

R

rabbit coniglio (8)
radio radio (10)
rain pioggia (7)
to rain piovere (7)
raincoat impermeabile (14)
to rake rastrellare (7)
rather piuttosto (12)
to read leggere (8)
really proprio (13)
reason ragione (3)
to receive ricevere (8)
record disco (11)
red rosso (5)
refrigerator frigo(rifero), (9)
relative parente (7)
religion religione (6)
to remain restare (7)
to rent affittare (13)
to repeat ripetere (8)
to require richiedere (10)
to respond rispondere (8)
restaurant ristorante (2)
rest room gabinetto (6)
rice riso (9)
rich ricco (5)
right-hand destra (14)
road strada, via (14)
roast beef arrosto (6)
roasted arrosto (9)
Roman romano (13)
room camera (2)
to require richiedere (10)
rude sgarbato (8)
rug tappeto (2)
rule regola (15)
ruler riga (2)
to run correre (8)
Russian russo (5)

S

salad insalata (9)
salary stipendio (11)
salesclerk commesso (11)
salt sale (9)
sandals sandali (14)
sandwich tramezzino (9)
Santa Claus Babbo Natale (8)
Saturday sabato (7)
scarf foulard (14)
school scuola (6)
science scienza (6)
scooter motoretta (14)
scrimmage allenamento (6)
sea mare (7)
section zona (13)
to see vedere (6)
to sell vendere (8)
to send mandare (6)
sentence frase (11)
September settembre (7)
serious serio (8)
to serve servire (9)
service servizio (14)
seven sette (1)
seventeen diciassette (4)
seventy settanta (6)
she lei (3)
sheep pecora (8)
ship nave (10)
shirt camicia (5)
shoe scarpa (5)

shopping spesa (12)
short (height) basso (5)
short (length) corto (5)
shorts pantaloncini (5)
shoulder spalla (8)
shoulder bag zainetto (11)
shower doccia (10)
shy timido (8)
side parte (15)
sideboard (13) buffet
sidewalk marciapiede (11)
silverware posate (9)
to sing cantare (6)
singer cantante (11)
sink lavandino (13)
sister sorella (4)
six sei (1)
sixteen sedici (4)
sixty sessanta (9)
to skate pattinare (7)
to ski sciare (7)
skirt gonna (5)
sky cielo (5)
sky blue azzurro (5)
sleep sonno (3)
to sleep dormire (9)
sleepy (to be) avere sonno (3)
slow lento (13)
small piccolo (5)
small pizza pizzetta (9)
to smoke fumare (14)
snack merenda (9)
snack spuntino (6)
sneakers scarpe da tennis (8)
to snow nevicare (7)
so così (3)
soccer calcio (6)
sock calzino (5)
sofa divano (13)
soft morbido (6)
soft drink bibita (9)
son-in-law genero (4)
song canzone (6)
soon, early presto (1)
soup minestra (9)
Spain Spagna (5)
Spanish spagnolo (5)
to speak parlare (6)
to spend spendere (8)
  _time passare (10)
spinach spinaci (9)
spring primavera (7)
square (town) piazza (11)
square largo (14)
stadium stadio (8)
stage palcoscenico (11)
stain macchia (13)
stairway scala (15)
stamp francobollo (11)
state stato (8)
station stazione (11)
stationery store cartoleria (11)
stationery vendor cartolaio (11)
to stay restare (7)
steamboat vaporetto (13)
stepbrother fratellastro (4)
stepfather patrigno (4)
stepmother matrigna (4)
stepsister sorellastra (4)
stewed in umido (9)
still, yet ancora (10)
stingy avaro (8)
stocking calza (14)
stomach stomaco (3)
store negozio (8)
straight dritto (8)
strange strano (7)
strawberry fragola (9)
street via (14)
streetcar tram (10)
string bean fagiolino (9)
strong forte (8)
student (m) studente (2)
student (f) studentessa (2)
study studio (11)
to study studiare (6)
stupid stupido (5)
subway metropolitana (13)
sugar zucchero (9)
to suggest suggerire (9)
suitcase valigia (12)
summer estate (7)
sun sole (7)
Sunday domenica (7)
superior superiore (8)
supermarket supermercato (6)
supper cena (9)
surprised sorpreso (10)
sweater pullover (5)
swimsuit costume da bagno (14)
to swim nuotare (6)
swimming pool piscina (6)
Swiss svizzero (5)
Switzerland Svizzera (5)

T

table la tavola (9)
table il tavolo (8)

T-shirt maglietta (5)
tablecloth tovaglia (9)
takeoff decollo (14)
to take, get prendere (8)
tall alto (5)
tattoo tatuaggio (5)
tavern basement, cantina (13)
tavolo table (8)
taxi tassì (10)
taxi driver tassista (11)
to teach insegnare (7)
team squadra (6)
technology tecnologia (13)
technology ed. educazione tecnica (6)
telegram telegramma (7)
ten dieci (1)
thanks grazie (3)
that quello (8)
that is cioè (4)
theater teatro (11)
theirs loro (10)
then allora (7)
then, afterwards poi (7)
there lì (1)
they loro (3)
thing cosa (13)
to think pensare (10)
thin, skinny magro (5)
thirst sete (3)
thirteen tredici (4)
thirty trenta (4)
this evening stasera (7)
this questo (2)
three tre (1)
throat gola (3)
through attraverso (5)
Thursday giovedì (7)
ticket biglietto (6)
tie cravatta (14)
time tempo (10)
times per (x) (6)
tired stanco (10)
today oggi (7)
together insieme (6)
toilet tazza del gabinetto (13)
tomato pomodoro (9)
tomorrow domani (7)
tone-deaf stonato (11)
too, too much troppo (5)
tooth dente (3)
tour giro (12)
tower torre
toy giocattolo (13)
traffic light semaforo (14)
train treno (10)
tranquil calmo (8)
transportation trasporto (13)
travel viaggio (6)
to travel viaggiare (7)
tree albero (13)
trio trio (10)
trip gita, viaggio (7)
trolley bus filobus (13)
true vero (5)
tub vasca da bagno (13)
Tuesday martedì (7)
turkey tacchino (7)
to turn girare (14)
TV set televisore (5)
twelve dodici (4)
twenty venti (4)
twice as much doppio (14)
two due (1)

U

ugly brutto (5)
umbrella ombrello (7)
uncle zio (4)
under sotto (13)
to understand capire (9)
university università (4)
unpleasant antipatico (5)
upbringing educazione (6)
to use usare (6)
used usato (12)
useful utile (12)

V

vacation vacanza (8)
VCR videoregistratore (11)
veal vitello (9)
vegetable garden orto (7)
vegetables verdura (9)
vertical verticale (14)
very well! benissimo! (2)
very, much molto (7)
victory vittoria (6)
videogame videogioco (2)
view panorama (4)
violet viola (5)
violin violino (6)
visit visita (12)
to visit visitare (7)

W

to wait for aspettare (7)

waiter cameriere (11)
to want volere (11)
warehouse magazzino (10)
warm, hot caldo (3)
wastebasket cestino (2)
watch orologio (14)
water acqua (9)
we noi (3)
weak debole (8)
to wear indossare (14)
weather tempo atmosferico (11)
Wednesday mercoledì (7)
week settimana (8)
welcome! benvenuto! (2)
well bene (3)
what che, che cosa, cosa (2)
when quando (6)
where dove (3)
which (one) quale (8)
while mentre (9)
white bianco (5)
who, that che (2)
who? chi? (1)
why, because perché (6)
wife moglie (4)
to win vincere (8)
wind vento (7)
window finestra (2)
  _**ticket** sportello
wine vino (9)
winter inverno (7)
winter coat cappotto (14)
wish voglia (3)
with con (10)
wolf lupo (13)
woman donna (15)
word parola (8)
work lavoro(13)
to work lavorare (7)
world mondo (10)
to write scrivere (8)
wrong torto (3)

Y

year anno (3)
yellow giallo (5)
yes sì (2)
yesterday ieri (7)
you tu (3)
you (pl.) voi (3)
young giovane (5)
young man ragazzo (10)
yours tuo (4)
yours (pl.) vostro (10)

Z

zoo zoo (7)

INDEX